School Foodservice Management

School Foodservice Management

————Fourth Edition————

Dorothy VanEgmond Pannell

Director, Food Services
Fairfax County (Virginia) Public Schools

VNR VAN NOSTRAND REINHOLD
————————— New York

Van Nostrand Reinhold
115 Fifth Avenue
New York, New York 10003

Van Nostrand Reinhold International Company Limited
11 New Fetter Lane
London EC4P 4EE, England

Van Nostrand Reinhold
480 La Trobe Street
Melbourne, Victoria 3000, Australia

Nelson Canada
1120 Birchmont Road
Scarborough, Ontario
Canada M1K 5G4

16 15 14 13 12 11 10 9 8 7 6 5 4 3 2 1

Library of Congress Cataloging-in-Publication Data

VanEgmond Pannell, Dorothy.
    School foodservice management / Dorothy VanEgmond Pannell. — 4th
ed.
        p. cm.
    Rev. ed. of: School foodservice. 3rd ed. 1985.
    Includes index.
    ISBN 0-442-31959-2
    1. Food service management. 2. School lunchrooms, cafeterias,
etc. I. Title.
TX911.2.M27V36   1990
642′ .5′068—dc20
                                                            89-16551
                                                            CIP

To Jerry Pannell, who came into my life at an important time and has challenged my thoughts and brightened my look to the future.

Contents

Preface

This book may be considered the sequel to *School Foodservice*, which was first published in 1974. Radical changes in the food industry, and particularly in school foodservice, over past five years have challenged the skills of managers in the field. Meeting those challenges is the theme of *School Foodservice Management*.

The effects of the changes will be increasingly felt within the next five years. Labor shortages, more knowledgeable customers, heightened nutrition awareness, media coverage, technological change, competition from management companies, food shortages, increased accountability, and escalating costs have combined to force changes upon management. This book examines each of these issues carefully and gives special attention to several new areas of concern, including lowering sodium and fat content in foods served in schools, dealing with financial crises, competing with management companies, and meeting the press.

Chapter 1 addresses most of the basic regulations and laws that one should know to determine whether the foodservice program can operate under the federally subsidized program guidelines. Specific applications are discussed in the relevant chapters. In the appendixes, the relevant National School Lunch Program regulations are reproduced for the reader's reference.

Since there are many good sources of information on nutrition, principles of food preparation, and food specifications, these subjects are not discussed in any detail. Instead emphasis is placed on the areas that are unique to school foodservices and the troublesome areas that will be challenging management in the 1990s.

Many people have contributed to this book. I wish especially to thank the staff at the Food and Nutrition Information Center of the National Agricultural Library in Beltsville, Maryland.

My thanks also go to my colleagues, especially Gloria Johnson, Gloria Beddingfield, and Cathy Lina, and to my employer, Fairfax County Public Schools, and to Marlene Gunn, R.D., Director of the Child Nutrition Programs, Mississippi State Department of Education.

I gratefully acknowledge permission granted for the use of illustrations and quotes throughout the text. My special thanks and appreciation to my family and friends, for their patience and encouragement.

1

Introduction to School Foodservice

HISTORY

School foodservice is a growing industry with annual expenditures in excess of $14 billion. It is the third largest foodservice industry today and will continue to expand if it is able to meet some of the growing needs for foodservice in communities. The local school foodservice has the opportunity of becoming a community nutrition center as the food needs of the elderly and preschool children increase.

Serving food at school began with the volunteer efforts of the Children's Aid Society of New York in 1853. In the early years of the twentieth century two books, *Poverty* (Hunter 1904) and *The Bitter Cry of the Children* (Spargo 1906), brought to public attention the hunger and malnutrition that existed in this country. Hunter estimated that at least 10 million persons were living in poverty in 1904. He observed that poverty's misery falls most heavily upon children. Hunter also estimated that in New York City alone, 60,000 to 70,000 children "often arrived at school hungry and unfitted to do well the work required." Spargo described case after case of deplorable poverty in New York City.

The people feeding children lunch in the early 1900s were primarily volunteer groups. Soon, however, many schools over the country assumed responsibility for serving lunches. In 1921 Chicago claimed it had "the most intensive school lunch system in America." All its high schools and 60 of its elementary schools were serving lunches paid for or authorized by the Chicago Board of Education.

By 1918, lunch of some type was being provided in schools in approximately one quarter of the larger cities. However, it could hardly be compared to the lunch program today. School lunch programs expanded during the Depression, when for the first time federal funds were appropriated for such programs. The first federal funds came from the Reconstruction Finance Corporation in 1932 and 1933. These paid labor costs for preparing school lunches in several towns in southwestern Missouri. By 1934 the funding had been extended to 39 states.

The Works Progress Administration (WPA), created in 1935, assigned women in needy areas to jobs in the school lunch program. This resulted in school lunch programs becoming relatively organized and being supervised by each state. Some standardization of menus, recipes, and procedures resulted. By 1941 the WPA program was operating in all

1

Table 1-1.   Population Change for Five Age Groups, 1980-2000 (population in millions)

Age Groups	1980	1990	2000
Children			
Under 5	16.4	19.2	17.6
5-9	16.6	18.6	18.8
Youths			
10-14	18.2	16.8	19.5
15-19	21.1	17.0	19.0
20-24	21.6	18.6	17.0

Source: Census Bureau projections 1985.

states, the District of Columbia, and Puerto Rico. Some 23,000 schools were serving an average of nearly 2 million lunches daily and employing more than 64,000 people.

In 1942 surplus foods and federal funds were being used by 78,841 schools to serve some type of food to over 5 million children. Often the foods came directly from the local farms to the schools. During World War II, however, federal assistance was cut and commodities were no longer available. The number of schools serving lunch declined to 34,064 during this period.

The program quickly recovered following World War II. The passage of the National School Lunch Act in 1946 made it possible to provide 4.5 million children lunch at school. This legislation provided funding that year of $231 million for the National School Lunch Program.

The peak in number of children served at school under the National School Lunch Program was in fiscal year 1979, when 27 million children were served in 94,300 schools and residential institutions. Millions of other children were being served under unsubsidized programs. Due to declining school enrollment (Table 1-1) and the implementation of the Omnibus Budget Reconciliation Act, a budget-cutting law, there was a decline in the number of school lunches served during the 1980s. Enrollment is expected to rise in the 1990s among the younger age groups, as can be seen from Table 1-1.

NATIONAL SCHOOL LUNCH PROGRAM

The National School Lunch Program (**NSLP**) was signed into law in 1946 by Harry S. Truman. It became a law primarily because (1) during physical examinations for military service many young men had been found to be malnourished, (2) there was a need for an outlet for agricultural commodities produced by flourishing farms after World War II, and (3) lunch at school was needed for learning to take place. The purpose was stated in the introduction to the law: "... as a measure of national security, to safeguard the health and well-being of the Nation's children and to encourage the domestic consumption of nutritious agricultural commodities and other food. . . . "

During the mid-1960s there was great interest in Congress regarding nutrition and poverty in various parts of the country. As a result, the Child Nutrition Act of 1966

(Public Law 89-642) was passed. It provided the first substantial funding for needy children's meals, guidelines for identifying the needy, and a pilot breakfast program.

During the 1970s Hubert Humphrey (Democrat of Minnesota) in the Senate and Carl Perkins (Democrat of Kentucky) in the House of Representatives introduced legislation for the first time to make the school foodservice program a "Universal Food Service and Nutrition Education Program." The bills have never made much progress because of the high price tag and the difficulty of determining what a universal program would actually cost.

The child nutrition programs are popular with Congress, which rejected the annual budget cuts recommended by the president during most of the 1980s. The program has provided nutritious meals to countless undernourished children over the years either free or at reduced prices, as can be seen in Table 1-2. The "paid" meals provided under the National School Lunch Program are usually priced from 25 to 75 cents less than at schools not participating in the NSLP as a result of the subsidy and volume.

Any public or nonprofit private school (high school level or under) is eligible to participate in the NSLP, except in the case of private schools with tuition of more than $2,000.

The National School Lunch Program is administered by the United States Department of Agriculture (**USDA**) at the federal level and by state departments of education. Cash reimbursement and commodity assistance are provided to nonprofit foodservices that agree to carry out federal regulations. Federal funding over the years is shown in Table 1-3.

The payment and commodity rates by type of meals in the 1989-1990 school year are shown below:

Paid	$0.1475
Free	1.5325
Reduced-Price	1.1325
Commodities* (all lunches)	0.1325

Schools qualifying and serving more than 60 percent of their students lunches at free or reduced prices quality for severe needy rates, which were an additional 2 cents per lunch in 1989-1990.

These rates have increased annually based on the Consumer Price Index for food away from home, except in 1981, when the Omnibus Budget Reconciliation Act (Public Law 97-35) was implemented, as shown in Table 1-4. As long as there is a huge federal deficit, these programs will be threatened annually by budget cuts. The paying child's subsidy is at the greatest risk. The NSLP and other child nutrition programs are mandated by entitlement laws that have been exempted from the Gramm-Rudman deficit-cutting legislation of the 1980s.

Under these programs needy children are provided meals free and at reduced prices. The free and reduced-price meal eligibility is determined based on federal poverty

---

*Entitlement commodities only. Bonus commodities, which are foods acquired by the Department of Agriculture through price support and surplus removal programs, may be available to supplement this amount.

Table 1-2. National School Lunch Program Participation and Meals Served

Fiscal Years	Number of Schools[a] (thousands)	Participation (9-Mo. Avg.) (millions)				Total Meals Served (millions)				Percent F/RP of Total
		Free	Reduced	Paid	Total	Free	Reduced	Paid	Total	
1969	74.9	2.9	b	16.5	19.4	507.7	b	2,860.5	3,368.2	15.1
1970	75.6	4.6	b	17.8	22.4	738.5	b	2,826.6	3,565.1	20.7
1971	79.9	5.8	0.5	17.8	24.1	1,005.7	b	2,842.6	3,848.3	26.1
1972	83.3	7.3	0.5	16.6	24.4	1,285.3	b	2,686.8	3,972.1	32.4
1973	86.4	8.1	0.5	16.1	24.7	1,363.9	38.5	2,606.4	4,008.8	35.0
1974	87.6	8.6	0.5	15.5	24.6	1,432.8	45.3	2,503.5	3,981.6	37.1
1975	88.9	9.4	0.6	14.9	24.9	1,545.4	92.5	2,425.1	4,063.0	40.3
1976	88.6	10.2	0.8	14.6	25.6	1,650.2	138.0	2,359.7	4,147.9	43.1
1977	91.3	10.5	1.3	14.5	26.2	1,696.4	209.0	2,344.6	4,250.0	44.8
1978	93.8	10.3	1.5	14.9	26.7	1,659.3	248.7	2,386.1	4,294.1	44.4
1979	94.3	10.0	1.7	15.3	27.0	1,623.4	277.9	2,456.1	4,357.4	43.6
1980	94.1	10.0	1.9	14.7	26.6	1,671.4	308.0	2,407.6	4,387.0	45.1
1981	94.0	10.6	1.9	13.3	25.8	1,736.7	311.7	2,162.2	4,210.6	48.6
1982	91.2	9.8	1.6	11.5	22.9	1,621.6	261.7	1,871.7	3,755.0	50.2
1983	90.6	10.3	1.5	11.2	23.0	1,713.5	252.9	1,836.9	3,803.3	51.7
1984	89.2	10.3	1.5	11.5	23.3	1,701.7	248.0	1,876.5	3,826.2	51.0
1985	89.4	9.9	1.6	12.1	23.6	1,656.6	254.5	1,979.0	3,890.1	49.1
1986	89.9	10.0	1.6	12.2	23.8	1,678.0	257.0	2,007.5	3,942.5	49.1
1987	90.2	10.0	1.6	12.4	24.0	1,656.1	259.0	2,024.8	3,939.9	48.6
1988	90.6	9.8	1.6	12.8	24.2	1,652.9	262.6	2,118.1	4,033.6	47.5

Source: U.S. Department of Agriculture, *Annual Historical Review of FNS Programs, Fiscal Year 1988.*

[a]Residential child care institutions (eligible to participate since FY 1977) are included. Schools alone are: FY 1977—88,800; FY 1978—90,700; FY 1979—90,800; FY 1980—90,400; FY 1981—89,000; FY 1982—87,200; FY 1983—86,800; FY 1984—85,400; FY 1985—85,500; FY 1986—85,900; FY 1987—86,200; FY 1988—86,200.

[b]Included with free meals.

Table 1-3. Federal Cost of All School Food Programs (millions of dollars)

Fiscal Years	NSLP Section 4	NSLP Section 11[a]	NSLP Total Cash	School Breakfast	Special Milk	Total Cash	Commodities Entitlement[b]	Commodities Bonus	Commodities Total	Total Federal Cost
1969	162.0	41.8	203.8	5.4	101.3	310.5	272.0	—	272.0	582.5
1970	168.0	132.2	300.2	10.8	101.2	412.2	265.2	—	265.2	677.4
1971	224.7	307.5	532.2	19.4	91.2	642.8	277.3	—	277.3	920.1
1972	225.7	513.0	738.7	24.9	90.3	853.9	312.1	—	312.1	1,166.0
1973	225.7	656.4	882.1	34.6	90.8	1,007.5	331.0	—	331.0	1,338.5
1974	409.0	676.4	1,085.4	59.1	49.2	1,193.7	316.1	—	316.1	1,509.8
1975	463.4	825.6	1,289.0	86.1	122.9	1,498.0	423.5	—	423.5	1,921.5
1976	513.0	978.5	1,491.5	113.7	138.5	1,743.7	418.6	—	418.6	2,162.3
1977	560.1	1,010.2	1,570.3	148.6	150.0	1,868.9	540.8	—	540.8	2,409.7
1978	618.0	1,190.3	1,808.3	181.2	135.3	2,124.8	485.3	57.6	542.9	2,667.7
1979	684.6	1,299.1	1,983.7	231.0	133.6	2,348.3	675.3	69.6	744.9	3,093.2
1980	772.4	1,507.0	2,279.4	287.8	145.2	2,712.4	765.5	139.0	904.5	3,616.9
1981	708.6	1,672.0	2,380.6	331.7	100.8	2,813.1	578.9	316.3	895.2	3,708.3
1982	421.3	1,764.1	2,185.4	317.3	18.3	2,521.0	426.2	330.8	757.0	3,278.0
1983	446.2	1,955.6	2,401.8	343.8	17.4	2,763.0	426.8	374.1	800.9	3,563.9
1984	470.9	2,036.8	2,507.7	364.0	16.0	2,887.7	440.5	386.9	827.4	3,715.1
1985	497.9	2,080.5	2,578.4	379.3	15.8	2,973.5	456.0	345.2	801.2	3,774.7
1986	524.1	2,190.4	2,714.5	406.3	15.5	3,136.4	445.7	376.2	821.9	3,958.3
1987	541.5	2,255.7	2,797.2	446.8	15.5	3,259.5	448.5	439.6	888.1	4,147.6
1988	574.9	2,344.9	2,919.8	483.7	19.0	3,422.5	462.7	340.6	803.3	4,225.8

Source: U.S. Department of Agriculture, *Annual Historical Review of FNS Programs, Fiscal Year 1988.*

[a]Includes Commodity Schools (cash).

[b]Includes cash-in-lieu of commodities and Commodity Schools.

Table 1-4.　National School Lunch Program National Average Payment and Commodity Rates by Type of Meal (cents per lunch)

Periods	Paid Section 4	Free Sections 4 and 11	Reduced Price Sections 4 and 11	Commodities All Lunches
07/73-11/73	8.00	53.00	43.00	7.00
11/73-12/73	10.00	55.00	45.00	7.00
01/74-06/74	10.50	57.75	47.75	7.00
07/74-12/74	11.00	60.50	50.50	10.00
01/75-06/75	11.75	64.25	54.25	10.00
07/75-12/75	12.25	66.75	56.75	11.00
01/76-06/76	12.50	69.25	59.25	11.00
07/76-12/76	13.00	71.50	61.50	11.75
01/77-06/77	13.25	73.25	63.25	11.75
07/77-12/77	14.00	77.00	67.00	12.75
01/78-06/78	14.50	79.50	69.50	12.75
07/78-12/78	15.25	83.50	73.50	13.75
01/79-06/79[a]	15.75	87.25	77.25	13.75
07/79-12/79[b]	17.00	93.25	83.25	15.75
01/80-06/80	17.75	97.25	87.25	15.75
07/80-12/80	18.50	102.00	92.00	15.50
01/81-06/81[c,d]	16.00	99.50	79.50	13.50
07/81-08/81	17.75	109.25	89.25	11.00
09/81-06/82[e]	10.50	109.25	69.25	11.00
07/82-06/83	11.00	115.00	75.00	11.50
07/83-06/84	11.50	120.25	80.25	11.50
07/84-06/85	12.00	125.50	85.50	12.00
07/85-06/86	12.50	130.25	90.25	11.75
07/86-06/87	13.00	135.50	95.50	11.25
07/87-06/88	13.50	140.50	100.50	12.00
07/88-06/89	14.00	146.25	106.25	12.25

Source: U.S. Department of Agriculture, *Annual Historical Review of FNS Program, Fiscal Year 1988.*

[a]During January 1, 1979-December 31, 1980, the reduced price could be up to 10 cents less than indicated depending upon state pricing policies.

[b]Alaska has been reimbursed at lunch rates equal to 162 percent of the national average payment rates since July 1, 1979.

[c]Hawaii has been reimbursed at lunch rates equal to 117 percent of the national average payment rates since January 1, 1981.

[d]Between January and August 1981, payment rates were 2.5 cents higher for those school food authorities which served 60 percent or more of their lunches free or at a reduced price in the second prior school year.

[e]After September 1981, payment rates were 2.0 cents higher for school food authorities which served 60 percent or more of their lunches free or at a reduced price in the second prior school year.

guidelines, which are revised annually and published in the *Federal Register* in February or March for the following school year. The same poverty guidelines are used for the Food Stamp Program as for the school lunch and breakfast programs. Participation in the National School Lunch Program dropped from a high of 27 million in 90,800 schools in fiscal year 1979 to 22.9 million in 87,200 schools in fiscal year 1982. With declining enrollment and the 1981 budget cuts, participation has increased only slightly since (see Table 1-2).

In order to qualify for cash reimbursement and commodity assistance, numerous federal regulations must be implemented by a school district or a single school. (See the appendix for the text of the regulations.) The main regulation centers around meal requirements, handling of the free and reduced-price meal applications, and meal accountability. The relevant regulations will be addressed in each of the following chapters.

NATIONAL SCHOOL BREAKFAST PROGRAM

Breakfast was provided at school for the very needy long before a program became law. Sometimes it was at the expense of the lunch program, and in many instances the money for food in the morning came from donations. The Child Nutrition Act of 1966 established funding for a pilot breakfast program, which was made permanent in 1975.

Over one third of the schools (34,400 in 1989) that participate in the NSLP participate in the breakfast program as well, serving an average of 3.8 million a day in 1989. Free and reduced-price meals account for over 87 percent of the breakfasts served in 1989.

A few states (such as Massachusetts and Texas) have mandated the National School Breakfast Program. Generally the mandate is that breakfast be provided in any school where the number of free and reduced-price lunches served exceeds a specified percent of those served, usually between 30 and 40 percent.

The benefits of breakfast to students have been proven in several studies. One of the most quoted is the study in 1973, when a team of researchers from Tufts University School of Nutrition and Boston City Hospital conducted a study of 1,023 school children in Lawrence, Massachusetts. They found significant increases in test scores and less tardiness among children who received school breakfast than those who did not.

Some of the reasons the breakfast program has not grown any larger in some parts of the country are: (1) the school transportation system does not deliver students in time for breakfast, (2) administrative personnel are not available for supervision, (3) there is a lack of interest on the part of students, (4) foodservice personnel are not available to serve breakfast, (5) the reimbursement rates are not adequate to cover the cost, and (6) some administrators do not believe that breakfast is the responsibility of the schools.

The federal reimbursement rates for free, reduced-price, and paid meals escalate annually and are indexed to change as the Consumer Price Index for food away from home changes. The income eligibility guidelines for free and reduced-price meals for the lunch and breakfast programs are identical.

Additional funding is available for schools designated as "severe need," which are those serving in excess of 40 percent of their lunches free or at a reduced price.

The costs of preparing and serving breakfast must equal or exceed reimbursement rates, or rates are adjusted accordingly. The state departments of education provide school districts with current federal rates of reimbursement for the breakfast program. For example, in the 1989-1990 school year, federal reimbursements are as follows:

Paid breakfast	$0.175
Non-severe need, reduced-price	0.56
Non-severe need, free	0.86
Severe need, reduced-price	0.72
Severe need, free	1.02

Commodities for the breakfast program were eliminated in 1981. In 1989-1990 the reimbursement rates were increased by 3 cents (in addition to escalation increases) to assist in improving the nutritional quality of meals served. The breakfast program has begun to grow, with the greatest increase in paid meals. The program is meeting a need for children of working parents.

DONATED COMMODITY PROGRAM

Two types of commodities are provided to schools for the National School Lunch Program: (1) "entitlement" commodities based on the number of meals served multiplied by the annual per meal commodity rate (see table 1-4), and (2) "bonus" commodities, which are additional foods acquired through the price support and surplus removal programs. Bonus commodities are made available to "commodity schools only," as well as state-operated institutions.

Commodity value, like the cash reimbursement, increases annually based on changes in the Consumer Price Index for food away from home. The USDA acquires foods for donation under three authorizations:

1. **Section 6** (National School Lunch Act of 1946)
2. **Section 32** (Public Law 320 as amended in 1936)
3. **Section 416** (Agricultural Act of 1949)

Table 1-4 shows the commodity rates from 1973 through 1989 for the entitlement commodities. The bonus commodities vary according to the market and how much the school district can use. In the 1970s and through most of the 1980s, there were surplus dairy products that government officials thought would never be used. These products were distributed to schools as bonus commodities and in unlimited quantities. With the increased popularity of pizza and the distribution of these products to the needy and drought victims, the "unlimited" supply was used up by 1988. All of a sudden the world market price was above the surplus removal price paid by the USDA. In July 1988 the USDA cut back on cheese and dry milk allocations to the schools and limited the quantities schools could receive.

Requirements of the Commodity Program

Schools receiving commodities are required to submit inventory reports during the school year to the department within the state responsible for distribution. Schools are required to maintain records of the amounts received and used for a period of three years plus the current year. The USDA foods cannot be sold or traded. It is the duty of the school receiving the commodity to inspect the delivery, noting the amount received and the condition of the food before signing the receipt. The school is then held responsible for properly storing and using the commodity.

Federal regulations allow a school district to refuse up to 20 percent of the total value of a commodity and receive substitute commodities. Most school districts do not utilize this federal regulation to their full advantage. Often the lead time between notification and receipt does not allow for any refusals. Some commodities are unpopular in parts of the country and difficult for school districts to use. Processing of commodities as a way to obtain variety and flexibility and utilize more donated foods is discussed in chapter 7.

Alternatives to the Commodity Program

Schools and food distributors had various complaints in the 1970s and 1980s about commodities relating to quality, delivery, quantities, timing, size and type of packaging, waste, and other problems. Some people argued that since the early 1930s, when the commodity program was started, foodservice at schools had changed, but that the commodity program had not kept pace with the changes. For example, commodities are usually delivered in the raw state and some school districts do not have the equipment and/or labor to prepare meals from raw ingredients. For some it is no longer cost effective to accept a commodity that will require excessive labor hours to prepare or an unpopular food item that will negatively affect participation.

As a result of the complaints, Congress authorized a study to be made of alternatives to the commodity program. During the 1978-1979 school year, eight school districts took part in a one-year pilot program and received all cash from USDA's budget for their lunch programs in place of donated commodities. A study done by Kansas State University and financed by the National Frozen Food Association found that schools could get more out of the money available and serve lunches that cost less if they received cash instead of commodities. The study projected a potential annual savings of $162 million in 1979 if this program were extended nationwide.

Pro-commodity groups argued that cashing out commodities would defeat the whole purpose of the agricultural support programs. Also, the sample was very small. As a result, during the spring of 1980 the "voucher" system, or "commodity letter of credit" (**CLOC**) system, was promoted by the National Frozen Food Association and some school districts. Congress listened and passed legislation to fund a small national study to test two alternatives—CLOC and cash. Ninety-six school districts participated in the three-year study: there were 32 CLOC, 34 cash, and 30 control commodity sites.

The impact of the different alternatives on school districts and on the stock of surplus food was analyzed. The sites receiving CLOCs proved that a voucher system could work effectively with the smallest to the largest school districts. Those testing CLOCs saw that their main advantage to the school districts is that the system is flexible and permits the purchase of the food product (generic food that USDA designates as price support or surplus) in the form the local school district can use best. For example, a CLOC for "apples" can be used to purchase fresh apples, canned apples, canned apple pie filling, canned applesauce, apple turnovers, and so on.

Sixty school districts opted through legislation to continue following the study to receive the alternative they tested. Also, all the schools in the state of Kansas have received cash for entitlement commodities since the late 1970s.

The future of the commodity program and its alternatives is hard to predict since it is a sensitive political issue. A lot will depend on the farm policy of the country during the 1990s.

SPECIAL MILK AND KINDERGARTEN MILK PROGRAMS

The Special Milk Program was first authorized in 1954, and in 1966 it was made a part of the Child Nutrition Act. The program provided subsidy for milk purchased by children in addition to the milk served as a part of lunch and breakfast. For example, if a school purchased milk for 9.1 cents per half-pint in 1972, the child would pay 4 cents and the federal subsidy would be 5 to 6 cents. In 1980 funding was drastically cut, and from 1981 to 1986 the Special Milk Program was restricted to schools and institutions that did not participate in any other child nutrition program.

In 1986 Congress authorized subsidizing milk for kindergarten children who did not have the option of breakfast or lunch at school. The milk is to be provided free to students who qualify for free meals. The milk served "paying" students (those not qualifying for free) is subsidized by an established rate, which is determined annually (1989-1990 rate was 10.25 cents). The subsidy for the free milk covers only the cost of the milk from the dairy. The school district must cover the cost of labor to handle the milk, storage, and paper supplies.

SPECIAL NEEDS OF CHILDREN

Handicapped Children

Handicapped children's nutritional needs at school are to be met through the National School Lunch Program in accordance with Public Law 94-142, with only slight menu modification. However, schools are not required to provide special diets for any students. (See the National School Lunch Program regulations in the appendix for meal pattern adjustments that can be made in menus.)

In accordance with Public Law 94-142, both public and private education programs are prohibited from discriminating in the operation of foodservice programs. The slight modifications to the meals are to be made at no extra charge to the students whose handicaps restrict the diet. If the child has a medical request for food substitutions that the school foodservice does not have available, the parent may have to furnish the food. States may have additional regulations, and it is always wise to check with the state supervisor for such requirements.

Children with Allergies

Allergies are becoming more common among students. Regulations governing the National School Lunch and Breakfast programs do allow for food substitutions for individual students with medical or other special dietary needs when supported by a statement from a recognized medical authority. The statement should include recommended alternate foods. When a state supervisor or other auditors representing USDA review the school foodservice in a district, they will ask to see the statements. As far as federal regulations are concerned, a statement can be used so long as the student is in school and does not have to be updated annually. The state regulations should be checked.

Head Start Children

Head Start children enrolled in the school district may receive a breakfast and/or lunch under the National School Lunch and Child Nutrition programs. However, the school district's contract with the state must include preschool-age children. It is important to determine if the meals can be claimed in the monthly state reimbursement report for the school district or if the Head Start Program must be treated as a separate entity (like a contract, which is discussed in chapter 15). State regulations differ as to how the claim for reimbursement is handled.

MEETING REGULATIONS

At the local level, each school food authority (**SFA**), which is the entity signing the National School Lunch and Child Nutrition programs contract with the state, is responsible for meeting the federal and state regulations of the programs that the school district is participating in. The relevant federal regulations are provided in the appendix and addressed in the checklist in Figure 1-1. Under AccuClaim, the federal accountability regulation, school districts are being required to review their school foodservices using a specific checklist.

PRESENT AND FUTURE TRENDS

Foodservice in the public and private schools takes many forms; however, over 90 percent of the schools that qualify have elected to participate in the National School Lunch Program because of the funding provided.

Many private schools cannot qualify for the NSLP because of the tuition they charge. Some administrators of schools that do qualify prefer to be in total control of their schools and their lunch programs and do not elect to participate. The same is true of a few public schools, usually high schools. Some select to receive commodities only and not have all the regulations to carry out, known as "commodity only schools."

Though this book will focus on carrying out the regulations of the NSLP and the related federally authorized programs, the information and procedures are applicable to any institutional foodservice. Basically, this book covers how to run a cost-effective, successful foodservice, meeting the challenges of the 1990s.

Enrollment in the schools is not expected to grow substantially during the first half of the 1990s (Table 1-1), nor is federal funding for the Child Nutrition Programs expected to increase substantially. In spite of enrollment, the foodservices operated in the schools throughout the country have an opportunity to grow by expanding into other areas of service (see chapter 15).

The challenges facing the school foodservice industry in the 1990s include tighter budgets, labor shortages, customers who are more demanding and knowledgeable, tougher federal audits (referred to as **AccuClaim**), and stiff competition. The commercial management companies and school district managements will be in competition as financing of

Yes	No
——	——	1. Has the annual contract with the state department of education been executed?
——	——	2. Is a copy of the school district's policy statement for provision of free and reduced-price meals on file in each school?
——	——	3. Has the application for free and reduced-price meals been distributed to all students?
——	——	4. Are the free, reduced-price, and paid students treated the same?
——	——	5. Are nondiscrimination posters displayed where students can see them?
——	——	6. Are only students who qualify for free or reduced-price meals receiving them?
——	——	7. Are the applications for free and reduced-price meals that are approved complete and in accordance with regulations?
——	——	8. Is verification of an approved sample of the free and reduced-price meal applications being completed annually?
——	——	9. Has an appropriate hearing procedure been developed and implemented for use if the family does not agree with the action taken on the free and reduced-price meal application?
——	——	10. Are ticket posters displayed in the school if tickets are used?
——	——	11. Is a procedure used for obtaining an accurate meal count by category—free, reduced-price, and paid?
——	——	12. Are the school's financial data and meal counts consolidated monthly and submitted by the twentieth of the following month (or in accordance with the state's requirements)?
——	——	13. Is the purchasing procedure used in compliance with state and federal regulations?
——	——	14. Is a monthly physical inventory being taken?
——	——	15. Are commodities and purchased foods being stored properly? Off the floor? At the correct temperature?
——	——	16. Do the menus planned meet the meal pattern?
——	——	17. Are whole milk and lowfat milk available to all students as choices?
——	——	18. Is "offer-versus-serve" carried out in senior high schools? At other levels at the option of the local school district?
——	——	19. Is an "offer-versus-serve" poster displayed where students can see it?
——	——	20. Is a medical statement on file for every student receiving a substitute for milk as a part of the federal school lunch or breakfast program?
——	——	21. Is food waste low?
——	——	22. Are leftover foods being handled properly?
——	——	23. Are all foods served or sold in the cafeteria area sold by the school foodservice program with the profits from the sales going to the program?.
——	——	24. Is the temperature of all cold food kept at 40° F. or below?
——	——	25. Is the temperature of all hot food kept at 150° F. or hotter?
——	——	26. Is the temperature of all refrigeration being recorded at a minimum of three times a week?
——	——	27. Are production records completed daily?
——	——	28. Is there parent involvement and is it documented?
——	——	29. Is there student involvement and is it documented?
——	——	30. Are all foods in the storage area labeled, dated, and covered properly?
——	——	31. Are cleaning supplies stored separately from food?
——	——	32. Is only one lunch and/or breakfast per student counted for reimbursement?
——	——	33. Are records kept and available for audit for the three previous years?
——	——	34. Is the lunch priced as a unit?
——	——	35. Are all components of the breakfast program offered?
——	——	36. Is the fund balance no greater than three months' operating cost?
——	——	37. Is the school foodservice fund kept separate from other school funds?
——	——	38. Is interest earned by the fund credited to the fund?
——	——	39. Are school foodservice funds used only for the benefit of the school foodservice program?
——	——	40. Is the adult meal price sufficient to cover cost and at least equal to the federal and state subsidies for the free lunch?
——	——	41. Do all adults, except foodservice employees, pay for meals?

FIGURE 1-1. Checklist for meeting regulations.

school foodservice becomes more of an issue. School district management of foodservice will be handicapped by high pay scales and the high cost of fringe benefits.

Regardless of who manages the school foodservice programs, the successful program will have to be customer oriented and cost effective and able to utilize technology effectively.

BIBLIOGRAPHY

American School Food Service Association. 1983. "Child Nutrition Programs: A Legislative History." *School Foodservice Journal* 37(6): 62-71.

Briggs, H. L., and Constance C. Hart. 1931. "From Basket Lunches to Cafeterias—A Story of Progress." *Nation's Schools* 8:51-55.

Dwyer, J. T., M. F. Elias, and J. H. Warren. 1973. "Effects of an Experimental Breakfast Program on Behavior in the Late Morning." Master's Thesis, Harvard School of Public Health, Cambridge, Mass.

Fairfax, Jean. 1968. *Their Daily Bread.* Atlanta, Ga.: McNelley-Rudd Printing Service.

Food and Nutrition Service. 1970. *Chronological Legislative History of Child Nutrition Program.* Washington, D.C.: U.S. Department of Agriculture.

Gunderson, G. W., ed. 1971. *The National School Lunch Program: Background and Development.* FNS 63. Washington, D.C.: U.S. Department of Agriculture.

Hunter, R. 1904. *Poverty.* (Reprinted, 1965, as *Poverty: Social Conscience in the Progressive Era.*) New York: Harper & Row.

Kotz, N. 1969. *Let Them Eat Promises: The Politics of Hunger in America.* Englewood Cliffs, N.J.: Prentice-Hall.

National Archives and Records Administration. 1987. *Code of Federal Regulations,* parts 210 to 299. Washington, D.C.: The Office of Federal Register.

National Education Association. 1989. *The Relationship between Nutrition and Learning: A School Employee's Guide to Information and Action.* Washington, D.C.: National Education Association.

Pollitt, Ernesto, Mitchell Goisovitz, and Marita Gargiulo. 1978. "Educational Benefits of the United States School Food Program: A Critical Review of the Literature." *American Journal of Public Health* 68(6): 477-81.

Popkin, Barry M. 1982. *The National Evaluation of School Lunch and Breakfast.* Chapel Hill, N.C.: University of North Carolina.

Spargo, J. 1906. *The Bitter Cry of the Children.* New York: Macmillan.

U.S. Department of Agriculture (USDA). 1983. *The National Evaluation of School Nutrition Programs: Final Report.* Vols. 1 and 2. Washington, D.C.: U.S. Government Printing Office.

———. 1988a. "National School Lunch Program: Accountability; Proposed Rule." *Federal Register:* 7CFR, part 210 (September 9, 1988). Washington, D.C.: U.S. Government Printing Office.

———. 1988b. "National School Lunch Program Revision; Final Rule." *Federal Register:* 7CFR, part 210 (Aug. 2, 1988). Washington, D.C.: U.S. Government Printing Office.

————. 1989. *Annual Historical Review of FNS Programs, Fiscal Year 1988.* Washington, D.C.: USDA.

U.S. General Accounting Office. 1980. *Major Factors Inhibit Expansion of the School Breakfast Program.* Washington, D.C.: U.S. General Accounting Office.

VanEgmond-Pannell, Dorothy, and School Food and Nutrition Research Committee. 1987. *The School Foodservice Handbook: A Guide for School Administrators.* Reston, Va.: The Association of School Business Officials International.

2

Financial Management

THE IMPORTANCE OF MANAGING FINANCES

The first step in managing a financially successful operation is to know the financial objectives and goals of the school board. Is the foodservice program to be self-supporting? Or, is it more important that the prices charged students be kept very low?

The next step toward managing a financially successful operation is to have a good accounting system. An accounting system that provides accurate data on a timely basis is essential for management to be able to "manage finances." It is of little value to a person trying to "manage tight finances" to receive data five months after the expenditures are incurred. With the slim margin that most school foodservices have to run on, it is essential for the information to be accurate and in a form that can assist management in making decisions. Computerization of the different financial functions (discussed in chapter 14) will be necessary in the 1990s for school foodservice to survive.

There are uniform systems of accounting for restaurants, hotels, and clubs, but no one universal guide for school foodservice has been provided since the cost-based accounting manuals provided by USDA in the early 1970s. Some state departments of education (North Carolina, South Carolina, and New York, for example) have supplied guidance materials and established standards for financial management of the school foodservice account. With some modifications, the *Uniform System of Accounting for Restaurants* (1986), published by the National Restaurant Association, is a usable guide for school foodservices.

As a result of the lack of a uniform guide, the financial information provided foodservice managers/supervisors varies greatly from school district to school district. If the finance officer for the school district is handling the school foodservice account too, the account may not get the attention needed. It is a small fund in comparison with the school district's general fund and may not be considered that important (so long as there is no financial problem), when in fact, it is one of the most challenging to manage.

The kind of information needed for an enterprise account generating its own income is very different from what is needed for a budgetary fund. The school foodservice fund parallels an enterprise account, in that foodservice produces goods and provides services and charges for the goods and services and should be handled as an enterprise account.

When the school district is receiving federal and state funds for the school foodservice program, the accounting system has specific federal requirements to meet. In order to meet the federal requirements, the accounting system should:

- Provide accurate meal counts by category (free, reduced-price, and paid) at the *point of sale*
- Ensure that those served a free or reduced-price meal are eligible
- Ensure that the school foodservice is in compliance with state and federal program requirements
- Ensure that the school foodservice funds (which include federal funds) are safeguarded against unauthorized, improper, or wasteful use or disposition
- Comply with federal and state regulations in purchasing
- Provide a system whereby the revenues, expenditures, and all other fund transactions are properly managed, recorded, and accounted for
- Maintain files for the previous three years

FINANCIAL REPORTS

According to Tidwell (1986), the three financial statements needed by an enterprise account, such as the school foodservices, are (1) a balance sheet, (2) a statement of income (accrual income) or profit and loss, and (3) changes in fund. Accrual base accounting is a method of tabulating revenue earned and expenses accrued. The accrual income statement indicates the financial position for any given period in time. It shows the amount of cash earned and the amount of food, labor, supplies, and so forth that is actually used. Cash base accounting reflects the cash in the account at the time of the month the account is closed out. The accrual income statement will show how a school foodservice is doing financially when credit is extended and the program usually has an outstanding federal reimbursement.

Balance Sheet

A **balance sheet** is the basic financial statement, which shows the financial condition of the fund at a given point and compares current balances with balances at the end of the prior year (Fig. 2-1). It reports assets, liabilities, and net worth at the end of the accounting period (generally a month). This report shows cash on hand (including the value of inventory). A school district may or may not include the value of equipment as an asset.

The *revenue* (*assets*) includes cash, accounts receivable, inventories, prepaid expenses, and fixed assets. *Expenditures* (*liabilities*) include accounts paid during the accounting period, accounts payable, accrued payroll, and taxes payable.

	FY 1989	FY 1988
ASSETS		
Current assets		
Cash	$ 171,516	$ 166,957
Investments	114,989	67,437
Accrued interest receivables	—	7,111
Other miscellaneous receivables	—	29
Due from other governments	—	31,272
Inventory	79,755	83,403
TOTAL CURRENT ASSETS	$ 366,260	$ 356,209
Equipment		
Total	179,178	175,357
Less accumulated depreciation	112,317	101,545
NET EQUIPMENT	$ 66,861	$ 73,812
TOTAL ASSETS	$ 433,121	$ 430,021
LIABILITIES AND FUND BALANCE		
Liabilities		
Accounts payable	$ 274	$ 1,164
Fund Balance		
Retail earnings	432,847	428,857
TOTAL LIABILITIES AND FUND BALANCE	$ 433,121	$ 430,021

FIGURE 2-1. Balance sheet. This type of report form received, the Certificate of Excellence in Financial Reporting by School Systems awarded by the Association of School Business Officials (ASBO).

Profit and Loss Statement

A **profit and loss statement** (referred to as a statement of income or operating statement) shows the financial results at the end of an accounting period—usually the end of each month. The profit and loss statement provides (1) the costs of goods and services, (2) summary of the income or revenue, and (3) net income (Fig. 2-2).

The Financial Accounting Standards Board (1980) defines revenues as "inflow of assets" and expenses as "outflow of assets." The bottom line reflects either a gain (profit) or a loss. Large school districts with central office staffs may wish to show the labor costs for the office under administrative expenses rather than in labor costs.

Comparisons of data—current month with previous month and previous year—are very useful. Comparison analysis with last year's participation in the program and revenue will show when unusual increases or decreases should be of concern. The highest participation may be during December, January, and February. The cost of labor may be highest in September and June because of the days when employees are paid without revenue (holidays, inservice training, "set up" time prior to opening, and "clean up" time prior to closing). Comparative percentage analysis is more meaningful than straight figures for many managers and supervisors. It is important to know what percentage of the income is being used for food and for labor. It is helpful to compare these analyses with those of other school districts.

For Month of   December 1988

School: Roberts School District

Earned Revenue

Student Lunches, Elementary	$10,002.90	
Student Lunches, Secondary	10,010.70	
Adult Lunches	2,076.60	
Special Function	1,087.70	
Kindergarten Milk	400.10	
Subsidies:		
Federal Cash Reimbursement	8,102.36	
State Cash Reimbursement	80.00	
Interest	30.50	
A la Carte Sales	4,809.70	
TOTAL EARNED REVENUE		$36,600.56

Accrued Expenditures

Food	$16,998.11	
Labor (including fringe benefits)	15,098.27	
Supplies/Paper Goods	1,168.30	
Other	1,429.17	
TOTAL ACCRUED EXPENDITURES		$34,693.85
NET GAIN (LOSS)		$ 1,906.71

FIGURE 2-2. Profit and loss statement for a school district.

Profit and loss statements by school are needed on a monthly basis (Fig. 2-3). The profit and loss statement by location will provide the manager incentives for improving. Also, management can do a comparison of similar sized schools and determine exactly where the problems are if one of the schools is operating at a deficit (Fig. 2-4). If a school is operating at a deficit, preparing a daily or weekly profit and loss statement will help pinpoint problems.

Statement of Changes

A statement of financial position or fund balances (Fig. 2-5), known as a **statement of changes**, provides a summary of the fund to date, showing changes in working capital from one year to the next.

School: Oakview High   Month: December   19 88

	For Month	Percent of Income	Year to Date	% of Income
REVENUE ACCOUNT				
Student breakfasts				
Paid	$ 112.50	0.4	$ 487.50	0.4
Reduced-price	90.00	0.3	387.00	0.3
Student lunches				
Paid	15,000.00	48.8	65,000.00	45.2
Reduced-price	180.00	0.5	11,700.40	8.0
Adult meals	525.00	1.7	2,275.00	1.6
Federal reimbursement	6,048.00	19.7	26,208.10	18.3
State subsidy	837.00	2.7	3,627.46	2.5
Local subsidy	418.50	1.4	1,813.50	1.3
A la carte sales	6,375.00	20.7	27,625.00	19.2
Other sales	425.00	1.4	1,435.60	1.0
Commodity rebates	697.50	2.3	3,022.50	2.0
Other income	50.25	0.1	290.00	0.2
TOTAL REVENUE	$30,758.75	100	$143,872.06	100
EXPENDITURES				
Food Costs				
Beginning inventory	$ 4,921.40		$ 4,970.20	
+ Food purchased	13,478.00		58,404.66	
− Ending inventory	5,240.50		5,240.50	
TOTAL FOOD COSTS	$13,158.90	42.8	$58,134.36	40.4
Paper supplies	1,230.35	4.0	5,431.52	3.8
Labor costs				
Payroll	$10,995.91	35.7	$47,948.94	33.3
Fringe benefits	3,298.77	10.7	14,320.67	10.0
TOTAL LABOR COSTS	$14,294.68	46.4	$62,269.61	43.3
Operating expenses				
Cleaning supplies	$ 768.96	2.5	$ 3,383.42	2.4
Maintenance	320.00	1.0	1,250.00	0.9
Administrative costs				
Office supplies	28.00		201.10	
Delivery charges	27.00		320.60	
Travel	12.00		49.00	
Date processing	25.00		125.40	
TOTAL ADMINISTRATIVE COST	$ 92.00	0.3	$ 696.10	0.4
TOTAL EXPENDITURES	$29,864.89	97.0	$131,165.01	91.2
PROFIT (LOSS)	$ 893.86	3.0	$ 12,707.05	8.8

FIGURE 2-3. Profit and loss statement by school.

	Oakview High School		Jefferson High School		Central High School	
	$	%	$	%	$	%
REVENUE						
Student breakfast	$ 202.50	0.7	—		—	
Student lunch	15,180.00	49.3	$11,250.00	41.7	$18,375.00	47.0
Federal reimbursement and commodity rebates	6,745.50	22.0	10,963.00	40.7	2,246.05	5.7
State/local	1,255.50	4.1	1,716.12	6.4	541.40	1.4
A la carte sales	6,375.00	20.7	2,502.00	9.3	14,480.00	37.0
Other income	1,000.25	3.2	507.50	1.9	3,500.00	8.9
TOTAL REVENUE	$30,758.75	100.0	$26,938.62	100.0	$39,142.45	100.0
EXPENDITURES						
Food cost	$13,158.90	42.8*	$11,852.99	44.0*	$15,500.41	39.6*
Labor cost	14,294.68	46.4	12,903.62	47.9	16,635.54	42.5
Paper supplies	1,230.35	4.0	1,212.24	4.5	1,996.26	5.1
Administrative costs	92.00	0.3	107.75	0.4	156.57	0.4
Operating costs	1,088.96	3.5	1,050.61	3.9	1,409.13	3.7
TOTAL EXPENDITURES	$29,864.89	97.0	$27,127.21	100.7	$35,697.91	91.2
PROFIT (LOSS)	$ 893.86	3.0	($188.59)	(0.7)	$3,444.54	8.8
COMMODITY VALUE						
Beginning inventory	$ 9,500.00		$ 8,700.90		9,880.00	
+ Commodities received	2,460.00		2,200.80		2,510.00	
− Ending inventory	7,744.11		7,891.15		7,904.10	
COMMODITY VALUE USED	$ 4,215.89		$ 3,010.55		$ 4,485.90	

*Percent of purchased food cost

FIGURE 2-4. Comparison analysis of school profit and loss.

Allowable Profits

Though school foodservice is considered a nonprofit foodservice, it is not a good management practice to take this literally. Since federal funding is on a reimbursement basis and may be received six to eight weeks after a meal is served, it is advisable to maintain a two- to three-month operating balance. This enables a school foodservice to meet payrolls and pay vendors on a timely basis. Federal regulations limit the funds in the account at the end of a school year to three months of operating cost, except when major equipment replacement is planned.

	FY 1989	FY 1988
SOURCES OF WORKING CAPITAL		
Operations		
Net income	$ 3,315	$33,585
Depreciation not requiring an outlay of funds	14,295	14,352
TOTAL SOURCES OF WORKING CAPITAL	17,610	47,937
USES OF WORKING CAPITAL		
Purchase of fixed assets	7,146	21,299
NET INCREASE IN WORKING CAPITAL	$10,464	$26,638
ELEMENTS OF NET INCREASE (DECREASE) IN NET WORKING CAPITAL		
Cash and investments	$51,634	$ 2,247
Receivables	(31,300)	2,623
Accrued interest receivable	(7,112)	(4,571)
Inventories	(3,648)	25,374
Accounts payable	890	965
NET INCREASE IN WORKING CAPITAL	$10,464	$26,638

FIGURE 2-5. Statement of change.

REVENUE MANAGEMENT

Sources of Revenue

The revenue or income for a school foodservice usually comes from four or five sources: federal (cash reimbursement and commodity value), state, and possibly local subsidies, interest earned, and customer payment. In 1989 slightly over 50 percent of the students participating in the National School Lunch Program paid for their meals (that is, they did not qualify for free or reduced-price meals). Table 2-1 provides an example of the

Table 2-1. Income Received for a Lunch

	Paying Student		Reduced Price	Free	
Source	Elementary	Secondary	Student	Student	Adult
Cash sales	$1.25	$1.35	$0.40	$0.00	$1.75
Federal cash	0.14	0.14	1.0625	1.4625	0.00
Commodity value	0.18	0.18	0.18	0.18	0.00
State cash	0.057	0.057	0.057	0.057	0.00
Local funds	0.00	0.00	0.00	0.00	0.00
Total income	$1.627	$1.727	$1.6995	$1.6995	$1.75

income received for a lunch, which includes price charged customers, and federal, state, and local subsidies.

A la carte sales provide substantial income in some school districts, particularly in high schools. Other services, such as day care meals, senior citizen meals, and special functions, provide revenue (see chapter 15). None of these services should operate at the expense of the federally subsidized school foodservice program.

Pricing Food and Services

In accordance with the federal regulations, the lunch and breakfast under the National School Lunch and Child Nutrition programs must be priced as a unit. Individual food items may be sold a la carte or separately. Prices charged for the lunch and breakfast, unfortunately, are often a local political issue.

The items sold a la carte and services provided in addition to the federally subsidized lunch and breakfast should be priced so that they do not compete with the lunch or breakfast program. Most school districts price a la carte and other services to make a profit, which is used to subsidize the school lunch and breakfast programs.

There is an "art" to pricing, which the restaurant industry knows well, and it should be used in school foodservices. It is a combination of intuition, knowledge of customers and competitors, and knowing the real cost of the product being priced. Some call it using "the psychology of pricing," which means arriving at a price the customer will pay without great resistance. It is important that the customer not perceive the price as too high. On the other hand, if it is too low, the customer may perceive food as being of low quality or having something wrong with it.

Pricing should be competitive with the surrounding school districts and no more than charged at local restaurants, convenience stores, and grocery stores. School foodservices are expected to charge less for an a la carte item than is charged by commercial foodservices. Too rapid or too large a price rise can result in huge drops in participation. Timing is crucial. It is better to raise prices over the school break (summer) than in the middle of the month or school year. The quantity and quality should not be reduced, nor should the menus be negatively changed at the time an increase goes into effect.

According to a USDA study (1982), participation decreases 1 percent for every cent the price of lunch increases. However, this may not always be true. Timing and other happenings influence the reaction to a price increase.

There are a number of methods used in the foodservice industry for arriving at the price to charge. The "actual pricing methods" (Miller 1980) is probably the safest, since it considers all costs of producing and serving the item, which are discussed later in this chapter. Many commercial foodservices use a "food-cost-percentage markup." Since labor costs may be consuming more than 50 percent of the school foodservice income, it is important that labor-intensive items include sufficient costs for that labor. Otherwise, an item may really be costing more than priced using the food-cost-percentage markup method. If the price that management needs to charge in order to cover cost and obtain the profits desired is too high for the students to pay, management needs to decide: (1) Can we afford to sell the item for less than it cost (bearing in mind that no other program should be run at a cost to the National School Lunch Program)? (2) Can costs be reduced? (3) Do we offer the item as a **loss leader**?

A loss-leader is an item priced at cost or even below for a reason. It may be an item that needs to be moved (because it has sold too slowly or has a brief shelf life), it may be a "come on" that will encourage purchasing something else (go-togethers), or it may be a nutritional item that management wants to promote, such as fresh fruit and yogurt.

Adult Meal Prices

What should an adult be charged? The guidelines have been loose over the years. However, in 1988 USDA did provide some written guidelines to the states, as follows:

> *Breakfasts and lunches served to teachers, administrators, custodians, and other adults must be priced so that the adult payment in combination with any per-lunch revenues from other sources designated specifically for the support of adult meals (such as state or local fringe benefit or payroll funds, or funding from voluntary agencies) is sufficient to cover the overall cost of the lunch, including the value of an USDA entitlement and bonus donated foods used to prepare the meal. If cost data are not available, the minimum adult payment should reflect the price charged to students paying the school's designated full price, plus the current value of federal cash and donated food assistance (entitlement and bonus) for full-price meal.*

A la Carte Prices

A la carte sales include any items sold in addition to the unit-priced breakfast and lunch. Some school districts have limited a la carte sales to milk and items on the menu. However, more and more school districts are finding that a la carte sales provide revenue needed to stay in business and provide funds for subsidizing the school lunch program. A la carte sales may be a service that is needed by students who cannot afford or do not want an entire meal, particularly in high schools. Federal competitive food regulations and state regulations specify what can be sold (see chapter 4).

Any items sold a la carte should be carefully priced, so that they are not in competition with the lunch and breakfast programs' unit prices. A la carte prices should be determined based on (1) product cost, (2) prices charged by commercial competitors, and (3) how much the customer will pay (the value of the product to the customer).

When setting a la carte prices, it is helpful to group items at a particular price—for example, all vegetables at 50 cents a portion, all similar-sized cookies at 25 cents each. Group pricing of items is easier for the customer and the cashier to remember. Even when using a programmable cash register, it is more efficient to limit the number of differently priced items.

EXPENDITURE MANAGEMENT

Usually expenses are categorized as direct and indirect. Direct expenses are related to the services provided, such as food, paper supplies, and the labor involved in preparation and service. Indirect expenses are those not directly a part of the services provided, such as maintenance of equipment, cost of running the central foodservice office, printing, utilities, and so on.

The charges that a school district expects the foodservice program to pay vary greatly across the country. For the most part, they are limited to the most identifiable costs incurred in providing the service. In most cases, custodial services, maintenance of equipment, and all utilities are paid for by the school district's budget. In a few cases, school district-managed foodservice programs are expected to pay all costs, including a prorated charge for utilities and custodial, maintenance, personnel, and financial services. In these school districts the foodservice programs are expected to cover a greater share of the costs than if a management company operated the foodservice program. (Contract management is discussed in chapter 6.) In the case of the management company, some of the indirect costs may be returned to the school district at the end of the school year, if there is a "profit" for the year.

Any profits that accrue to the school foodservice fund can be used only for the school foodservice programs and cannot be transferred to other school operating funds.

Costing Food and Service

For management to know the cost of each service and each product may be impractical. Management, however, does need to know costs in order to make such decisions as whether to add a new food product to the menu or how much to charge for a service provided. In actual costing, the following should be calculated:

- Direct labor cost associated with the production of the food or providing the service
- Ingredient (food and supplies) costs required to produce the finished product or service
- Proportionate share of all other costs to operate (fixed cost, administrative cost, management salaries, miscellaneous cost of operating)

To determine the "cost of operating" or "fixed cost" may mean adding together all expenditures besides direct labor, food, and supplies (including expenditures in the summer months). In order to charge this against each product and service, it may be useful to determine the cost of operating per dollar of revenue and use this rate to arrive at the pro rata share for each service. In this way the operating cost is charged proportionately.

This may be far more than a school foodservice manager or supervisor wants to know; however, these costs do need to be considered. Subjective pricing of products and services can be dangerous. One can be fooled into believing a food item or service is costing less than it does.

Actual product cost is needed in order for management to make decisions such as determining

- If a food item should be purchased already prepared *or* should be prepared by foodservice employees (Note: When using this data for deciding to purchase pre-prepared items, labor costs must be eliminated to realize savings.)
- Price to be charged for a product or service, such as a la carte prices to be charged for a food product or the price per person for a special banquet

Table 2-2.   Determining Unit Prices of Raw Food Products to Be Used in Costing Recipes

Item	Purchase Unit	Purchase Price	Unit	Unit Cost
Flour, all purpose	50 lb.	$60.00	lb.	$1.20
Macaroni	20 lb.	8.30	lb.	0.42
Sugar	50 lb.	17.63	lb.	0.36
Applesauce (6/10)	Case	10.48	can	1.75
Apricots, halves (6/10)	Case	28.05	can	4.68
Peaches				
halves (6/10)	Case	25.35	can	4.25
slices (6/10)	Case	21.09	can	3.52
Beans, green (6/10)	Case	14.70	can	2.45
Corn, yellow (6/10)	Case	22.93	can	3.83
Peas, green (6/10)	Case	19.50	can	3.25
Cocoa (5 lb)	Case	8.80	lb.	1.76
Cornstarch (24/1)	Case	11.40	lb.	0.48
Pickle relish (4/1)	Case	11.55	gal.	2.89
Potatoes, French fries (27 lb.)	Case	8.86	lb.	0.33
Beef, ground (with TVP)	20 lb.	15.74	lb.	0.79
Cheese, American (30 lb.)	Case	40.50	lb.	1.35
Strawberries, frozen (6½ lb.)	Package	6.05	lb.	0.93

- Whether management can support the prices charged (in the public sector, a manager often has to have good documentation for making a decision)
- If the product or service should be continued
- If the price of lunch and breakfast should be increased or decreased

Management needs to decide if the dollar value of USDA-donated commodities will be used or whether the commodities will be considered "free." Since donated commodities available at a given time change, the value is shown here as a cost, in which case, the value of the donated commodities will also be considered as income. When pre-costing menu items, the price per unit of raw food products and supplies must be determined (Table 2-2) in order to cost recipes (Fig. 2-6). To maintain an up-to-date, pre-costed menu will require a computer (see chapter 14). Pre-cost information is useful in menu planning; however, what something really costs, the "post-cost," is the cost that is important in pricing or determining whether the product can be served. The use of a perpetual inventory or a good requisition system is needed to provide this information.

It is not easy to arrive at the "real cost" or the post-cost because there are so many variables. What is the pre-cost of preparing and serving a lunch? What is the real cost of preparing and serving a lunch? If the pre-cost and post-cost are very different, management needs to find out why and reduce the differences.

The New York State Department of Education (1987) provides instructions for determining the cost of a lunch when other services are provided (Fig. 2-7).

TACO SALAD BAR

Chili with USDA-donated Beef

Number portions: 336 ⅓ cup   Portion Cost: $0.064
Recipe yield: 7 gal.   Total Cost: $21.434
Portion: ⅓ cup, 3 oz   Preparation Time: 45 min/7 gal
Plan group: Meat/meat alternate

Cook utensil: Kettle
Cook time: 30 min
Cook temp: 170° F

Food File Number	Ingredient Name	Quantity	Item Cost
156	Textured vegetable protein	14 oz	$0.411
0	Water	2½ cup	
520	Beef, ground USDA	5 lb	5.756
17	Onions, dehydrated	1 cup	0.182
157	Flour, all purpose	1 cup	0.042
0	Water	1 cup	
76	Beans, kidney	4½ gal	9.950
122	Chili powder, ground	10 Tbsp	0.499
85	Tomato paste	1 gal	4.593
0	Water	2 qt	

Instructions

---

1. Add water to textured vegetable protein.
2. Brown beef, onions, and reconstituted textured vegetable protein; drain.
3. Make a paste of flour and water; add to meat; stir constantly.
4. Add beans, chili powder, tomato paste, and water to meat mixture. Simmer until internal temperature reaches 170° F.
5. Transfer into soup crock for service. Reduce heat to prevent thickening. (Add water to thin.)

FIGURE 2-6. A costed recipe.

The two largest expenditures will be food and labor. To determine the percentage of food costs, divide the cost of food by the total revenue:

$$\frac{\text{Cost of food}}{\text{Revenue}} = \text{Food cost \%}$$

To determine the percentage of labor costs (payroll plus fringe benefits), divide the cost of labor by the total revenue:

$$\frac{\text{Labor cost}}{\text{Revenue}} = \text{Labor cost \%}$$

EXPENSES
Labor:

Salaries	$19,106.04
Fringes	16,285.31

Food:

Value of food used (Purchased only)	36,055.42

Other:

Value of mat. & supp. used	2,264.09
Warehousing	
Equipment	2,304.72
Management company fee	
Miscellaneous	219.67
TOTAL CUMULATIVE EXPENSES	$76,235.25

DEDUCTIONS
If applicable:
Breakfast program expenses

Food cost	NA
+ Labor cost	NA
+ Misc. cost	NA
= Total breakfast program expenses	NA

A la carte expenses

Sales	$14,650.27	
− Profit (est. 50%)	7,325.14	
= A la carte costs		$7,325.13
TOTAL DEDUCTIONS		− 7,325.13
NET LUNCH COST		68,910.12

$$\frac{\text{Net Lunch Cost}}{\text{Number of Lunches Served}} \qquad 40{,}039$$

= AVERAGE COST PER LUNCH (excluding commodities)	$ 1.721

Average income per lunch	$ 1.6421
− Average cost per lunch	1.7210
= Loss/gain per lunch	$−.0789

FIGURE 2-7. Cost per lunch worksheet (sample). (*Source:* New York State Department of Education 1987.)

The New York State Department of Education's financial training manual (1987) recommends that food cost be 40 percent, labor cost 50 percent, miscellaneous cost 5 percent, and fund balance at 5 percent. The food cost in this case does not include the value of commodities.

BUDGET

A budget is a plan for financial management of an account. It helps a manager to forecast the outcome for the year if the budget is followed. By comparing the projections and actuals on a monthly basis, a manager can determine if the budget is going to be met. A convenient form for budget analysis is shown in Figure 2-8.

The budget should be a plan of revenue and expenses based on estimates and results, if the projections are met. The budget is an important management tool because it

- Provides a constant reminder of projections, throwing up red flags to identify potential problems (If estimated income is not being generated monthly, then expenditures should be down, or a deficit beyond what was planned may result.)
- Sets performance standards for management
- Provides bases for comparison (monthly profit and loss can be compared to budget)
- Controls erratic expenditures
- Helps a manager determine if a program can afford to make an expenditure (e.g., purchase a piece of equipment, or attend a national convention)

Many centralized school districts do a district-wide budget (the "top down" approach) without individual schools being involved in the budget process. When a budget is developed at the top and "passed down" for implementation, top management is totally responsible for meeting the budget. Therefore, it is desirable for a school district made up of more than one school to start with the individual school's budget—the "bottom up" approach. The latter approach provides a separate budget for each school foodservice and then rolls all the budgets up into one budget for the district. Most commercial foodservice operations use a bottom up approach. The lower the level, the greater is the feeling of ownership and the more the involvement and help in meeting the budget on the part of the school-based manager and employees.

Usually budgets are prepared a year in advance and involve several processes before final approval (Fig. 2-9). Based on an "educated guess" that far in advance, the estimated figures may be way off because of unexpected changes in cost.

According to Hess and VanEgmond-Pannell (1987), some of the factors to be considered in making revenue projections and expenditure estimates are:

Historical data
Economic indicators
Demographic changes (school openings or closings and new housing in area)
Projected enrollment
Effects of menu changes
Changes in operating procedures

	Aug.	Sept.	Oct.	Nov.	Dec.	Jan.	Feb.	Mar.	Apr.	May	Jun.	Total
No. Serving Days	0	19	20	18	16	18	19	23	14	22	11	180
Actual	0	19	20	18	16	17	19	23	14	22	12	180
% Days	0	10.5	11.1	10	8.9	9.4	10.5	12.8	7.8	12.2	6.7	100
$ Income	0	$22,448	$22,264	$17,296	$16,008	$16,560	$20,240	$21,712	$12,696	$23,736	$11,040	$184,000
Actual	0	$22,205	$22,023	$17,108	$15,834	$16,380	$20,020	$21,477	$12,558	$23,479	$10,921	$182,005
% Income	0	12.2	12.1	9.4	8.7	9.0	11.0	11.8	6.9	12.9	6.0	100
$ Exp.	$8,500	$16,150	$17,680	$15,130	$12,920	$15,810	$14,960	$20,230	$14,110	$21,930	$12,580	$170,000
Actual	$8,950	$17,005	$18,610	$15,931	$13,604	$16,647	$15,752	$21,301	$14,857	$23,091	$13,246	$178,994
% Exp.	5.0	9.5	10.4	8.9	7.6	9.3	8.8	11.9	8.3	12.9	7.4	100
$ Labor	$2,856	$6,783	$7,140	$6,283	$5,141	$6,783	$6,426	$8,425	$6,355	$9,139	$6,069	$71,400
Actual	$3,007	$7,142	$7,518	$6,616	$5,413	$7,142	$6,766	$8,871	$6,691	$9,623	$6,391	$75,180
% Labor	4.0	9.5	10.0	8.8	7.2	9.5	9.0	11.8	8.8	12.8	8.5	100
$ Food	$3,485	$6,831	$7,597	$6,761	$6,064	$6,691	$6,203	$8,364	$6,134	$8,294	$3,276	$69,700
Actual	$3,701	$7,253	$8,067	$7,179	$6,439	$7,105	$6,587	$8,881	$6,513	$8,807	$3,478	$74,010
% Food	5.0	9.8	10.9	9.7	8.7	9.6	8.9	12.0	8.8	11.9	4.7	100
$ Other	$2,159	$2,536	$2,943	$2,086	$1,715	$2,336	$2,331	$3,441	$1,691	$4,427	$3,235	$28,900
Actual	$2,242	$2,610	$3,025	$2,136	$1,752	$2,400	$2,399	$3,549	$1,653	$4,661	$3,377	$29,804
% Other	7.5	8.8	10.2	7.2	5.9	8.1	8.1	11.9	5.5	15.6	11.3	100

FIGURE 2-8. Budget analysis form.

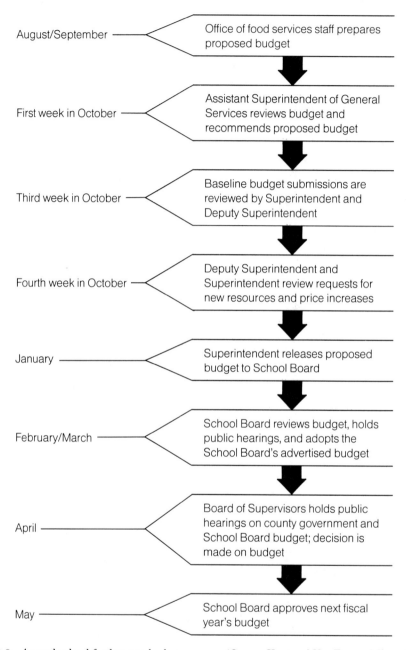

FIGURE 2-9. Annual school foodservice budget process. (*Source:* Hess and Van Egmond-Pannell 1987.)

Goals and plans
Changes in food and labor costs
Changes in state and federal legislation
Meal price changes
Operational changes

Since the estimates and projections have so many variables, it is important that the budget be updated in the late summer before the school year begins and again after the trends in participation and costs have been set (around December). It is not possible to predict the variables a year ahead with 100 percent accuracy—how many students will be served a day, what the federal reimbursement rate will be, and what the cost of food will be. When a price increase is involved, the estimated number that will be served (a decrease in participation can be expected) is important to revenue as well as expenditures. When these factors are known, the budget should be adjusted.

There are two basic methods of preparing a budget: zero-base and traditional financial budgeting. Zero-base budgeting assumes no function or expense is absolutely required and all must be justified. This means determining income by extending out the numbers and dollars (e.g., the number of lunches served for year $\times$ the amount of the federal reimbursement).

With the traditional financial budget, it is assumed that all the activities of the previous year are necessary and a "base line" is provided. Generally the budget is a projection of costs based on the percentage of increase or decrease over the previous year. Normally this is the method used; however, it is wise to check the figures occasionally by using the zero-base method.

The steps to planning a budget are as follows:

1. Forecast participation and sales
2. Forecast federal reimbursements and other subsidies
3. Forecast all other income
4. Forecast the percentage increase (or decrease) in food cost
5. Forecast the increase (or decrease) in labor cost based on raises and staffing
6. Forecast equipment needs and other costs

Some basic questions a manager and supervisor should ask are the following:

- What is the daily revenue (including reimbursements)?
- Will the daily income multiplied by the serving days equate to what is in the budget?
- How much does one day of labor including fringe benefits cost? What is the average cost of one hour of labor?
- What percentage of the income is spent for labor?
- How much do management's salaries cost? How much does central office staff in a centralized foodservice cost? What percentage of the labor cost goes for management?
- How much are overhead and other costs in dollars? What percent of the income?

Along with the yearly budget, forecasting revenue and expenditures over the next five years is important to long-range planning. This can give management enough warning of upcoming problems that action can be taken to correct them. With increases in labor costs, which occur annually in most school districts, and the rising costs of fringe benefits, lunch price increases need to be annual. The traditional 5- and 10-cent increases may not be enough. It is not a good business practice to run at a deficit unless the operating balance provides more than enough to operate for one to two months.

ESTABLISHING BREAK-EVEN POINTS

It is important under this concept of managing finances for the foodservice supervisor/director and each manager to know the answer to this question: How many meals must the school district foodservice or an individual school serve each day and how many dollars must the daily deposit be? This may be a different way of looking at finances for most in school foodservice; however, break-even points and number of customers are successfully used in restaurant management. This section takes the break-even formula taught by Professor Mickey Warner, Florida International University, and applies it to school foodservices.

The daily break-even point (**BEP**) can be established for the school district and for each of the schools. Since the controlling of cost and increasing of sales are most effected at the school level, ending the school year with a small profit can best be accomplished by involving the managers of the individual schools in the process. The following example is of a high school in a centralized school district.

To determine a break-even point for the school (and school district) the following basic formula (Warner 1989) is used:

$$\frac{\text{fixed cost ($\$$)}}{100\% - \text{variable cost} \% = \text{contribution margin (CM\%)}} = \text{break-even point}$$

The *fixed cost* (**FC**) is always expressed in dollars and includes: management salaries and fringe benefits, telephone service, depreciation (if currently being used by school district in profit and loss), utilities (if applicable), and office supplies. To be included are the costs that stay relatively constant regardless of whether a school serves, for example, 600 or 700 lunches.

The *variable costs* (**VC**) are costs that vary with the number served, such as for food, paper, and detergent costs. Hourly employees, or the staff employees, usually vary with the number served (particularly if schools are staffed based on meals per labor hour); therefore, the staff employees' salaries and fringe benefit costs would be considered variable costs.

When establishing a break-even point for the individual schools, the labor cost for the foodservice central office and those expenses that are charged to the central office must be charged against the schools—as overhead costs. A decision to be made is whether this cost will be "fixed" or "variable." Considering overhead as a fixed cost is easier to compile. Annually the central office can allocate the costs based on the previous year's activity. The percentage of the total costs to be charged to each school can be based on meals served or dollars. If the a la carte sales contribute much to the revenue, then the percentage should be based on dollars. For example, if the school district's revenue for the

SAMPLE ANALYSIS OF A FINANCIAL STATEMENT
High School

Item	$	%	Fixed $	Variable
Revenue for Year	$250,000	100.0		
Food Cost	100,000	40.0		40.0%
Labor Cost				
Management Salaries	16,000	6.5	$16,000	
Hourly Labor	66,500	26.6		26.6
Fringe Benefits				
(30% × labor cost)	24,750	9.9	4,800	8.0
Total labor	$107,250	43.0		
Direct Expenses:				
Paper Goods	10,000	4.0		4.0
Cleaning Supplies	6,250	2.5		2.5
Telephone and Utilities	7,500	3.0	7,500	
Office Supplies and				
Data Processing Serv.	6,000	2.4	6,000	
Overhead (17% of				
Central Office Cost)	8,500	3.3	8,500	
Misc. Costs	1,500	0.6	700	0.3
Total Direct Expenses	$39,750	15.8		
Total Cost	$247,000	98.8	$43,500	81.4
Total Profits	$ 3,000	1.2		

FIGURE 2-10. Determining fixed and variable costs.

year was $1,450,000, the percentage of overhead costs a high school in that school district (with a revenue for the year of $250,000) would be charged is ($250,000 ÷ $1,450,000 = .17) 17 percent. If the number served is going to be used to determine the percentage share of overhead that is to be charged to each school, then the total meals served in the school district and the total number of meals served by each school are to be used.

To utilize the "break-even formula," list all the costs and put the dollar costs in the appropriate column—fixed and variable. Total the dollars in the fixed column and determine the percentage of the revenue each of the variable costs is, as shown in Figure 2-10.

Using the break-even formula (Warner 1989), the break-even point can be obtained, as follows:

$$\frac{FC}{100\% - VC = CM} = BEP$$

$$\frac{\$43,500}{100\% - 81.4\% = 18.6\%} = \$233{,}871 \text{ break-even point}$$

The annual break-even point should be further broken down to a manageable amount — the month's or day's break-even point. To obtain the month's break-even point, divide the annual break-even point ($233,871) by 9 or the number of months the school foodservice serves ($233,871 ÷ 9 = $25,985.67). To obtain the day's break-even point, divide the annual break-even point by 180 or the number of days the school foodservice serves ($233,871 ÷ 180 = $1299.29). In order to reach a profit goal for the year, establish the goal and add it to fixed cost. In the above example, the break-even point would be $250,000 per year or $1,388 per day.

To determine how many customers must be served each day to end the year with a $3000 profit, determine the average amount each customer spends (customer check), then dividing the number of customers into the daily revenue ($1300.00 is the average revenue for the day ÷ by 682 average customers = $1.90 customer check).

In the preceding example the revenue included federal reimbursement, which is necessary to see the whole picture. To determine what the daily bank deposit should be, the federal reimbursement will need to be backed out of the break-even point.

Controlling the variable costs at the established percentage is a part of making this work (in the example used in Fig. 2-10, food cost at 40 percent of the break-even point; hourly labor cost at 26.6 percent; paper supplies at 4 percent; cleaning supplies at 2.5 percent; and miscellaneous cost at 0.3 percent). Using the preceding example, we now show what the average daily costs should be:

Food cost: $519.72
Hourly labor cost: $345.61
   (fringe benefits not included)
Paper supplies: $51.97
Cleaning supplies: $32.48
Miscellaneous cost: $3.89

AUDITS

In 1987, the Office of the Inspector General (**OIG**) reported to Congress that there were massive overclaims on the part of the local school districts. On the average, OIG found nearly a $7,000 overclaim for each school reviewed. As a result of this report, Congress has directed USDA to tighten its controls.

In an effort to ensure that the accountability system used in the school districts is meeting the objectives of Congress and in an effort to reduce the cost of the child nutrition program, Congress ruled in 1988 that federal regulations were to be adhered to more strictly. The assessment, improvement, and monitoring system (**AIMS**) review, a state review system required by USDA, was determined inadequate and failed to detect meal count deficiencies and overclaims. The system of audit that resulted is called **AccuClaim,** which is a modification of AIMS. AccuClaim imposes requirements of audit on both the states and the local school districts. Implementation began in late 1988.

Basically the purpose is to improve accuracy and accountability in the counting of school meals served and the claiming of those meals for federal reimbursement.

Under AccuClaim, local school food authorities have the responsibility to

- Perform at least one on-site review of each school every school year, to evaluate the meal counting and claiming procedures
- Compare the number served in each category against the school's eligible population (minus an attendance factor)
- Report at the end of October the number of children approved for free and reduced-price meals

State agencies will be comparing number claimed monthly against number approved and present (using an attendance factor). In addition, the reviews will be performed by the state on those schools claiming a large number of meals served free and reduced. Action will be taken against the school or school district when violations exceed $100, even the first time the violation occurs, whereas in the past the school or school district was given an opportunity to correct violations or errors the first time. (The checklist in Fig. 1-1 will be helpful to the manager concerned with meeting these regulations.)

Compliance Requirements

It is important to emphasize that AccuClaim audits are intended to determine if the school foodservice program is in compliance with federal and state requirements. It is important that the meal count and cash collection systems provide an accurate claim for reimbursement. McMullen (1989) offers criteria for a model meal count system:

- *Guidance, including written detailed instructions on the operation of the meal count system, is developed and provided to all responsible personnel.*
- *All personnel involved in the meal count system are knowledgeable and can adequately perform their duties and responsibilities.*
- *All applications have been approved in accordance with the regulations and in a timely manner.*
- *Category determinations are accurately recorded on the master roster and maintained throughout the year.*
- *Tickets, tokens, I.D.s, etc. and master roster accurately reflect the student's eligibility for free, reduced or, paid meals.*
- *Reimbursable meals are clearly identifiable.*
- *All meals are correctly counted at the point of service and recorded by category.*
- *The cash collection system for reimbursable meals and other sales ensures that appropriate amounts of cash are collected and recorded for each sale category.*
- *A cash reconciliation system is used that: (1) determines on a daily basis whether cash collected reconciles with meal counts as recorded; (2) ensures that all differences are documented; (3) ensures that corrective action is taken where needed.*
- *A system is in place to safeguard cash and tickets, tokens, I.D.s, etc. from loss, theft, or misuse.*
- *Reports of daily meals and cash collected are complete and are compiled for the Claim for Reimbursement.*

- *Edit checks for individual schools are implemented to identify potential problems in the meal count system.*
- *Periodic monitoring and technical assistance are provided for each school to ensure compliance with the approved meal count system.*

If a child is receiving free meals and the auditor determines that the application is not complete or incorrectly acted upon, the school district must return the federal reimbursement for the free meals received the entire school year or for the number of days a meal was served to the date of audit. Under AccuClaim a school district will be required to audit internally. The Appendix provides the text of the regulations relating to auditing.

BIBLIOGRAPHY

Dillmer, Paul R., and Gerald G. Griffin. 1984. *Principles of Food, Beverage, and Labor Costs Controls for Hotels and Restaurants.* 3d ed. New York: Van Nostrand Reinhold.

Donatello, Aaron. 1983. "Pricing for Your Target Market." *Restaurants USA* 3(8): 24-25.

Eshbach, Charles E. 1970. *Foodservice Management.* 3d ed. Boston, Mass.: CBI Books.

Financial Accounting Standards Board. 1980. *Statement of Financial Accounting Concepts No. 3—Elements of Financial Statements of Business Enterprises.* Stamford, Conn.: FASB.

Hess, John P., and Dorothy Van Egmond-Pannell. 1987. "Budgeting for Food Service Operations." *School Business Affairs* 53 (11): 35-37.

Kahrl, William L. 1974. *Foodservice on a Budget.* Boston, Mass.: Cahners Books.

Kasavana, Michael L. 1984. *Computer Systems for Food Service Operations.* New York: CBI Books and Van Nostrand Reinhold.

Kehoe, Ellen. 1986. "Educational Budget Preparation: Fiscal and Political Considerations." In *Principles of School Business Management,* edited by R. Craig Wood. Reston, Va.: Association of School Business Officials International.

McCullen, George. 1989. "AccuClaim Means Better Accountability." *School Food Service Journal* 43(2): 44-45.

Miller, Jack. 1980. *Menu Pricing and Strategy.* New York: Van Nostrand Reinhold.

National Restaurant Association. 1986. *Uniform System of Accounting for Restaurants.* Washington, D.C.: National Restaurant Association.

"National School Lunch Program: Accountability." 1989. *Federal Register* 54(58): 12575-12583.

Ninemeier, Jack D., and Raymond S. Schmidgall. 1984. *Basic Accounting Standards.* The L. J. Minor Foodservice Standards Series, vol. 3. New York: Van Nostrand Reinhold.

South Carolina Department of Education. 1986. *Nutrition Education and Management Training for School Food Service Personnel: Accounting and Reporting.* Columbia, S.C.: South Carolina Department of Education, Office of Food Services.

Southeast Regional U.S. Department of Agriculture. 1988. *The AccuClaim Handbook: Implementing a Model Meal Count System.* Atlanta, Ga.: U.S. Department of Agriculture.

State of New York Department of Education. 1987. *Financial Management: Training for School Food Service Personnel.* Albany, N.Y.: The University of the State of New York and the State Department of Education.

Tidwell, Sam B. 1986. "Educational Accounting Procedures." In *Principles of School Business Management*, edited by R. Craig Wood. Reston, Va.: Association of School Business Officials International.

U.S. Department of Agriculture. 1973. *School Food Service Handbook for Uniform Accounting.* Washington, D.C.: U.S. Government Printing Office.

————. 1975. *Financial Management—Cost-Based Accountability.* Washington, D.C.: U.S. Government Printing Office.

VanEgmond-Pannell, Dorothy, et al. 1987. *The School Foodservice Handbook: A Guide for School Administrators.* Reston, Va.: Association of School Business Officials International.

Warner, Mickey, 1989. "Break-Even Analysis and Profit Volume Charting: Function and Use for Restaurant Managers." Presentation at the National Restaurant Association Convention in Chicago.

3

Systems: Types of Foodservice Operations

FOOD SYSTEMS

According to Webster, a system is "a set or arrangement of things so related or connected as to form a unity or organic whole." The elements that comprise a foodservice system are: purchasing, receiving, storing, issuing, preparing, cooking, serving, and cleaning up.

In a conventional or traditional school foodservice the kitchen that prepares and cooks the food is on site. School foodservice does more raw ingredient cooking than do college and university foodservices, primarily because many of the USDA-donated commodities are in the raw form.

In a multi-unit foodservice operation, the preparation may be done at another school, in a "central kitchen," or at a "commissary."

Minor and Cichy (1984) classify foodservice systems "on the basis of the degree to which the use of processed foods takes place." The four categories of foodservice systems used in this volume are based on where the food is processed:

1. Conventional system: food preparation from raw ingredients on the premises
2. Convenience system: maximum amount of processed foods
3. Ready-food system: food production on the premises, chilled or frozen for later service
4. Central kitchen system (sometimes referred to as a satellite system or commissary system): production in a central location with distribution to schools and other service outlets

CONVENTIONAL FOOD SYSTEM

The conventional food system or on-site production of food is the most prevalent system across the country; however, it is not the most prevalent among intercity school districts and large suburban school districts. Rural school districts usually use the conventional system of preparing and serving food because of geographic location and preference. This may even mean cooking and baking foods using raw ingredients and all reusable dishes. It is the most expensive system; however, if costs are within the desired range and desired quality can be maintained, the conventional food system may be the preferred system for a school or school district.

The advantages of the conventional food system as described are the following:

- The manager can determine the ingredients (e.g., sodium, additives, and preservatives) in the product.
- The system provides more full-time jobs for the community.
- The manager can utilize USDA-donated commodities in the form received.

Disadvantages to the conventional food system are as follows:

- It is less efficient with lower productivity than other systems.
- Labor costs are higher.
- Better-trained employees are required—a good cook and a good baker—for good-quality products to be produced.
- Products may not be of the type or quality today's students prefer.

CONVENIENCE FOOD SYSTEM

As labor costs increase, labor shortages plague the industry, and labor turnover leaves some school districts without skilled labor, the convenience food system becomes an attractive option. Dungan and Lacey (1969) define a convenience food as "a menu item in a preserved state that with objective finishing instructions, allows the serving of the menu item without need for skilled cook or baker to assure customer acceptance of that item." Many school foodservices that consider themselves as users of the conventional system serve a number of convenience items.

Convenience food is usually higher in cost than the sum of the ingredient costs. Labor is "stored" in the product. Therefore it is important when increasing the use of convenience foods that the increase be related to a reduction in labor hours.

The convenience food system may involve assembling sandwiches made with bakery bread, presliced sandwich meats, and cheese; and providing portion "pak" mayonnaise with them. Hamburgers are made from bakery buns and pre-charcoal-broiled hamburger patties that have been reheated. Pizza is premade and portioned and requires heating to melt the cheese. The chicken is prefried and requires heating.

Formal banquets can be served with this system. Many specialty restaurants have considerable numbers of convenience items on their menus, such as spinach souffle, pepper steak with gravy, and chicken Napoleon.

Convenience food systems need a lot of storage space (mostly in the freezer), an assembly area, an oven for heating, and space for serving (preferably a serving line). The advantages are (1) more consistent quality, (2) in many instances better quality, (3) lower labor costs, (4) reduced need for skilled employees or training, and (5) increased productivity.

Convenience foods can be purchased in two basic sizes: single serving and bulk quantity. With the aseptic or "tetra brik" packaging process, which is just catching on in this country, it is possible to have more shelf-stable products. Ocean Spray Cranberries was one of the first companies to use aseptic packaging in this country. The system was first designed and used in Sweden in 1961.

READY-FOOD SYSTEM

With the ready-food system, foods are produced on the premise and packaged for later use, either in a chilled state or frozen. Cook-freeze and cook-chill systems are two ready-food systems used frequently in hospital foodservice; they are catching on in schools. Preparing ahead is a way to "store" labor in a single unit foodservice. Within the single unit, the cook or baker prepares ahead and/or for serving more than once. For example, vegetable soup can be prepared for serving 25 to 30 days ahead or for serving on several different days during that time.

Cook-Chill System

The cook-chill system is a time-tested and USDA-approved approach to food production on site or for transporting to other sites. In this system, food products are cooked in a kettle, then pumped (if quantities are large) or poured into flexible casings or special polyethylene bags while still hot (180°F). The bags are closed, then chilled in an ice water bath or tumble chiller to drop the product temperature from 180°F to 38°F in 30 to 60 minutes. The time required will depend on the food product's viscosity. The USDA requires that the temperature be reduced within 2 hours. This type product has a safe refrigerated shelf-life of up to 45 days.

Groen, a Dover Industries Company, has been a leader in the cook-chill field with its CapKold System. Public schools in Portland, Oregon, Norfolk, Virginia, and Los Angeles, California, as well as Kodak headquarters in Rochester, New York, offer good examples of properly equipped cook-chill systems. Some key pieces of equipment needed in the kitchen are listed below (Humes 1988).

1. Steam kettle: size ranges from 75 to 400 gallons, but most commonly used is 100 gallon size; typical cost is $42,000.*
2. Pumping station: fills 6-9 bags of food per minute; pumps directly from kettle; typical cost is $45,000.*
3. Tumble chiller: holds from 75 to 150 gallons of product; recommended with ice builder; typical cost is $56,000.*
4. Ice builder: makes from 5,000 to 30,000 pounds; can run at night for lower rates; typical cost is $16,000.*

A computer system is desirable for tracking food from purchasing to inventory and doing cost accounting. Kodak's foodservices using CBORD's computer software program (CBORD, Inc., Ithaca, NY) to produce an internal requisition system charges the kitchens receiving the food from this inventory.

---

*Note: prices were quoted in 1988.

A 30,000-square-foot space will house sufficient equipment to process food for 100,000 meals a day. The storage facilities will require as much space or more.

Some of the advantages of this system are the following:

- Flexibility in timing of preparation: allows preparation in down-time periods and planning of workload.
- Cost-effectiveness: provides more efficient use of employees' time and equipment (usually can reduce labor hours by 20 percent) and can reduce food costs since only what is needed has to be heated for use.
- Quality of food: captures food at its peak and maintains food quality better than holding food for long periods at hot temperatures.
- Food safety: ensures that food is safe if prepared and handled correctly.
- Nutritional value: maintains the nutritional value of the food for a longer period of time for more nutrients (when the product is transported chilled versus hot).
- Less pressure: by preparing ahead, reduces stress level in the kitchen.
- Ease in preparation for use: allows food to be reheated rather quickly because of the density of the product.
- More variety possible: enables a small staff to offer variety and choices daily.
- Efficiency of transport: allows food to be transported the day before or whenever is best for the school. The weight of the transported product is manageable.

Some disadvantages of this system are listed below.

- Specialized equipment: requires special equipment for doing the job properly.
- Specialized training: requires that employees be well trained.
- Refrigeration: In addition to an ice source or tumble chiller, increased refrigeration is usually needed.

Food is reheated in the storage bags in steam kettles in water, in compartment steamers, on top of the range, or in the oven. Items like macaroni and cheese can be prepared together or separately, then combined in steamtable pans on the day of service. Cheese topping can be added and the product heated in the oven.

CENTRAL PRODUCTION OR SATELLITE FOOD SYSTEM

In the early 1970s when expansion of the school breakfast and lunch programs was at its peak, central kitchens and commissaries became necessary to meet the needs of some school districts. A *central kitchen* or *commissary* is defined as any kitchen where preparation of food is done for serving in several other locations. The schools receiving the food prepared at the central kitchen are referred at as *satellites, receiving kitchens, or finishing kitchens.*

The multi-unit commercial foodservice industry, where profit on the bottom line is of great importance, switched from the true conventional system to a type of centralized production in the 1970s. The cost of labor, labor shortages, and high employee turnover will make the conventional system even less attractive and centralized preparation of some type more attractive in the 1990s.

A central kitchen may be preparing and portioning food into individual meals for service (these meals may be hot, ready to serve, or require heating), or preparing the food in bulk for serving on location. Both individual meals and bulk food may be transported hot or cold.

Points to be considered in locating a central kitchen are (1) the length of haul to receiving schools, (2) breakdown problems relating to plant and vehicles, (3) expansion needs, and (4) accessibility to primary traffic routes for deliveries.

Some existing high school kitchens serve as central kitchens. Using the large kitchen of a senior high has worked particularly well for small school districts (serving 4,000 or fewer children), when the satellite schools, usually elementary schools, are within a short distance. Columbia City, Maryland, built its schools with this plan in mind and has realized significant capital outlay savings. The kitchen in Yorktown Senior High in Arlington, Virginia, was turned into a preparation kitchen or central kitchen for 11 elementary schools.

In the 1990s, when employee productivity and labor shortages will be of increasing importance, the central kitchen will be a solution for many school districts. Productivity can be increased by five to eight times the conventional system production rate. On average an on-site production system will produce between 10 and 18 meals per labor hour. The central facility in the Dayton (Ohio) School District produces 100 to 110 meals per labor hour. Based on an hourly wage of $9.00 (including fringe benefits), the on-site kitchen's labor could be costing as much as 80 cents a lunch compared to 8 cents per meal when produced in a central facility.

There are other advantages to the central kitchen facility. A reduction in cost of food and supplies can be achieved, better controls can be put into place and maintained, and more standardization of quality can be maintained in the school district.

When and Why the Satellite System is Used

On-site production kitchens are often converted to receiving kitchens and a satellite system when 300 or fewer meals are served at one location. When building a new school, constructing a finishing kitchen rather than a traditional on-site preparation kitchen will save $50,000 plus in equipment and reduce space needs by 35 percent. The savings in producing a lunch will depend on the method of transporting food and the efficiency of the operation. Other reasons for using this system include the following:

- Facilities and/or equipment are not adequate to continue to produce food at every site.
- Costs of labor consume more than 50 percent of the income (or revenue).
- Labor shortages and heavy turnover are problems.
- Better quality and quantity controls are desired.

Method of Transporting Food

Transporting in Bulk

Transporting food in bulk is one of the oldest and most widely used methods for moving prepared food from the point of preparation to the point of serving. The oldest means is by insulated containers — heated food carriers and cold food carriers — to the receiving school where the food is ready to portion and serve. In recent years the cook-chill method of transporting food in bulk (see above) has become very popular in schools as well as hospitals. Both methods allow for service at the receiving kitchen resembling on-site preparation. Frequently the students and parents are not aware that the food was not prepared in their own school's kitchen.

The bulk method may be chosen over a preplated method by a school district for the following reasons:

- Kitchen facilities are available at the receiving school.
- Staff is available for serving.
- The school district wants as little change as possible in the foodservice provided.
- The method can reduce some costs.
- Less equipment is needed than for an on-site production kitchen.

Transporting in Hot and Cold Carriers (Inflight Food)

During transportation, cooked, ready-to-serve food is maintained at serving temperature. It is usually transported within two to three hours following preparation. Timing is important to maintaining a good-quality product at the proper temperature.

Well-insulated and electrically heated food carriers are necessary for bulk transporting of hot foods. Carriers are available that will hold, for example, five 12- × 20- × 2½-inch pans and three 12- × 20- × 4-inch pans. Utility carriers, used with eutectic plates for keeping food cold, are available that hold 12- × 20-inch and 18- × 26-inch pans. The carriers can be obtained with wheels or fitted with dollies for ease in handling. Food is generally transported in the steamtable pans or sheet pans from which the food can be served.

At the receiving school, students may be served from a serving line, cafeteria-style, picking up their tray, milk, silverware, and napkin. This method requires little labor and equipment at the receiving school.

Since the proper temperature is crucial to the safety of the food as well as its quality and taste, there is not a lot of flexibility in the time between production and transporting to serving. Before food is sent to the satellite schools, the temperature and quantity of each item should be recorded, and the managers at the satellite schools will need to record the temperature upon arrival and confirm that the quantities sent are correct. A sample record for use with the bulk system is shown in Figure 3-1.

The bulk system offers the advantage of maintaining a personal atmosphere in the serving of food, characteristic of on-site preparing and serving. Also, portions can be adjusted to the student's size and **offer versus serve** can be carried out very easily.

Preplated Meals

Preplated meals may be ready to eat or need reheating. There are several versions of the preplated hot and/or cold meals. Several of the methods used by school districts are described below.

Preplated Meals—Ready to Eat

In the preplated ready-to-eat method, hot and cold foods are delivered ready to serve, without reheating. A Styrofoam or aluminum tray may be used. Food will stay hot for up to

SCHOOL _____ DATE _____

TEACHER A LA CARTE   FOOD ITEM

Name

_____	_____	MEAL COUNT TELEPHONED IN BY
_____	_____	RECEIVING SCHOOL:
_____	_____	Student Lunch
_____	_____	Hot Lunches: _____
_____	_____	Salad Lunches: _____
_____	_____	Super Sack Lunches: _____
_____	_____	Adult Lunch
_____	_____	Hot Lunches: _____
_____	_____	Salad Lunches: _____
_____	_____	Super Sack Lunches: _____
_____	_____	A la Carte _____
		TOTAL: _____

Components of Meal	Serving Size	PRODUCTION KITCHEN Completes Columns 1 and 2		RECEIVING KITCHEN Completes Columns 3, 4, and 5		
		Column 1 No. of Servings Transported	Column 2 Departing Temp.	Column 3 Receiving Temp.	Column 4 No. Served	Column 5 No. of Servings Left Over
Entree:						
Vegetables/ fruit						
Bread or Rolls:						
Dessert:						
Other:						
		Initial _____		Initial _____		

Complete 2 copies: Return 1 copy to the production kitchen at the end of the day and retain 1 copy in the receiving kitchen.

FIGURE 3-1. Sample satellite school record for use with bulk transporting system.

three hours in these trays, when kept in insulated tote boxes; however, it is recommended that food be served within two hours. Some foods do not transport well (e.g., French fries) and menu mixes have to be carefully planned.

Service can go rather fast and will require few or no employees at the receiving school. The biggest complaints are that the heat is not held and the menu is limited.

Good communications between the preparation kitchen and the receiving school are always essential in any type of satellite system in order to avoid waste.

Preplated Meals—to Be Reheated

Preplated meals usually have a cold tray and a hot tray. These may be produced by the school district in a central kitchen or at a large production kitchen, or they may be purchased prepared. The hot tray may be in the frozen or chilled state and require reheating, whereas the cold tray is ready to serve and needs to be kept cold if containing any perishable foods.

The receiving school will need refrigeration and an oven. This system uses all disposable service and eliminates the need for a dishwasher machine. It has the following advantages over the on-site production kitchen:

- Schools with limited kitchen facilities can serve hot lunches.
- Less space and equipment are required.
- The system cuts operating costs, increases productivity, and uses less labor.
- Faster service can be provided.

Cold-Pack Lunch System

The brown bag lunch is the most common example of the cold-pack method. When this method is used to provide lunches to students, the sanitation aspects will limit what can go into the lunch, how long it can be held, and at what temperature it must be held.

Introducing any one of these systems, other than conventional on-site preparation, will require good communications. Any time a new system for providing food is started in a school—particularly when it is replacing on-site preparation—the school administration, parents, and students have to be receptive for it to work well. Not all of the systems described in this chapter will work for all situations. Each fits a different need.

BIBLIOGRAPHY

American School Food Service Association. 1984. "The Curtain Goes Up." *School Food Service* 38(5): 142-51.

Dungan, A., and S. Lacey. 1969. *Cornell Hotel and Restaurant Quarterly* 10(6): 50.

Durocher, Joseph. 1988. "Cook/Chill System." *Restaurant Business* 87(9): 180, 182.

Fairfax County Public Schools. 1989. *Food Service Manual.* Fairfax, Va.: Fairfax County Public Schools.

Hitchcock, M. J. 1980. *Foodservice Systems Administration.* New York: Macmillan Publishing Co.

Humes, Stephen J. 1988. "Figuring the Payback on Cook-Chill." *Foodservice Director* 1(12): 31.

King, Paul. 1988a. "Changing with the Times." *Food Management* 24(10): 63, 66.

———. 1988b. "Cook/Freeze Succeeds in Hawaii." *Food Management* 24(9): 55-56.

Khan, Mahmood A. 1987. *Foodservice Operations.* New York: Van Nostrand Reinhold.

Livingston, G. E., and Charlotte M. Chang, eds. 1979. *Food Service System: Analysis, Design, and Implementation.* New York: Academic Press.

Minor, Lewis J., and Ronald F. Cichy. 1984. *Foodservice Systems Management.* New York: Van Nostrand Reinhold.

Thorner, Marvin Edward. 1973. *Convenience and Fast Food Handbook.* New York: Van Nostrand Reinhold.

Winslow, Edward. 1988. "Has Cook/Chill's Time Come?" *Food Management* 24(9): 64.

4

Planning Menus and Food Offerings

TRENDS AND HEALTH CONCERNS

From all indications there will be a lot of emphasis on nutrition and content of food during the 1990s. Student customers (or their parents) will be better informed and will be more interested in what they are eating than in previous years. "Truth in menu" will become more important than ever.

During the 1970s and more so during the 1980s, school foodservice had a reputation (not necessarily deserved) for being loaded with saturated fat and sodium. The USDA-donated commodities, consisting mainly of unlimited quantities of butter, ground pork, and cheese, encouraged the image.

The pendulum has swung since the 1960s and early 1970s, when two teaspoons of butter and whole milk were requirements of the meal pattern, to the late 1970s and most of the 1980s, when lowfat milk was a required offering.

In 1985 Congress listened to the milk lobbyists and passed legislation that *required* schools to offer whole milk again, as a beverage. Those concerned about good nutrition were shocked by the passage of this legislation. Much progress had been made by school foodservice toward influencing students to drink lowfat milk as a result of the 1979 regulation requiring that lowfat, unflavored milk be offered as a beverage with lunch. Excess butterfat was becoming a problem for the dairy industry; therefore the whole milk requirement became law.

Dietary Guidelines for Americans, published by the Department of Health and Human Services and USDA in 1980, recommends increasing starch and fiber in the diet and avoiding too much fat, sodium, sugar, and alcohol. According to the USDA, the reason that these guidelines were directional rather than quantitative was that there is insufficient scientific data to support specific target levels of fat and sodium for children. The Recommended Dietary Allowances (**RDAs**) even state calories in a range. As an example, a school-age child's energy needs may range from 1,300 to 3,900 calories per day.

FACTORS TO BE CONSIDERED IN PLANNING MENUS

The menu is the single most controlling factor in any foodservice operation, especially the lunch menu in school foodservice. It would be ideal if the kitchen layout were planned

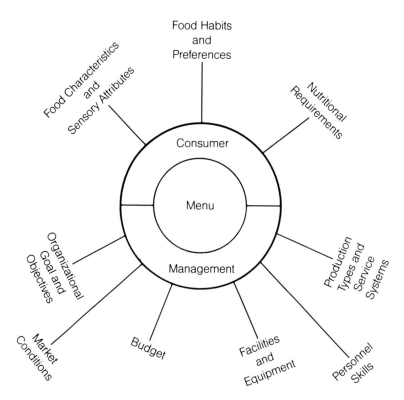

FIGURE 4-1. Factors to be considered in menu planning for a foodservice operation. (*Source:* Khan 1987.)

around the menus and the equipment purchased for the menus to be prepared; however, this is seldom the case. Certainly menus should be planned before food is purchased, the labor needs are determined, and the price of the meal to the customer is decided. Planning menus requires a great deal of knowledge about the operation.

The basic considerations are summarized by Khan (1987) and shown in Figure 4-1. When planning menus, the following factors should be considered: nutrition and federal regulations, particularly the school lunch and breakfast patterns; food habits and preferences; whether choices will be offered; the amount of money available; facilities and equipment in the kitchen; the number of employees and their skills; the type of service; food supply (including USDA-donated commodities); school district objectives and goals; and food characteristics and aesthetics. These topics are discussed below, primarily as they relate to breakfast and lunch menu planning.

NUTRITION AND FEDERAL REGULATIONS

The goal of the National School Lunch Program's meal pattern is to meet the nutritional needs of its customers. Nearly one-half of the students who eat lunch at school qualify for free or reduced-price meals, and for many of those students the lunch at school may be the only nutritious food they eat in a day. The Physician Task Force on Hunger in America

(1985) reported that domestic hunger is "the most serious threat to the health of the nation; it is a public epidemic that affects some 20 million Americans."

On the basis of nutrient intake data, students who participate in the school lunch program have superior meals to those not participating. Congressional studies show that the school lunch program does this more efficiently than providing additional cash benefits to the families.

With the increased interest in nutrition, this aspect of menu planning is expected to receive more emphasis by the customer in the coming years. The basic guidelines used by school foodservice menu planners are the school lunch meal patterns or, in a few cases, the nutrient standards. Since increased emphasis is being placed on lowering cholesterol and decreasing sugar and sodium in the diet, foods rich in these are discussed below.

The National School Lunch Meal Patterns

The National School Lunch Meal Patterns were developed and implemented in 1980, as a part of the guidelines of the National School Lunch Act, replacing the "Type A" lunch pattern. The lunch meal patterns have been revised three or four times since then (see Fig. 4-2). In order for a school district to claim meals for reimbursement, the school foodservice must carry out the school lunch meal pattern requirements. Like the five food groups, the school lunch meal patterns provide a simplified way of planning nutritionally adequate meals.

The school lunch meal patterns state minimum portion sizes for the four age groups: group I—ages 1-2; group II—ages 3-4; group III—grades K-3, ages 5-8; and group IV—grades 4-12, age 9 and over. For group V, *recommended* (not required) quantities are given for grades 7-12 students (age 12 and over). Group IV quantities will meet the requirement for all age groups. Group IV will provide approximately one-third of the daily RDAs for all nutrients for a student between the ages of 10 and 12 years. The school lunch meal patterns encourage varying the portion size according to the different needs of children.

Some schools plan their menus based on nutrient standards and the nutritive content of foods. Unless a school district has the state department of education's approval to use nutrient standards, the school lunch meal pattern guidelines must be met also.

The following features of the school lunch meal patterns and the accompanying regulations should be noted:

- Minimum quantities of the four lunch components (five foods) are stated for four age/grade groups.
- Preschoolers can be served in two sittings.
- If the choice is made to serve the larger portions of group V, smaller portions should be made available for those who prefer less; however, minimum quantities for that age/grade must be offered.
- All age groups must be offered all four components (five foods, at the minimum quantity specified) in order to meet the meal requirements.
- **Offer versus serve*** is required in high schools but may be extended to other age groups as a local option.

---

*Students are offered a complete meal but they may choose to select only three or four of the five items offered.

U.S. Department of Agriculture, National School Lunch Program

USDA recommends, but does not require, that portions be adjusted by age/grade group to better meet the food and nutritional needs of children according to their ages. If portions are adjusted, Groups I-IV portions are minimum requirements for the age/grade groups specified. If portions are not adjusted, the Group IV portions are the portions to serve all children.

Food Components	Food Items	Minimum Quantities				Recommended Quantities	Specific Requirements
		Preschool		Grades K-3	Grades 4-12	Grades 7-12	
		ages 1-2 (Group I)	ages 3-4 (Group II)	ages 5-8 (Group III)	age 9 and over (Group IV)	age 12 and over (Group V)	
MEAT OR MEAT ALTERNATE (quantity of the edible portion as served)	**A serving of one of the following or a combination to give an equivalent quantity:**						• Must be served in the main dish or the main dish and only one other menu item.
	Lean meat, poultry, or fish	1 oz	1½ oz	1½ oz	2 oz	3 oz	• Vegetable protein products, cheese alternate products, and enriched macaroni with fortified protein may be used to meet part of the meat or meat alternate requirement. Food and Nutrition Service fact sheets on each of these alternate foods give detailed instructions for use.
	Cheese	1 oz	1½ oz	1½ oz	2 oz	3 oz	
	Large egg(s)	½	¾	¾	1	1½	
	Cooked dry beans or peas	¼ cup	3/8 cup	3/8 cup	½ cup	¾ cup	
	Peanut butter or other nut or seed butters	2 Tbsp	3 Tbsp	3 Tbsp	4 Tbsp	6 Tbsp	
	Peanuts, soy nuts, tree nuts, or seeds, as listed in program guidance, meet no more than 50% of the requirement and must be combined in the meal with at least 50% of other meat or meat alternates. (1 oz of nuts/seeds = 1 oz of cooked lean meat, poultry, or fish.)	½ oz = 50%	¾ oz = 50%	¾ oz = 50%	1 oz = 50%	1½ oz = 50%	
VEGETABLE OR FRUIT	2 or more servings of vegetables or fruits or both to total	½ cup	½ cup	½ cup	¾ cup	¾ cup	• No more than one-half of the total requirement may be met with full-strength fruit or vegetable juice. • Cooked dry beans or peas may be used as a meat alternate or as a vegetable, but not as both in the same meal.
BREAD OR BREAD ALTERNATE	Servings of bread or bread alternate	5 per week	8 per week	8 per week	8 per week	10 per week	• Enriched macaroni with fortified protein may be used as a meat alternate or as a bread alternate, but not as both in the same meal. NOTE: *Food Buying Guide for Child Nutrition Programs, Program Aid No. 1331* (1984), provides the information for the minimum weight of a serving.
	Must be enriched or whole-grain.	minimum of ½ serving per day	minimum of 1 serving per day	minimum of 1 serving per day	minimum of 1 serving per day	minimum of 1 serving per day	
	A serving is a slice of bread or an equivalent serving of biscuits, rolls, etc., or ½ cup cooked rice, macaroni, noodles, other pasta products or cereal grains, or a combination of any of the above.						
MILK (as a beverage)	Fluid whole milk and fluid unflavored lowfat milk, skim milk, or buttermilk must be offered.	¾ cup (6 fl oz)	¾ cup (6 fl oz)	½ pint (8 fl oz)	½ pint (8 fl oz)	½ pint (8 fl oz)	

FIGURE 4-2. School lunch patterns. (*Source:* USDA 1987.)

- The bread alternates include enriched or whole-grain rice, macaroni, noodles, and other pasta.
- The bread requirement is for a minimum of one serving a day and a total of eight servings per week. The weight and portion sizes become important to meeting the bread and bread alternate requirement.
- Nuts and seeds can be used to meet 50 percent of the meat and meat alternate requirement.
- The milk requirement states that flavored milk may be offered as a choice but a student must be offered the choice of whole milk and an unflavored lowfat milk (skim milk, buttermilk, or lowfat milk).
- Choices from a variety of foods should be offered children to meet their needs better, appeal to their likes, and introduce them to new foods.
- Fruit and vegetable juices will meet no more than one-half of the fruit and vegetable requirement.
- The fruit and vegetable requirement must be met with at least two sources.
- It is recommended that iron-rich foods be offered frequently, as well as foods high in vitamins A and C.
- It is recommended that the quantity of fat, salt, and sugar be controlled.

There are many points to consider when using the school lunch meal pattern in planning menus. The goals are to ensure that the nutritional needs of the children are met within the guidelines set and that students will eat the food offered.

Protein-rich foods are expensive and may consume one-third or more of the food dollar. For economy reasons, a combination of meat, poultry, or fish and one of the less expensive meat alternates such as eggs, dry beans or peas, or peanut butter may be used in meeting these nutritional needs. The use of soy protein to meet a part of the protein requirement is a practical solution to rising food costs. Soy protein can be used to meet up to 30 percent of the meat and meat alternate component. The economy of this is discussed in chapter 10.

When using the school lunch meal patterns for compliance with the National School Lunch Act, the menu planner needs two guides: *Food Buying Guide for Child Nutrition Programs* (U.S. Department of Agriculture 1984), which provides the yields of food by purchased units; and *Menu Planning Guide for Child Nutrition Programs* (U.S. Department of Agriculture 1983a). The *Menu Planning Guide* provides good instructions for carrying out the lunch patterns and for good menu planning.

School Breakfast Patterns

The federal breakfast program requires that a breakfast contain the following as a minimum:

½ pint of fluid milk (as a beverage or on cereal or both)
½ cup of fruit or vegetable or fruit juice or vegetable juice
2 servings of bread or bread alternate *or* 2 servings of meat or meat alternate *or* 1 serving of bread or bread alternate and 1 serving of meat or meat alternate.

Studies of the breakfast program had shown that the breakfast pattern needs more protein and iron-rich foods than had been specified. Congress increased the reimbursement for the breakfast program by 3 cents in 1989 for the purpose of increasing the protein and iron-rich foods. The breakfast pattern was revised in 1989.

SPECIAL NUTRITIONAL CONCERNS

Present awareness about food safety and the potential link between diet and disease have made it more important than ever that the menu planner consider these concerns. Although the controversy over restricting fats and sodium during the growing years has not been settled, it is good business for the menu planner to develop menus that provide a moderate or controlled amount of these nutrients.

In an effort to encourage manufacturers to reduce saturated fat and sodium levels in foods, the American Heart Association awards a seal of approval. This seal is on processed food products that meet the nutritional criteria outlined in its *Nutrition and Your Health: Dietary Guidelines for Americans.*

Another health concern is obesity. In addition to fighting heart problems, scientists at the National Institutes of Health have declared obesity to be a killing disease in America (IFMA 1985).

According to the Department of Agriculture, there have been significant changes in Americans' food habits over the last 10 years. There has been an increase in consumption of leaner types of foods, such as fish and poultry. People have responded to the information on diet and disease, as can be seen by changes per capita consumption of certain foods (USDA 1987).

- Lowfat milk increased from 6.4 pounds per year to 77.8 pounds.
- Whole milk decreased from 251.7 pounds per year to 132.9 pounds.
- Yogurt increased from 0.3 pounds per year to 3.2 pounds.
- Butter decreased from 6.9 pounds per year to 5.1 pounds.
- Fresh broccoli increased from 0.4 pounds per year to 1.9 pounds.
- Eggs decreased from 40.3 pounds per year to 33.1 pounds.
- Chicken increased from 30.7 pounds per year to 53.9 pounds.
- Sugar decreased from 97.3 pounds per year to 71 pounds.

The National Restaurant Association (1984) noted a drop in the sale of beef by 36.8 percent and an increase in main-dish salads by 90.8 percent. However, an American School Food Service Association survey (1987) did not show the same trend in school-planned menus. Beef was being served one to two times per week in 49.4 percent of the schools, whereas chicken was being served one to two times per week in 22.7 percent of the schools (Table 4-1). These figures may reflect the fact that beef was a plentiful USDA-donated commodity that year and chicken was not.

The primary special nutritional concerns currently affecting school foodservices are fats and sodium, discussed below.

Fats

The American Academy of Pediatrics is advising doctors for the first time to test for blood cholesterol among children with family histories of premature heart attacks or high

Table 4-1.   Most Frequently Served School Foods

Item	Percent Serving 1-2 Times/Week
Meat	
Beef	49.4
Chicken	22.7
Produce/fresh	
Carrots	34.8
Tomatoes	32.8
Celery	29.5
Lettuce	28.7
Cabbage	24.4
Produce/cooked	
Beans (not dried)	46.6
Corn	45.3
Potatoes (French fried)	44.5
Potatoes (boiled, baked, mashed)	36.7
Tomatoes	23.7
Fruits	
Applesauce	48.9
Peaches	47.9
Mixed fruit	40.5
Pears	37.4
Oranges	34.4
Apples	33.1
Pineapple	27.0
Bananas	20.1
Grains	
Pasta	31.0
Dry Cereal	21.1

Source: American School Food Service Association 1987.

cholesterol levels. Public health officials are considering 140 to 150 milligrams the desirable level for children. The American Academy of Pediatrics recommends that children get no more than 40 percent of their total calories from fat. However, if total fat intake drops below 30 percent of needed calories, children may not be consuming enough calories to sustain normal growth.

Calculating fat calories, using 1,800 calories as the total daily intake, is done as follows:

Step 1. 35% of 1,800 (1,800 × .35) = 630 calories from fat
Step 2. Every gram of fat provides 9 calories. Divide 630 calories by 9 to determine how many grams of fat.

$$\frac{630}{9} = 70 \text{ grams of fat}$$

Step 3. Divide the grams for fat over the day—an average of 10-20 grams at breakfast, 25-30 for lunch, and 25-30 grams for dinner.
Step 4. Calculate the caloric content of the food and the fat content, and pay special attention to those fats with high cholesterol content.

Much of the controversy centers around the four different types of fat, which are described below. Sources of each of the fats, shown in Tables 4-2 and 4-3, may be useful to the menu planner.

1. *Saturated* fat tends to increase blood cholesterol levels. It comes from animal fats and palm and coconut oils. It is recommended that the menu calories be limited to 10 percent from saturated fats. Most American food processors have removed tropical oils from their products.

2. *Polyunsaturated* fat lowers blood cholesterol. It comes from vegetables such as corn, safflower, and sesame seeds, and from fish.

3. *Hydrogenated* fat is processed to convert oil to saturated fat.

4. *Monounsaturated* fat lowers blood cholesterol. It comes from olive and peanut oil.

Cholesterol, which is found only in animal foods, elevates blood cholesterol when consumed in excessive amounts.

Table 4-2.   Percentage of Polyunsaturated and Saturated Fats in Foods

Type of Oil or Fat	% Polyunsaturated Fat	% Saturated Fat
Safflower oil	74	9
Sunflower oil	64	10
Corn oil	58	13
Mayonnaise-type salad dressing	53	14
Italian dressing	58	14
Thousand Island dressing	55	16
Blue cheese dressing	54	19
Soybean oil	40	13
Margarine		
soft (tub)	42	16
hard (stick)	32	18
Peanut oil	30	19
Vegetable shortening	20	32
Lard	12	40
Olive oil	9	14
Beef fat	4	48
Butter	4	61
Palm oil	2	81
Coconut oil	2	86

Sources: Facts about Blood Cholesterol, U.S. Department of Health and Human Services, Public Health Service, National Institutes of Health Publication no. 85-2696 and *Eating the Moderate Fat and Cholesterol,* The American Heart Association (1988).

Table 4-3.   Quantity of Cholesterol Found in Foods

Food	Cholesterol (mg)
Fruits, grains, vegetables	0
Oysters (cooked, about 3½ ounces)	45
Scallops (cooked, about 3½ ounces)	53
Clams (cooked, about 3½ ounces)	65
Fish, lean (cooked, about 3½ ounces)	65
Chicken and turkey, light meat (skinned and cooked, about 3½ ounces)	80
Lobster (cooked, about 3½ ounces)	85
Beef, lean (cooked, about 3½ ounces)	90
Chicken and turkey, dark meat (skinned and cooked, about 3½ ounces)	95
Crab (cooked, about 3½ ounces)	100
Shrimp (cooked, about 3½ ounces)	150
Egg yolk, one	270
Beef liver (cooked, about 3½ ounces)	440
Beef kidney (cooked, about 3½ ounces)	700

Source: Facts About Blood Cholesterol, U.S. Department of Health and Human Services, Public Health Service, National Institutes of Health Publication no. 85-2696.

Sodium

Sodium is a fundamental nutrient, but because of the attention it has gotten, some think that it is bad. Much is being learned about the medical effects of a high-sodium diet, and the school meals should give the student the option of a diet with a moderate amount of sodium or whatever amount is considered safe for the student. As with fat, the RDAs do not specify exact quantities for sodium. It is known that some groups of people suffer from sodium deficiencies, while others are oversensitive to excess quantities. Foods high in sodium include cured and smoked foods; cold cuts, hot dogs, and sausages; canned vegetables and vegetable juices; canned and dehydrated soups and broths; canned meat and fish; pickled foods; and salted crackers, snacks, and nuts.

Dealing with Current Nutritional Concerns

During the 1990s it will be important that school foodservices create in the minds of customers and parents a reputation for serving good, high-quality, safe, nutritious food. Some of the ways that this positive image can be obtained are through expert menu planning, efficient and proper preparation practices, and effective advertising of what has been done. Some very basic practices should be changed:

• Discontinue the use of fatback pork meat and lard in the preparation of breads and pie crust and in seasoning vegetables. Avoid purchasing prepared foods such as pie crust and bakery products that have lard and tropical oils as ingredients.

- Cut down on hidden calories supplied by large quantities of butter as well as sugar and other sweeteners.
- Discontinue the use of high-sodium soups and mixes (such as salad dressings and gravies); pressure the food industry to provide products with acceptable levels of sodium by organizing school foodservices as an industry.
- Avoid salt-cured foods.
- Use more fresh fruits and vegetables; when using canned fruits, specify those packed in natural juices or light syrup.
- Request nutritional analysis from a reputable laboratory on processed foods such as mixes, pizza, burritos, and cookies. Know what is in the food served.

Allergies

Food allergies are either being diagnosed earlier or there is an increase in the number of school-age children with food allergies today in comparison to the 1970s. The most common allergy that school-age children have is to milk. Other common allergies to natural foods are soy, wheat, and peanut allergies.

In order for a breakfast or a lunch, under the National School Lunch Program, to qualify for federal reimbursement, the meals must meet the meal pattern requirements, or the foodservice manager must have a statement on file from a medical authority stating what the child is allergic to. A stated acceptable replacement is also helpful. This is because when the school foodservice is audited or reviewed by federal or state personnel, the foodservice manager will need to support substitutions being made with such statements for each child.

In addition to allergies to natural food products, many people are allergic to the chemicals in the preservatives, additives, artificial colorings, and artificial flavorings put into food. Also, a number of pesticides cause reactions. Monosodium glutamate (MSG) is a chemical that people are commonly allergic to. MSG is used to accentuate the flavor, and it may cause the so-called "Chinese restaurant syndrome," whose symptoms are dizziness, headache, facial pressure, and a burning sensation on the back and the neck.

A menu planner cannot find any food to which some person is not allergic, except for perhaps refined sugar. Thus a manager may be asked by parents for a list of menu items that contain certain ingredients. Ingredient lists on all food products may be required by the foodservice director from manufacturers and processors in bid specifications. This information may be needed to assist the allergic child in identifying foods he or she cannot eat.

FOOD PREFERENCES

The food habits and beliefs of different religious groups, the cultural differences of the students, and the fads of the time need to be considered by menu planners. By 1995 minorities are projected to make up more than 50 percent of the students participating in the school lunch program in most major cities. If there is a large Asian or Mexican population, the food likes and dislikes of the cultures will need to be considered. If there is a large Jewish population in the community, it will be important to consider whether the product purchased was prepared under Kosher standards. Though a public school caters to all, it is a good menu-planning practice (and good business) to consider the population it hopes to serve.

Student preferences play an important part in satisfaction with the foodservice. Food preferences can be defined as the food selected when options are made available. Figure 4-3 shows the factors that influence a student's food preferences. Those factors include (1) intrinsic characteristics—color, texture, flavor, quality, and the method of preparation; (2) extrinsic characteristics—the environment, expectations (for example, a banquet is expected to be good); (3) biological, physiological, and psychological—age, sex, appreciation, perception, and appetite; (4) personal—familiarity, expectation, importance, influence of peers, mood, and emotion; (5) socioeconomic—acceptance, prestige, and conformity; and (6) cultural and religious—including religious restrictions (for example, Muslims

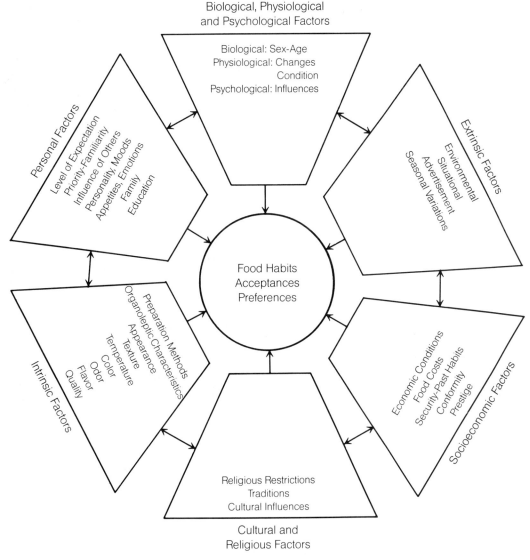

FIGURE 4-3. Factors affecting food habits, acceptance, and preferences. (*Source:* Khan 1987.)

and Jews restrict pork and pork products). Khan (1987) provides an excellent discussion of each of these factors.

TYPES OF SERVICE

Cafeteria Style

Cafeteria style service is by far the most common, and at one time may have been the only type used. Generally the employees serve the food onto plates or trays as the students move in front of the serving area. For many years in most school districts there was a set menu for the day. Before "offer versus serve" became a law in 1978, all parts of the menu for the day were served onto the plate, even if the student was protesting "I don't want any of that."

Today there are a number of innovative ways of carrying out the cafeteria style of service. Scramble cafeteria-style service uses several separate stations, serving different items. Students go from one station to another making their selections and exit by the cashier. This style has varying degrees of success. In fact, it can appear to an observer to be an unorganized approach.

Self-service was new in the last half of the 1980s, but it has gained popularity, particularly in southeastern states such as North Carolina and Tennessee. In these arrangements, students are served buffet style from a cafeteria line. Even elementary school children handle this style beautifully in the schools where administration and teachers are involved in the program.

Self-service will continue to be a popular trend. It is popular in part because of the labor shortage. The other advantage to students serving themselves is that when they are a part of the decision-making process, they do not blame the foodservice worker for the selection they make. It also allows preportioning of foods.

Self-Service Bars

Self-service bars became popular in the early 1980s as a result of the customer's desire to make selections, and it was to the foodservice industry's advantage because of high labor costs and the beginning of a labor shortage. Self-service bars caught on and have flourished in school foodservices with students at all age levels. The types of bars and the percentage of school districts providing bars (American School Food Service Association 1987) are:

Type of Bar	Percent
Salad	75.3
Snack	46.6
Dessert	45.8
Sandwich	40.0
Breakfast	31.4
Baked potato	30.8
Taco/ethnic	30.4

Bars may be planned to meet the school lunch meal pattern if "offer versus serve" is carried out. In order for a salad bar to qualify for meal reimbursement, all the components of a lunch must be offered and the student must take at least three of the food items.

Several types of specialty salad bars have been successfully used by school foodservices. These include (1) the taco salad bar (discussed later in this chapter); (2) the potato bar, serving a large baked potato with various toppings; (3) the sandwich bar or deli bar, with a choice of meats and cheese served by the ounce or number of slices; (4) the pasta bar, with different toppings; (5) the breakfast bar, with cereal in a large salad bowl and fruits and nuts as toppings; and (6) the dessert bar, serving ice cream or cake with toppings.

There are many attractive pieces of equipment for salad bars, however, some schools have successfully turned a regular serving line into a salad bar. The important thing is that there be a sneeze guard and the food be kept cold—for sanitation reasons as well as for customer appeal.

Self-service should be carefully costed out to determine if it is better to offer the bars a la carte or as a meal. This is discussed further later in this chapter.

Fast Foods

"Fast foods" denotes a type of service; however, it has also become synonymous with hamburgers and other types of sandwiches, pizza, and French fries. This type of food is very popular with students today. Regrettably, these foods are all thought to be high in fat and salt and are still considered by a few to be "junk foods."

Len Fredrick, Director of Food Services for the Las Vegas, Nevada School District in the 1970s, was one of the first in the school lunch program to deviate from the traditional. He developed the fast food concept to fit the school lunch program and meal pattern. Fredrick (1977) commented, "It continues to puzzle me that a school foodservice director persists in thinking that a school lunch operation can't be 'super efficient, a real money saver,' and still 'feed youngsters something that's good and that's good for them." He referred to his lunch as "Type A Combo." It was basically a choice of sandwiches, French fries, sandwich fixings (lettuce, tomatoes, and so on), and a choice of milk, including an enriched or vitamin-fortified milk shake. It provided one-third of a student's RDAs, according to Fredrick.

Since 1977 fast food menus have become a nationwide trend because of the popularity of the foods. It appears that the philosophy of school foodservice managers and principals seems to have the most influence over whether there will be a fast food menu offered.

TYPES OF MENUS

Standard Menu

A standard menu is a no-choice menu that meets the school lunch meal or breakfast patterns. This was the most common menu until the 1980s, when menus with choices were introduced in many school districts. When using no-choice, it is important to serve foods *most* students will like and eat—although it is impossible to plan one menu that all students will like. Older students particularly object to having someone else deciding what they will eat; therefore, a standard menu is more acceptable in elementary schools than in secondary.

The menu variety will have to be more limited when a standard (no-choice) menu is served. Unpopular items will cause fewer students to eat a school lunch, and if "offer versus serve" is not an option for elementary- and intermediate-age students, there will be heavy food waste.

The advantages of using a standard menu are (1) greater productivity and lower labor costs, (2) faster moving lines, (3) less equipment needed, and (4) ease in determining quantities of food needed.

Choice Menu

The choice menu takes careful planning and is more difficult to produce but has several advantages: (1) the number of lunches served usually increases; (2) plate waste decreases; (3) students complain less; (4) there is greater opportunity to meet students' nutritional requirements; and (5) more variety can be offered.

Care must be taken in offering choices within the meal pattern, since all combinations possible must meet school lunch meal pattern requirements. For example, potato chips cannot be offered as a choice with mashed potatoes, because potato chips are not considered a vegetable. In the sample menu shown in Figure 4-4, any combination will meet the requirements of the school lunch meal patterns.

Another consideration in planning a choice menu is that serving will take longer; however, with careful planning and portioning, some items for self-service choices can be managed. With the menu shown in Figure 4-4, the orange juice, fresh grapes, and dinner rolls can be portioned for self-service.

Offering choices is particularly desirable when an unpopular item is on the menu. This also will make it possible to increase the variety. Since vegetables are the least preferred food for most students, choices of vegetables can lessen plate waste and in turn

Choice of One:
Oven Fried Chicken
Pork Barbecue

Choice of Two:
Buttered Broccoli
Mashed Potatoes and Gravy
Orange Juice
Fresh Grapes

Dinner Rolls and Butter

Choice of One:
Lowfat Milk
Whole Milk

FIGURE 4-4. Example of a choice menu.

help meet nutritional goals. Providing choices usually reduces food complaints. It is common for people to complain about food, but a student who chooses what he or she will eat is less critical of the food.

Multiple Menu

Multiple menus are made up of more than one complete menu that students may select. Multiple menus are usually served on two different serving lines. High schools will frequently offer the popular sandwich/pizza (fast food) type foods on one serving line and more traditional foods on another line. Examples are shown in Figure 4-5.

These menus offer many combinations and are balanced nutritionally. Some school foodservices have been able to serve multiple menus with four or more choices successfully. However, this is probably unnecessary and may not be cost-effective.

Desserts may or may not be a part of the lunch menu. If cost is a factor, desserts should not be a part of the menu unless they contribute to the school lunch meal patterns or are served on a special day. Desserts can be sold a la carte for those who want them.

Since inactive teenage girls are often concerned with their weight, and their calorie needs are less than other more active students, it may be desirable to offer a salad plate that meets meal requirements if a salad bar is not available.

Salad Bar Menus

Salad bars can be presented as a lunch or offered for sale a la carte. If the salad bar (or any other self-service bars) is to meet the meal requirements, careful planning and supervision may be necessary. Consider the following when setting up a salad bar:

1. Meat and meat alternates are the most expensive part of the meal, and preportioning may be necessary to control cost.

2. Eight servings of bread and bread alternates a week may be slightly difficult to serve on the salad bar. Croutons, pasta products, and crackers add variety and contribute toward meeting the bread requirement.

Choice of One:	*Choice of One:*
Hamburger or Cheeseburger	Spaghetti with Meat Sauce
Pizza	Tuna Salad
Choice of Two:	*Choice of Two:*
French Fries	Tossed Salad with Dressing
Soup of the Day	Soup of the Day
Sandwich Fixings	Green Beans
Sliced Peaches	Sliced Peaches
Choice of One:	*Choice of One:*
Lowfat Milk	Lowfat Milk
Whole Milk	Whole Milk

FIGURE 4-5. Example of a multiple menu.

3. Controlling the portions must be considered. This may be done with the size of the bowl or plate to be filled, by number of scoops, or by weight. The bowl or plate capacity is probably the easiest.

4. A cashier should be stationed at the end of the salad bar, where the tray can be checked to ensure that the school lunch patterns are followed. Students have to take a minimum of three food items under "offer versus serve."

The cashier has to be alert and well versed in the school lunch meal patterns to determine if the foods taken are in sufficient quantities to meet school lunch meal patterns requirements (see Fig. 4-2). Some managers prefer portioning the meat and meat alternate to ensure that the component is met and to control cost. However, some school districts have found that when students are allowed to help themselves, the cost is not that much different.

An example of a popular taco salad bar setup is shown in Figure 4-6 (see the USDA guide *Menu Planning Guide for Child Nutrition Programs* [1983a] for details on meeting the meal requirements in a self-service situation). The meal is priced at $1.25 for elementary school, $1.35 for high school, and counts as a lunch under NSLP. The student can have all he or she can put in a 12-ounce bowl. The chili goes on top of the salad items. To keep costs down, the chili recipe was developed to utilize the maximum amount of textured vegetable protein permitted and more kidney beans than normally. The nacho chips come in bulk sizes and 1-ounce packages. It may be more cost-effective and less messy to use the packages. The chips do not count as a bread/bread alternate. The cost may be further reduced by using sour cream dressing rather than sour cream (the prepared product tastes almost identical). The popularity of this bar is so great that Fairfax County, Virginia, schools have had to open a second salad bar in many of the secondary schools when it is offered, which was once a week, extended to twice a week.

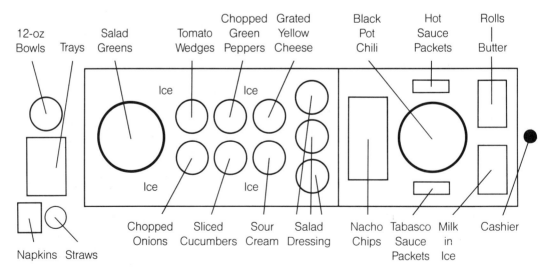

FIGURE 4-6. Self-service taco salad bar setup, priced at $1.25 elementary, $1.35 secondary. The meal counts as a lunch under the National School Lunch Program. (*Source:* Fairfax County, Virginia Public Schools.)

Suggested Salad Bar Offerings

A variety of foods can be offered in a salad bar. A five-day salad bar menu is recommended. This helps prevent sameness and provides a better guide to ordering. Four or more of the following can be offered for a variety of colors, shapes, and textures:

Bean sprouts	Cucumber slices
Chick peas	Broccoli florets
Cauliflower florets	Celery, chunks or chopped
Radishes, sliced	Spinach leaves
Julienne beets	Green peas
Carrots, sliced or grated	Beans, green, waxed, or kidney
Green pepper, sliced	Pickle chips

Offering two or more of the following daily will provide variety in meat/meat alternates. If "offer versus serve" is being carried out, the meat/meat alternate does not have to be proportioned.

Cheese, grated or cubed	Julienne turkey
Eggs, sliced or wedged	Macaroni salad (protein
Cottage cheese	fortified)
Chicken, tuna, or egg salad	Three-bean salad (made with
Julienne ham or salami	dry beans)
Canned salmon or tuna flakes	Peanuts

At least one serving of the following should be offered daily and eight servings in a week to meet requirements:

Enriched or whole-grain bread	Soft pretzels
Crackers	Croutons
Pasta products	Muffins
Bread sticks	

A choice of salad dressings should be offered.

BREAKFAST MENUS

In addition to the foods required by the breakfast pattern (see above), other foods, such as potatoes, bacon, doughnuts, butter or fortified margarine, and jelly, jam, honey, or syrup, may be served to help satisfy appetites and for the sake of variety. A breakfast bar for cereal and fruit/nut toppings is popular, although cost may be a prohibitive factor.

The breakfast and lunch menus should be coordinated so that the same foods are not on both menus the same day.

OTHER FACTORS AFFECTING MENUS

Amount of Money Available

In order to operate a sound foodservice, the amount of money available to be spent on food must be determined accurately, not left to guesswork. Recipes and menus need careful costing, as discussed in chapter 2.

In calculating food costs, it must be determined what percentage of income is to be spent on labor and other expenses and what percentage is to be spent on food in order to break even. For example, if the food cost is running 50 percent of income and the price of lunch is $1.50, the amount of money available for food is 75 cents. It should be determined how the 75 cents will be divided among the food items. If milk costs 15 cents per half pint, this would leave 60 cents to cover all the other foods in the menu. If the cost of one menu is greater than the amount of money available, the next day's menu can be under, so that it averages out.

Facilities and Equipment

It would be ideal if the equipment could be selected to fit the menus planned; however, this is seldom the order of events. In many instances menus will be determined by the equipment. If oven space is limited, a menu that includes baked potatoes, oven-fried chicken, and yeast rolls may be physically impossible. Also to be considered is whether the serving line will accommodate the food.

Staff: Number of Employees and Skill Levels

A balance from day to day in the amount of preparation required is desirable, so that the workload is not impossible one day and very light the next. The person planning the menus needs to be very familiar with how to schedule, how many labor hours are available, and how much preparation can be accomplished.

The skills and training of the staff may limit the menus. In any areas with heavy staff turnover and employees with low educational levels, menus will need to be simpler. Even with skilled staff, it may not be cost-effective for complex items such as stuffed eclairs to be on the menu, and it may be necessary to plan menus using some convenience foods.

Purchased Food Supplies and USDA-Donated Foods

The availability of food will limit menus, and the type and quantity of storage space available will influence the types of food that can be put on a menu. The season of the year will influence the prices of some foods. Produce prices will vary greatly over the year and in relation to the season; for instance, fresh strawberries may be affordable at the peak of their season but not at other times.

Schools participating in the National School Lunch Program will find that their menus are greatly influenced by USDA-donated foods, and sometimes this is not to the benefit of the program. In order to obtain the full value from USDA-donated foods and keep the price of the lunch to the students as low as possible, it is necessary to utilize the donated foods well. This may be the greatest challenge of menu planning. For the most part, USDA-donated foods are of good quality.

Processing of USDA-donated foods into other, more usable products will increase the variety and acceptability (see discussion in chapter 7). For example, frozen whole turkeys have limited use in planning favored lunches. Processing by a commercial manufacturer can convert the turkey into turkey ham, nuggets, hot dogs, turkey pot pies, and other varieties of cold cuts.

Aesthetics

"People eat with their eyes" is a saying that is very true. A meal can be nutritionally adequate and also contain favorite foods, but if it is not attractively served and visually appealing, it may not be eaten. When planning menu "eye appeal," the planner will use some basic principles used by an artist in obtaining good design.

MENU PLANNING

Successful menu planning takes time, concentration, reference materials, and knowledge. Menus should be planned far enough ahead so that orders can be placed and received. It is poor management to plan the menu by the day, depending on what is on hand. A few uncentralized school districts where the individual managers make all decisions and do all the jobs may still function on a day-to-day basis. This is not the norm, however. Certainly menus need to be planned a month in advance so that ordering can be cost-effective and efficient.

The menus of other school foodservices can be useful as guides and provide ideas. McDonald's and Pizza Hut have made the food choices of the student-age customer so universal that except for a few regional foods, one could plan a menu on that model that would be universally popular.

Reference materials that can be helpful in planning menus are *Quantity Recipes for Child Nutrition Programs* (USDA 1988), *Menu Planning Guide for Child Nutrition Programs* (USDA 1983a), *Food Buying Guide for Child Nutrition Programs* (USDA 1984), past records of participation, and lists of USDA-donated commodities on hand as well as other foods in inventory.

Once the menu has been planned, the planner should check to see that all the above listed factors have been considered (see the checklist, Fig. 4-7).

Cycle Menus

The process of menu planning can be made easier by using cycle menus. Children, particularly seventh and eighth grade age students, tend to like routine, and they like having their favorites often. Variety is not as important to students as to adults. A sample menu cycle is provided in Figure 4-8.

	YES	NO	COMMENTS/SUGGESTIONS
1. Are all components of the lunch/breakfast included each day?			
2. Are serving sizes sufficient to provide: A. meat or meat alternate as specified in the appropriate meal pattern?			
B. two or more vegetables or fruits or both?			
C. appropriate servings of enriched or whole-grain bread per week?			
D. fluid milk as a beverage?			
3. Is a VITAMIN A vegetable or fruit included at least twice a week?			
4. Is a VITAMIN C vegetable or fruit included 2 or 3 times a week?			
5. Are foods rich in IRON included?			
6. Are foods planned and included to satisfy the appetites of the age group?			
7. Are the combinations of foods pleasing and acceptable to this age group?			
8. Do lunches have a good balance of: A. *Color*—in the foods themselves or as a garnish?			
B. *Texture*—soft, crisp, firm?			
C. *Shape*—different size and shapes?			
D. *Flavor*—bland and tart, or mild and strong?			
9. Are most of the foods and food combinations ones children of this age have learned to eat?			

FIGURE 4-7. Menu checklist. (*Source:* USDA 1983a.)

In the Fairfax County, Virginia, school district, menus are planned as follows: a one-week cycle for fast food lines in high schools; a one-week cycle for chef salads and salad bars, with one or the other available in all schools each day; a four-week cycle for the basic lunch menu in all schools; and a one-week cycle for breakfast. Certain foods are always served on certain days within the four-week basic lunch menu. Serving favorite foods on particular days had become such an accepted practice that when it was changed, the director received letters and signed petitions from the PTA to put pizza back on Fridays. For high school students, who often do not keep up with the printed menus, the plan described in Table 4-4 very quickly becomes a memorized meal pattern.

	YES	NO	COMMENTS/SUGGESTIONS
10. Have children's cultural, ethnic, and religious food practices been considered?			
11. Is a popular food or dish planned for lunch which includes a "new" or less popular food?			
12. Are foods varied from day to day?			
13. Are different kinds or forms of foods (fresh, canned, frozen, dried) included?			
14. Are seasonal foods included?			
15. Have "new" foods or new methods of preparation been included occasionally?			
16. Can lunches be prepared and served successfully by employees in the time available?			
17. Are lunches planned so that some preparation can be done ahead?			
18. Is workload balanced among employees from day to day?			
19. Can lunches be prepared and served with facilities and equipment available?			
20. Is oven, surface-cooking or steam-cooking space adequate for items planned for each lunch?			
21. Can foods planned for each lunch be easily served?			
22. Will foods "fit" on dishes or compartment trays?			
23. Have USDA-donated foods been used to best advantage?			
24. Do high- and low-cost foods and lunches balance?			

FIGURE 4-7. *Continued.*

Since some dieticians think that it is desirable to avoid menus that repeat the same meals on the same days of the week, they go to great pains to ensure that this doesn't happen. Along with scrambling the menus, they try to include "healthy" foods. These efforts, as the preceding example shows, are not always popular with the students. Therefore, although the motives are admirable, business suffers.

Because of differences in food prices and availability, there are some advantages to planning the menu in three seasonal cycles: (1) September-October-November, (2) December-January-February, and (3) March-April-May-June.

Menu planning is a complicated process that controls all parts of the foodservice.

Monday	Tuesday	Wednesday	Thursday	Friday
3	4	5	6	7
B: Doughnuts Chilled Juice Milk L: Mexican Pizza or Chicken Salad w/Crackers Shredded Lettuce Chilled Applesauce Milk	B: Sausage Biscuit Apple Juice Milk L: Hot Ham/Cheese Sandwich or Hamburger Deluxe Sweet Potato Souffle Seasoned Green Beans Milk	B: Cheesy Eggs w/Toast Orange Juice Milk L: Chicken Nuggets or Meat Loaf Field Peas Fruit Cocktail Hot Roll Milk	B: Cinnamon Roll Choice of Juices Milk L: Super Taco or Submarine Sandwich Buttered Corn Lettuce & Tomato Milk	B: School Baked Muffin Chilled Fruit Milk L: Ft. Long Hot Dog w/Chili or Manager's Choice Potato Rounds Fresh Fruit Milk
10	11	12	13	14
B: Waffle w/Syrup Orange Juice Milk L: Crunchy Fish on Bun or Barbecued Pork Sandwich Baked Potato Crisp Coleslaw Milk	B: Cinnamon Bun Apple Juice–Milk BIRTHDAY LUNCH L: Ham Biscuit w/Macaroni & Cheese or Country Style Steak w/Biscuit Baby Lima Beans Sliced Peaches Cherry Cobbler–Milk	B: Buttered Biscuit w/Jelly Chilled Juice–Milk L: Vegetable Beef Soup Grilled Cheese Sandwich or Hamburger on Bun (Mustard/Mayo./Catsup) Fresh Apple Milk	B: Bacon 'N Cheese Biscuit Grape Juice–Milk L: Baked Chicken & Rice w/Roll or Tuna Salad on Lettuce w/Crackers Spicy Baked Apples Steamed Cabbage Milk	B: Grilled Cheese Chilled Fruit Milk L: Lasagna w/Roll or Turkey Club Sandwich Shredded Lettuce Buttered Mixed Vegetables Milk VALENTINE'S DAY
17	18	19	20	21
B: Cereal Chilled Juice Milk L: Sausage Pizza or Grilled Cheese Sandwich Seasoned Green Beans Fruit Cocktail Milk	B: Hot Coffee Cake Apple Juice Milk L: Cheeseburger on Bun or Chicken Nuggets w/Roll Shredded Lettuce Dill Chips Buttered Potatoes Milk	B: School Baked Muffin Orange Juice Milk L: Spaghetti w/Roll or Chef's Salad w/Roll or Crackers Tossed Salad Orange Wedges Milk	B: Buttered Toast w/Jelly–Grits Chilled Juice–Milk L: Super Taco or Hot Ham/Cheese Sandwich Lettuce & Tomato Buttered Corn Milk	B: Ham & Cheese Biscuit Chilled Fruit Milk L: Hot Dog on Bun w/Chili (Mustard/Catsup/Onions) or Quiche w/Roll Creamy Coleslaw French Fries Milk
24	25	26	27	14
B: Doughnut Chilled Juice Milk L: Cheeseburger on Bun or Corn Dog Mixed Vegetables Sliced Peaches Milk	B: Breakfast Buffet Milk L: Vegetable Beef Soup Peanut Butter and Jelly Sandwich or Chicken Fillet on Bun Fresh Apple Milk	B: Cinnamon Toast Applesauce Milk L: Lasagna w/Roll or Barbecue on Bun Spinach Salad Applesauce Milk	B: Fruit Danish Chilled Juice Milk L: Fried Chicken w/Roll or Manager's Choice Mashed Potatoes Green Peas Milk	B: Biscuit w/Jelly Fruit Cup Milk L: Crunchy Fish on Bun or Barbecued Pork Sandwich Crisp Coleslaw French Fries Milk

FIGURE 4-8. Four-week menu cycle. (*Source:* Wake County, North Carolina, Public Schools.)

68

Table 4-4.   Menu Pattern Used by a Large Metropolitan School
District in Planning Menus

Monday	Tuesday	Wednesday	Thursday	Friday
Sandwich-type food[a]	Mexican-type food[b]	Chicken or turkey[c]	Italian-type food[d]	Pizza or fish[e]

Selection of four to six items each day (select two) that include fresh fruit,
canned fruit, vegetable salad or vegetable soup, cooked vegetables or potatoes

Bread and bread alternates

Milk, low-fat, whole, and chocolate

[a]Burgers, hot dogs, steak subs, grilled cheese, peanut butter and jelly, ham and cheese
[b]Tacos, burritos, nachos
[c]Chicken nuggets, fried chicken, barbecued chicken, sliced turkey, turkey/chicken pot pies
[d]Spaghetti, lasagna, macaroni and cheese with little smokies
[e]French bread pizza; cheese, pepperoni, and sausage pizza; tuna fish salad sandwich;
batter-fried fish, and fishburger

There are many variables. Some of the advantages of cycle menus are that they (1) reduce time spent planning menus; (2) make it possible to develop an almost "perfect" set of menus; (3) standardize production, service, and purchasing; (4) make production forecasting more accurate; (5) enable staff to improve quality by perfecting routines and procedures; and (6) allow work schedules to be reused.

Student and Parent Involvement

Student committees can be involved in menu planning; however, it is probably not feasible or good business to involve them in planning all menus since so many factors should be considered. "Student-planned" menus served once a month usually give students enough feeling of involvement.

A student (and parent) group can act as adviser in menu planning, testing new foods, testing recipes, selecting qualities of foods to be purchased, and suggesting policy changes. Surveys conducted by student leaders can provide valuable information to menu planners. Menu planning should not be limited to the upper grade levels since elementary school students also enjoy this type of activity. When classes are studying a country, it is meaningful to provide a theme menu and tie it in with what has been learned in the classroom.

Frequency Charts

A frequency chart lists the number of times foods appear on the menu. Such charts, which provide a record for meats, vegetables, breads, fruits, and desserts, show at a glance which foods are repeated most often (see Fig. 4-9). If a food is repeated frequently on the menu, the reason should be that the item is popular and students will eat it.

	Week 1					Week 2					Week 3					Week 4				
	M	T	W	T	F	M	T	W	T	F	M	T	W	T	F	M	T	W	T	F
Beef:																				
Steak Sandwich																				
Tacos																				
Hamburger																				
Meat Loaf, Beef, and Pork																				
Lasagna																				
Spaghetti with meat sauce																				
Meat Ball Subs																				
Burritos, Beans, and Ground Beef																				
Roast Beef Sandwich																				
Chili on Taco Salad Bar																				
Sloppy Joe on Bun																				
Barbecued Beef Sandwich																				
Cheeseburgers																				
Nacho with Cheese and Chili																				
Cheese:																				
Macaroni with cheese																				
Grilled Cheese Sandwich																				
Cheeseburgers																				
Pizza, cheese topping																				
Grilled Ham and Cheese Sandwich																				
Burrito with Cheese Topping																				
Nacho with Cheese and Chili																				

FIGURE 4-9. Frequency charts, such as this one for a four-week cycle menu, are useful in planning and help avoid repetition.

	Week 1					Week 2					Week 3					Week 4				
	M	T	W	T	F	M	T	W	T	F	M	T	W	T	F	M	T	W	T	F
Pork:																				
BBQ Pork on Roll																				
Ham Slices																				
Meat Loaf, Beef, and Pork																				
Smoked Sausage Links																				
Smoked Sausage with Red Beans over Rice																				
Pizza, Ground Pork Topping																				
Poultry:																				
BBQ Chicken																				
Chicken Nuggets																				
Chicken or Turkey Salad																				
Oven Fried Chicken																				
Turkey and Dressing																				
Chicken or Turkey Pie																				
Grilled Ham (Turkey) and Cheese Sandwich																				
Seafood:																				
Bread Fish Sticks																				
Salmon Patty																				
Tuna Salad																				
Other:																				

FIGURE 4-9. *Continued.*

The frequency chart is helpful in determining the quantities of different foods that will be used during the cycle or year. This information is needed in estimating quantities for the bid process and for placing orders.

A LA CARTE OFFERINGS

A la carte offerings are usually limited at the elementary school level, whereas in high schools they range from limited to widely varied choices. The philosophy of the school

Monday		Tuesday	
Honeywheat Doughnut	1	Honey Oatmeal	1
Milk	½ Pint	Granola Bar	
or Juice	4 oz	Milk	½ pt
Napkin, Straw		or Apple Juice	4 oz
		Napkin, Straw	

Wednesday	
Fresh Fruit	½ cup
Select one:	
Apple	
Banana	
Grapes	
Melon	
Orange	
Milk	½ Pint
or Juice	4 oz
Napkin, Straw	

Thursday		Friday	
Popcorn	1 pkg	Cheese	1 oz
Milk	½ pt	Crackers	2 pkg
or Orange Juice	4 oz	Milk	½ Pint
Napkin, Straw		or Juice	4 oz
		Napkin, Straw	

FIGURE 4-10. Snack menu.

district will have a lot to do with the types of foods sold. As a cost-savings measure many school districts have taken desserts off the menus and sell them a la carte.

Vending of fruit-based drinks can provide a la carte offerings without labor on duty. Vending has much potential for growth especially in parts of the country where labor shortages are experienced. Vending machines can be merchandisers of good nutritious foods, such as fresh fruits, yogurts, salads, sandwiches, and fruit juices. It allows food-service to be available over extended hours when otherwise it would not be economically feasible.

OTHER FOOD OFFERINGS

Snack programs for kindergarten children and for Head Start and after-school "extended" day care programs can be a source of revenue for the school foodservice, and there may be a need for these services. Examples of simple, convenience-type foods that can be used for a snack program are shown in Figure 4-10.

BIBLIOGRAPHY

American Heart Association. 1984. *American Heart Association Cookbook.* New York: David McKay Co.

Birchfield, John. 1979. *Foodservice Operations Manual: A Guide for Hotels, Restaurants, and Institutions.* Boston, Mass.: CBI Publishing Co.

Carlson, B. 1986. "Analysis of Nutrition in the Hospitality Industry." Ph.D. Dissertation, Cornell University.

Dosti, Rose, Deborah Kidushim, and Mark Wolke. 1982. *Light Style: The New American Cuisine.* San Francisco, Calif.: Harper & Row.

Fredrick, Len. 1977. *Fast Food Gets an "A" in School Lunch.* Boston, Mass.: Cahner Books.

Jacobson, Michael, and Sarah Fritschner. 1986. *The Fast-Food Guide.* New York: Workman Publishing.

Khan, Mahmood. 1987. *Foodservice Operations.* New York: AVI and Van Nostrand Reinhold.

Leveille, G., M. Zabik, and K. Morgan. 1983. *Nutrients in Foods.* Cambridge, Mass.: Nutrition Guild.

Pouwels, Marie K. 1988. "The Battle over a la Carte." *Food Management* 24(9): 75.

Survey Reveals School Food Facts. 1987. *School Food Service Journal* 41(8): 17+.

U.S. Department of Agriculture (USDA). 1982. *Food 3: Eating the Moderate Fat and Cholesterol Way.* Chicago: American Dietetic Association.

———. 1983a. *Menu Planning Guide for Child Nutrition Programs.* PA 1260. Washington, D.C.: U.S. Government Printing Office.

———. 1983b. *Nutrient Standard Menu Planning Computer Coding Manual.* Washington, D.C.: U.S. Government Printing Office.

———. 1984. *Food Buying Guide for Child Nutrition Programs.* PA 1331. Washington, D.C.: U.S. Government Printing Office.

———. 1987. *School Lunch Patterns.* Washington, D.C.: Food and Nutrition Services, United States Department of Agriculture.

————. 1988. *Quantity Recipes for the Child Nutrition Programs.* Washington, D.C.: U.S. Government Printing Office.

U.S. Department of Agriculture and Health, Education and Welfare. 1980. *Nutrition and Your Health: Dietary Guidelines for Americans.* Washington, D.C.: U.S. Government Printing Office.

West, Patricia Hurst, and Kathryn M. Kolasa. 1984. *Menu Planning: School Food Service Training Manual.* Greenville, N.C.: East Carolina University.

Woodman, Julie G. 1985. *IFMA Encyclopedia of the Foodservice Industry.* 5th ed. Chicago: International Foodservice Manufacturers Association.

5

Organizational Structure and Personnel

ORGANIZATIONAL MANAGEMENT

As school foodservices grew from "soup kitchens" to full-fledged businesses, it became necessary for management to be more aware of organizational structure and personnel matters. This growth is illustrated by Caton and Nix (1986) in *I Can Manage: A Practical Approach.*

    The basic principles of management are the same for restaurants, hospitals, residence halls, and school foodservices. The larger the operation, the more complex the organization becomes. School foodservices range from those in small single-unit, decentralized schools serving less than 100 meals to foodservices in centralized city and county districts with 250 to 900 schools serving 100,000 to 800,000 meals per day.

    The purpose of an organization dealing with manpower is, according to West et al. (1977), "to accomplish with the efforts of people some basic purpose or objective with the greatest efficiency, maximum economy, and minimum effort, and to provide for the personal development of the people working in the organization."

    For an organization to function effectively and to grow, it must utilize all resources—people, materials, and facilities—to their fullest. The most challenging resource for many managers is people. To be effective, an organization must provide for maximum utilization of their capabilities. To accomplish this, the organization should follow general principles of good management that call for

- A clear line of authority established and understood by the employees
- Objectives and goals set and used as a measurement of success
- Responsibilities clearly identified for each member of the organization
- Effective leadership
- Timely provision of necessary materials and equipment

Line of Authority

The responsibility for the National School Lunch Program is given to the U.S. Department of Agriculture, which administers the program through seven regional offices and the individual states. Administration of the school foodservice programs is the responsibility of the state department of education in all states; however, that is about all the different states have in common. At the local level, the board of education is usually the overall governing body that enters into an agreement (annual contract) with the state department of education to carry out federal and state rules and regulations concerning school food programs. The agreement is made in order to receive federal and state cash reimbursements and USDA-donated foods.

The delegation of authority from federal government via the regional offices is shown in Figure 5-1. A local-level organizational chart should show the positions in the organization, the overall responsibilities of the various positions denoted in a general manner, and the relationship among departments and services (Fig. 5-2). Positions with the greatest authority are shown at the top of the chart, with those with the least authority at the bottom. A chart should make it clear to whom each person in the organization should report.

Positions and Job Descriptions

Once the basic plan of an organizational chart has been established and the line of authority is set, a job description is needed for each position. It should provide a general definition of the job to give management and the employee a clear understanding of what the job entails. Examples of job descriptions are shown in Figures 5-3 and 5-4.

The person responsible for running the kitchen is usually called the *manager* or *cook-manager* in a small school. The position may be referred to as a *lead person* in a satellite school or finishing kitchen.

Should other staff members have titles and be paid accordingly, or should all staff be paid at the same level? In a small kitchen (ten or fewer employees), the manager may need the flexibility to cross-train and move employees around to different jobs, in which case the different pay levels can be a problem. Establishing titles for job purposes without pay differences at the staff level gives more flexibility.

Objectives of Management

Management is responsible for planning, directing, and controlling the foodservice in a sound financial manner and for serving good, nutritious food as a part of the educational system. Some school foodservice programs have responsibility for nutrition education as well as foodservice. Although specific objectives and goals may differ from school to school, five important general objectives should be adopted by a school foodservice:

1. Operate on a sound financial basis.
2. Serve good-quality, nutritious food.
3. Teach good food habits.
4. Meet the needs of the students in a satisfying way.
5. Give employees an opportunity for personal development.

Management should (1) set the standards; (2) develop the objectives and goals; (3) make the policies; (4) do the planning and organizing; (5) communicate with the

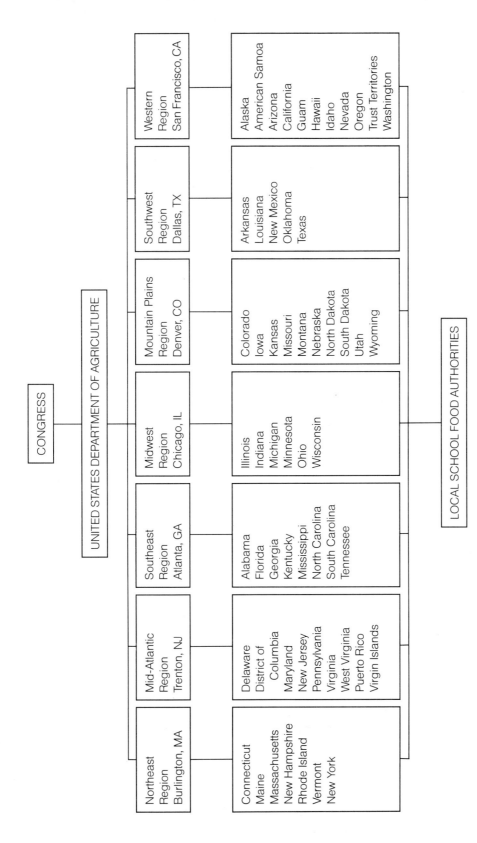

FIGURE 5-1. Organizational chart showing responsibility for administration of the National School Lunch Program.

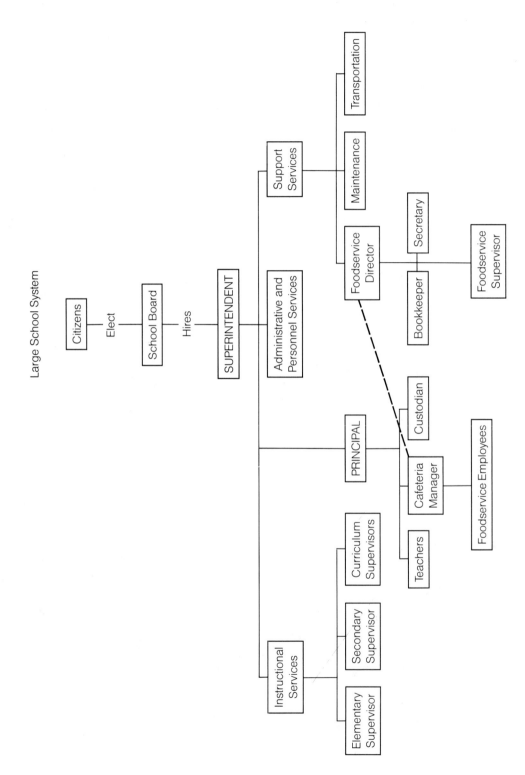

Large School System

FIGURE 5-2. Large school district organization chart.

Job Title: Foodservice Staff Employee or Assistant

Grade Step: II

Job Description: Prepare the main dish and vegetables.

General Duties: Is responsible for the preparation of the main dish and cooked vegetables. Prepares food for the serving line and keeps all foods on the serving line at lunchtime. Is responsible for the cleaning and maintaining of the small equipment, washing pots and pans when needed. Helps with the general preparation and serving of foods and the cleaning.

Requirements: Must be able to read and write English, to do simple arithmetic, and to follow oral and written direction. Must have the capacity to grasp and adjust to new and changing situations. (Manual dexterity and ability to work under pressure are desirable.) Must be neat in appearance and wear uniform-type clothing, hairnet or cap covering on hair, and comfortable, safe shoes. Must provide a health certificate verifying a negative tuberculin test.

Tools and Equipment: Uses scales for weighing ingredients and portion control, mixer, oven, range, steam cooker, steam-jacketed kettle, fryer, food chopper, slicer, vertical cutter-mixer, and other related tools and equipment.

Working Conditions: Works an average of thirty hours per week, Monday through Friday with school holidays, for ten months a year, in a well-lighted, ventilated, and comfortable kitchen. Must do much standing on feet and some lifting.

Supervision: Is responsible to the school foodservice manager. Supervises an assistant cook in a large school kitchen.

Personal Requirements: High school education or equivalency test. At least one year of experience in foodservice preparation.

FIGURE 5-3. Job description for a foodservice staff employee or assistant.

School Foodservice Manager

Description: Manages foodservice program in an individual school according to system policies, procedures, and methods. Cooperates with principal and teachers to promote Child Nutrition Program's educational values. Supervises and instructs foodservice personnel. Maintains high standards of food preparation and service with emphasis on appetizing appeal, maximum nutritive value, and flavor. Maintains high standards of sanitation and safety: records of cash, food, supplies, and equipment. Salary should be based on such factors as: number and type of meals served daily, percent participation, number of employees, and nature of responsibilities.

Education: High school diploma or equivalent needed. Specialized education and training in school foodservice management desirable.

Experience: Diversified experience in foodservice production and management with progressively more responsible positions.

FIGURE 5-4. Job description for a school foodservice manager. (*Source:* Mississippi State Department of Education 1987.)

foodservice employees, the customer, the public, the parents, the school administration, and the board of education; (6) control food quality; (7) control costs; (8) carry out the objectives and goals; (9) supervise and direct; (10) evaluate; (11) teach and encourage the growth of the foodservice workers; and (12) look out for the foodservice's welfare.

LOCAL FOODSERVICE ADMINISTRATION

There are two basic ways of administering the foodservice operation in a school district: centralized and decentralized. Though the trend is toward school-based management on the education side, more and more school districts are centralizing the foodservices. In some states the trend is toward merging small school districts to reduce administrative costs.

When the school district has a decentralized foodservice operation, each school administers its own foodservice. This may include menu, purchasing, interpretation of regulations, finances, personnel, and preparing state reports. However, many state departments of education require state reports to be combined into one report for the entire school district, and USDA-donated commodities are often distributed to the school district for dividing up.

When foodservice administration is centralized, a director or supervisor of foodservices is usually appointed to work under the general direction of the superintendent of schools or school business administrator. Centralized management means different things to different school districts. In some it means little more than that the accounting work and the monthly state report are done at one location, whereas in others it may mean centralized planning of menus, purchasing, warehousing, accounting and fiscal control, and personnel.

The advantages of centralized administration with the responsibility for all the various jobs related to operating school foodservices is that a more qualified person can be afforded, more purchasing power is obtained with larger volume, better organization and management of the program is possible, and principals have to spend less time tied up with foodservice matters. Centralized purchasing can result in significant financial savings. Not only is there a possible savings from prices paid, but savings can also be realized in labor. One person can plan the menu, meet with food companies, and purchase the food and supplies. This saves the manager time.

Director or Supervisor

The head administrator of school foodservice is often given the title of *director* in the large school districts. According to the American School Foodservices Certification Committee, "the director is one who plans, organizes, directs, administers the foodservice program in a school system according to policies established by the Board of Education."

In smaller systems, the person heading the school foodservice may be called a *supervisor.* In a large school district the supervisor is someone who works under the director. A supervisor is responsible for evaluating the programs, aiding the foodservice manager, and generally directing the individual foodservice units.

Table 5-1.   Administrative Staffing Guide for School Foodservice

Number of School Foodservices	Director	Supervisor[a]	Assistant Supervisor[a]
1-15		1	
16-30		1	1
31-40		1	2
41-60	1	3	
61-80	1	4	
81-100	1	6[b]	
101-125	1	7[b]	
126-150	1	8[b]	
151-175	1	10[b]	
176-200	1	12[b]	
201-225	1	14[b]	

[a]In a foodservice covering more than 40 schools, the supervision may be divided between supervisors and assistant supervisors.
[b]One of these positions should be designated as an assistant director position.

Span of Control

How many schools can one person supervise? When does a supervisor need an assistant or a director need another supervisor? The span of control will depend on what the supervisor/director is responsible for and the training and skills of the managers the person supervises. Table 5-1 provides a guideline for staffing at the supervisory level. The amount of time that a supervisor can and needs to spend in the schools is an important consideration. AccuClaim audits, which are discussed in chapter 2, will increase the need for supervision.

STAFFING AT INDIVIDUAL SCHOOLS

Foodservice at the school level will need someone in charge, regardless of how small the unit is. The profile of a school foodservice employee in the 1970s was a person who was 45 to 50 years old, a high school graduate, semiskilled, with 8 years of experience. The food-service employee in the 1990s will be slightly older because of a decline in available workers in the age range of 20-34 years (see Table 5-2), and more part-time employees will be needed in school foodservice. In many cases, the older employee will be retired from a job and working only part time at the local school to supplement income and to have something to do.

An accurate assessment of work to be done is required to determine the number of labor hours needed, or the productivity rate possible, in a foodservice operation. Productivity in the United States increased at an overall rate of 3 percent a year from 1950 through the mid-1960s. During the 1970s the increase slowed to 2 percent, and since then

Table 5-2.   Size of Labor Force by Age

Age	1986 (Actual)	2000 (Projected)
16-19	7,926,000	8,800,000
20-24	15,442,000	13,751,000
25-34	34,592,000	31,657,000
35-44	27,233,000	38,571,000
45-54	17,500,000	30,552,000
55-64	11,894,000	12,970,000
65 and over	3,010,000	2,394,000

Source: Bureau of Labor Statistics (1988).

it has been under 1 percent. School foodservice productivity changed very little in most school districts during the 1980s.

"Meals per labor hour" is most frequently used in school foodservice to determine productivity rate and the number of labor hours needed. The formula for determining the productivity rate of a school foodservice is as follows:

$$\frac{\text{Total meals served}}{\text{Total labor hours}} = \text{Meals per labor hour}$$

"Total meals served" may contain equivalencies for a la carte sales and other programs, such as breakfast. This is discussed later in this chapter. When determining how much staff is needed, determine the productivity rate desired for example, 16 or 18 meals per labor hour. Divide the meals (including equivalent meals) by the productivity rate. See Table 5-3 for suggested staffing guidelines. These guidelines are for a conventional system (on-site production using some convenience foods, such as bakery-purchased hamburger and hot dog rolls, prepared pizza, and some disposable dishes) and for a convenience system (discussed in chapter 3). The meals per labor hour are much greater for a satellite food system.

Another way of determining staff hours needed is by dividing servings by productivity rate desired (number of servings per labor hour). Mayo and Olsen (1985) state that "meals per labor hour" works only when all parts of the lunch are served. With the "offer versus serve" option, they recommend allocating labor based on portions served. They found that 71 to 73 servings per labor hour were the mean for producing food from raw ingredients. The formula they used follows:

$$\frac{\text{Total food servings}}{\text{Total labor hours}} = \text{Servings produced per labor hour}$$

Since most students take at least four menu items, the "meal per labor hour" still seems to be a fair way of determining labor hours. Figuring the staff based on portions as shown above equates to 15 to 18 meals per labor hour.

The Mississippi State Department of Education has set its standard between 12 and

Table 5-3.   Staffing Guidelines for On-Site Production

Number of Meal Equivalents[a]	Meals Per Labor Hour (MPLH)/Total Hours			
	Conventional System[b]		Convenience System[b]	
	MPLH	Total Hours	MPLH	Total Hours
Up to 100	8	9-12	9	9-11
101-150	9	12-16	10	11-14
151-200	10-11	16-17	12	14-16
201-250	12	17-20	14	16-18
251-300	13	20-22	15	18-20
301-400	14	22-29	16	20-25
401-500	14	29-35	18	20-28
501-600	15	35-40	18	28-34
601-700	16	40-43	19	34-37
701-800	17	43-47	20	37-40
800+	18	47+	21+	40+

[a]Meal equivalents include breakfast and a la carte sales. Three breakfasts equate to one lunch. A la carte sales of $3 equate to one lunch.

[b]Conventional system is preparation of food from raw ingredients on premises (using some bakery breads and prepared pizza and washing dishes). Convenience system is using maximum amount of processed foods (for example, using all bakery breads, prefried chicken, and preportioned condiments, and using disposable dinnerware).

15 meals per labor hour. In 1980 North Carolina established a staffing formula for no choice or limited choice from 9 meals per labor hour when serving 200, to 30 meals per labor hour when serving more than 1,500; and a formula for multi-plus-choice-programs of 8.75 meals per labor hour when serving 200, to 21 meals per labor hour when serving more than 1,500. North Carolina Department of Education further states: "At no time in using this guide should one allow more than 50% of income including benefits to be expended for labor." The New York School Food Service Division (State of New York, 1987) has also established 50 percent of income for labor cost as the maximum.

Unless the productivity rate of school foodservice increases, or new pay scales are instituted during the 1990s, labor costs in many school districts will force meal prices up to the point that students will be unable to afford a lunch at school.

Most school foodservices have added a great many convenience foods in the last 10 years, discontinuing a great deal of "from scratch" cooking, which should mean that less labor is needed. However, many choices have been added, requiring more labor hours than no-choice menus. The use of disposable dishes has increased, which should reduce the labor hours needed.

There are no magic formulas that can be applied to staffing all foodservices. The number of employees needed and the labor hours will be influenced by a number of factors, including the following:

1. *Type of foodservices operation:* On-site production, central kitchen operation, finishing kitchen operation, preplated meals, etc., require different amounts of labor. On-site production will usually have the lowest productivity and preplated meals the highest.

2. *Number of meals to be served at the location:* The smaller operation (serving under 200 meals) will have a higher labor cost percentage than an operation twice its size. The larger the operation, the higher the productivity can be.

3. *Menus:* The no-choice menu will take less labor than the choice menu, particularly in smaller schools.

4. *Type of food used:* Cooking from "scratch" with raw materials, or heavy use of convenience foods, or an arrangement somewhere in between must be carefully considered.

5. *Number and length of lunch periods:* The most common and workable schedule in high schools, for example, are three 30-minute lunch periods. Four or five lunch periods, or lunch periods over extended time mean more labor needed.

6. *Kinds and arrangement of equipment:* It will make a difference if the equipment is automated or manual. A compact, well-designed, and efficiently planned kitchen versus a too-large, awkward, poorly planned kitchen can mean increased productivity.

7. *Number of serving lines:* A serving line should be able to handle at least 100 students in 10 minutes. The more serving lines, the more employees needed. How many employees are needed on a serving line? It depends on how much self-service is utilized and how many foods are to be actually served. Good "back up" of serving lines is imperative to the speed and efficiency of the lines.

8. *Experience and training of employees:* Training in how to do the jobs efficiently and correctly, along with experience at doing the job, makes a difference in the number of employees needed.

9. *Supervision:* Supervision and direction in what to do and when can mean a better flow of work and more effective staff performance. The value of work schedules cannot be overemphasized in staffing as a management tool.

10. *Using disposables or washing dishes:* The time dish washing takes will depend a great deal on automation of dish washing and how many dishes are involved. The cost of dish washing, including labor, detergents, utilities, and replacement, should be compared to using disposables (Table 5-4).

Staffing a la Carte Sales

How much time it takes for a la carte service depends on the number of items offered, how much preparation is involved, the time frame in which sales occur, and the type of service involved (for example, individually prepared soft-serve ice cream cones will require more time than selling a fresh apple). Many schools bake cookies, pies, and cakes for selling a la carte, whereas other schools may purchase all the a la carte items already prepared for sale.

Two different methods may be used to arrive at a staffing formula. Twenty-five percent of the revenue from a la carte sales could be designated for labor if most of the food consists of convenience items and requires little preparation. A labor cost of 25 to 30 percent of the revenue is reasonable when most items are prepared (baked). For example, for $300 a la carte sales average per day:

$$\$300 \times .25\,(25\%) = \$75 \text{ can be spent on labor}$$

Table 5-4.   Cost Comparison of Washing
Dishes versus Using Disposable Dishes

	Cost of Washing	Cost of Disposables
Disposables	$0.009	$0.089
Labor[a]	0.08	0.005
Detergents	0.008	—
Replacement of dishes, equipment[b]	0.042	—
Utilities (estimated)	0.02	—
Total cost	$0.159	$0.094

Source: Fairfax County Public Schools 1988.
[a]$6.91 per labor hour (plus 25 percent fringe benefits).
[b]Replacement of entire set of dishes and silver in the period
of one year (trays not replaced) and depreciation on machine
over ten-year period was used.

To determine how many labor hours can be used, divide $75 by the average wages including fringe benefits:

$$\$75.00 \div \$11.75 \text{ per hour* } = 6.3 \text{ labor hours}$$

Another method is to convert a la carte sales to equivalent meals. Since a la carte items are usually priced to make a profit, the equivalent can be three to one (or $3 in a la carte sales equals one lunch). Using the example above, assuming 16 meals per labor hour, the labor needs would be determined as follows:

$$\$300 = 100 \text{ meals}$$
$$\$100 \div 16 = 6.25 \text{ labor hours}$$

The most exact method would be to determine the actual time required for preparing and selling a la carte items at a school with the desired labor costs.

Staffing for Breakfast

The amount of labor needed for a breakfast program depends on the number of meals served and how much preparation is needed. For a simple menu, a formula of 50 breakfasts per labor hour is workable. When the menu consists of a prepackaged cereal, toast, proportioned juice, and milk, very little labor is needed. Labor cost can be kept at a minimum by planning menus with baking that can be done with the lunch the day before.

---

*Includes all fringe benefits.

If the preparation and cleanup of breakfast is worked into the day with the preparation of lunch, income is increased without labor increases. Using disposables instead of dish washing may be an advantage if the labor is needed for only a short time and is unavailable for that period.

Many foodservices are able to add a breakfast program without increasing labor hours. This is an excellent way to increase productivity and revenue. Most on-site production foodservices with a reasonably smooth operation can adjust to the addition of a breakfast program with little difficulty.

Satellite foodservices may have a problem obtaining employees who will work for a 1-hour period to serve breakfast. It could result in paying labor for more hours than needed to serve breakfast.

DISTRIBUTION AND SCHEDULING OF LABOR HOURS

The number of labor hours available should be distributed throughout the work day among the number of people and at the times needed. A combination of part-time and full-time employees is usually the most efficient way of staffing a foodservice. The one-meal-a-day foodservice does not need cooks and bakers for 7 or 8 hours per day.

The productivity of foodservice workers is greatest during the first 6 hours of work and declines after that. Breaking down the labor hours and distributing them wisely over the work day will require "hands-on" experience. Wynn (1973) stated that in an elementary school, "no one except the manager needs to arrive more than three hours before serving time." In distributing the labor hours, the number of employees needed for serving should be first decided. (See examples in Figs. 5-5 and 5-6.)

When planning the schedule for the staff, the manager should determine the job assignments using the job descriptions and keeping each person's abilities in mind. It is necessary to schedule the specific jobs to be done within the time restraints. In order to ensure that all the jobs are completed at the correct time and nothing is omitted, the manager should plan daily work schedules.

Planning a work schedule means assigning workers to do specific jobs at particular times; all jobs and duties should be planned on a daily, weekly, monthly, or yearly basis. The purpose of a work schedule is to inform employees concerning the work to be done, their individual responsibilities, the sequence for each of their duties, and the time it should take to do the job.

Work schedules should be in writing and available to each employee. Some of the advantages of work schedules (VanEgmond-Pannell 1987) are that they

- Save time and energy; prevent employees from waiting around for someone to tell them what to do next.
- Help the kitchen run more smoothly and more efficiently; help increase employees' efficiency by setting deadlines.
- Make the job easier.
- Make it less likely that a job will not be done or will not be completed in time.

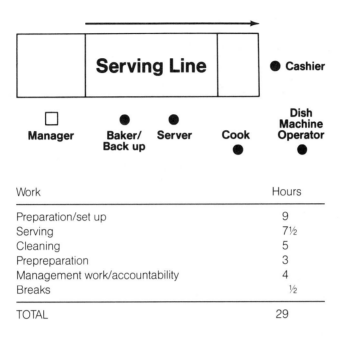

Assigned: 29 hours
Productivity rate: 17 meals per labor hour
Lunches served: 475 + 20 equivalent meals = 495
A la carte: $40 × 0.50 = 20

Work	Hours
Preparation/set up	9
Serving	7½
Cleaning	5
Prepreparation	3
Management work/accountability	4
Breaks	½
TOTAL	29

FIGURE 5-5. Staffing an elementary school foodservice.

- Help the foodservice staff feel more secure, knowing that the job can be done within the time available, and take more pride in their work.
- Distribute the workload more evenly and inform the staff as to who is responsible for each job.

Parkinson's Law that states "Work expands to fill the time available" is illustrated at a work place without work schedules and time limits. One hour of work can be stretched out to fill 2 hours. Time needs to be managed. Employees have to be motivated to be efficient and time-conscious.

An example of a work schedule for an elementary school that serves 400 complete lunches a day is shown in Figure 5-7. When planning work schedules, it is important to determine how much time (labor hours) is available to accomplish the work and then how many people are needed (or available) at serving time, which is usually peak time. The labor hours assigned should be divided among the employees according to the assignments. The hours (number and time of day) assigned an employee should be based on the job to be done.

Assigned: 45½ hours
Productivity rate: 20 meals per labor hour
Lunches served: 750 + 160 equivalent meals = 910
A la carte: $320 × 0.50 = 160 equivalent meals

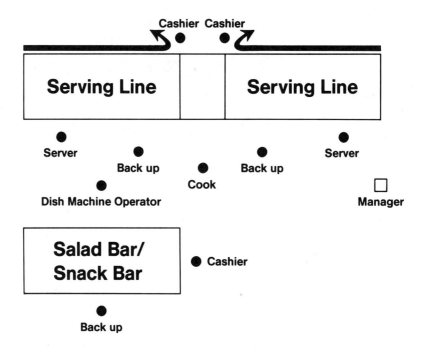

Staff	Shift	Hours
Manager	7:30–3:00	7
Cook	8:00–2:30	6
Assistant/back up	8:30–2:30	5½
Assistant/back up	8:30–2:30	5½
Cashiers (3)	10:00–1:00	7½
Salads/back up	9:00–1:30	4
Dish machine/clean	10:00–2:30	4
Servers (2)	10:00–1:30	6
TOTAL HOURS		45½

FIGURE 5-6. Staffing a high school foodservice.

Menu:	Lasagna Casserole	Buttered French Bread		
	Tossed Salad	Milk		
	Chilled Peach Halves			

TIME	Manager (7 hr)	6-hr Assistant	5-hr Assistant	4-hr Assistant
7:30-8:00	Make coffee for teachers			
8:00-8:30	Help with lasagna sauce	Prepare lasagna		
8:30-9:00	Lunch count— tickets		Dip up fruit and refrigerate	
9:00-9:30				
9:30-10:00	Teacher's salads		Wash vegetables for salad	
10:00-10:30	Cut bread and butter	Prepare bread crumbs for fried chicken tomorrow		Cut up vegetables for salad
10:30-11:00			Put out desserts	Set up line—napkins, straws, dishes
	Eat lunch	Eat lunch	Eat lunch	
11:00-11:30	11:15/Put food on steam table	Put food on steam table	Wash pots and pans	Mix salad for first lunch
11:30-12:00	Serving	Serving Set up for next line	Cashier Help in dishroom	Back up line Dishroom
12:00-12:30	Serving	Serving Set up for next line	Cashier Help in dishroom	Back up line Dishroom
12:30-1:00	Serving	Serving Put away food	Cashier break	Back up line Dishroom
1:00-1:30	Count money. 10 min break. Help clean tables	10-min break Clean tables	Clean steam table	Eat lunch
1:30-2:00	Prepare reports	Clean up		Clean dishroom
2:00-2:30	Place orders			Help with kitchen cleanup
2:30-3:00	Take topping out of freezer and put in refrigerator for tomorrow			

FIGURE 5-7. Work schedule for an elementary school serving 400 lunches. (*Source:* Dorothy Van Egmond-Pannell 1987.)

LABOR SHORTAGES AND TURNOVER

The shortage of foodservice employees at the low end of the pay scale and high turnover are two of the most challenging problems of the 1990s. Those factors will cause tremendous changes in the traditional kitchen and cause automation to flourish.

To figure the turnover rate, Buchanan (1973) provides the following formula:

$$\frac{\text{number of separations from job during year} \times 100}{\text{number of employees at midyear}} = \text{turnover rate \%}$$

$$\text{Example: } \frac{300 \text{ employees resigned} \times 100}{1075 \text{ employees}} = 28 \text{ percent}$$

BIBLIOGRAPHY

Buchanan, R. D. 1973. "Personnel." *School Foodservice Journal* 27(7): 32.

Bureau of Business Practice. 1981. *The Supervisor's Handbook of Productivity and Quality Meetings.* Waterford, Conn.: Bureau of Business Practice.

Caton, Jay, and Mary Nix. 1986. *I Can Manage: A Practical Approach.* New York: Van Nostrand Reinhold.

Fairfax School Food Services. 1988. *Comparison of Disposables versus Dish Washing.* Study done by Fairfax County, Va., Public Schools, Office of Food Services.

Knickrehm, Marie E., Rebecca Jo McConnell, and Claire Anne Tunkel Berg. 1981. "Labor Time Analysis: School Lunch Meal Pattern versus a la Carte Meal Service in a Public School System," *School Food Service Research Review.* 5(2): 85-89.

Mayo, Cynthia R. 1981. "Variables That Affect Productivity in School Food Services." Ph.D. diss., Virginia Polytechnic Institute and State University, Blacksburg.

Mayo, Cynthia R., and Michael D. Olsen. 1985. "Food Servings per Labor Hour: An Alternative Productivity Measure." *School Food Service Research Review* 11(1): 48-51.

North Carolina Department of Education. 1984. *Organization and Personnel Management.* Raleigh, N.C.: State Department of Education.

State of New York. 1987. *Financial Management: Training for School Food Service Personnel.* Albany: The University of the State of New York and the State Education Department.

VanEgmond-Pannell, Dorothy. 1987. *Focus: Management Skills for School Foodservice Managers.* Jackson: Mississippi State Department of Education, Child Nutrition Programs.

West, B., L. Wood, V. Harger, and G. Shugart. 1977. *Food Service in Institutions.* 6th ed. New York: John Wiley & Sons.

West, Patricia Hurst, and Kathryn M. Kolasa. 1984. *School Food Service Training Manual: Organization and Personnel Management.* Greenville, N.C.: East Carolina University.

Wynn, J. T. 1973. "Staffing Broward County Style." *School Foodservice Journal* 27(1): 44-54.

Zaccarelli, Brother Herman, and Jack D. Ninemeier. 1982. *Cost Effective Contract Food Service.* Gaithersburg, Md.: Aspen Systems Corporation.

6

Contract Management

MANAGEMENT COMPANIES

Commercial management companies began managing a few school foodservices in 1959; however, they were independent of the National School Lunch Program. They did not have the benefit of federal support—cash reimbursements and USDA-donated foods. In 1969 Congress passed legislation that allowed a commercial management company to contract with a school district to operate the foodservice; the school district could still qualify for National School Lunch Program funding (see the appendix). This legislation was a result of the White House Conference on Nutrition, which brought to light the poverty in the country and made it clear that, even with the National School Lunch Program, school districts were not meeting the needs of all children for a nutritious meal at school. It was thought that not all needy children could be fed without lifting the restrictions on commercial companies. Public Law 95-166 governs the management companies operating school foodservices (see Appendix A for regulations).

Management companies operated 8 to 10 percent of the school foodservice programs at the beginning of the 1990s; most of those are in the Northeast. This figure may double or triple by the year 2000. Management companies have not made greater inroads into the market mainly for the following reasons: (1) they have concentrated on hospital and inplant foodservice; (2) school district management has been very successful (school foodservices are generally run by people who are dedicated, live in the community, and are well trained in food and nutrition); (3) principals/administrators prefer to control their own school operations; and (4) the profit margin of most school foodservices is small.

For some companies to grow they will have to pursue the school market in the 1990s as other foodservice markets become saturated.

Why Contract Out School Foodservices?

According to Caton (1988), more and more administrators are asking, "Should we consider contracting out management of foodservice?" He said the reasons for the question vary, but that administrators are considering management companies primarily because of

- *Red ink at the bottom line*
- *Boards of education that cannot afford to use general funds to support foodservice programs*
- *Salary/benefits packages that exceed income*
- *Forgetting the foodservice mission of providing nutritious meals that satisfy customers*
- *Problems with personnel negotiations*
- *Worn-out equipment and not enough money to replace it*
- *Aggressive sales pitches by competitors, primarily food management companies that promise extra dollars with no hassles*
- *A communication gap between school foodservice administrators and supervisors*
- *Complacency among rank-and-file school foodservice employees*

Other motivating factors that may arise include the following: (1) The manager has resigned and no suitable replacement has been found; (2) labor costs have been driven too high by low productivity and/or yearly raises in salaries and fringe benefits for all school district employees; (3) current management has failed and is resistant to change; (4) students, parents, and/or administrators demand service that cannot be provided with the present staff and equipment.

There are instances when school administrators should consider an alternative and determine whether it would provide equal or better foodservice at less cost to the community. Some school districts are spending considerable amounts subsidizing the program.

In some cases the decision to contract out management of the foodservice may be a political decision made by a school board (as appeared to be the case in Colorado Springs in the mid-1980s) or the result of a philosophical belief that the management of support services can be handled better by the business world.

The following quiz, given by the Marriott Corporation's School Food Services Department representatives to promote contract management, illustrates how a management company thinks it can resolve a school district's problems.

1. *Is your precious management time being wasted by foodservice problems?*
2. *Are you trying to hire another foodservice manager again?*
3. *Are you or your staff overburdened by foodservice record keeping for state and federal reports?*
4. *Are student participation and satisfaction in your foodservice program going down while the lunch time profits of the surrounding fast food restaurants and markets are going up?*
5. *Are you tired of the red ink at the bottom line of your foodservice budget?*

If your answer is "YES" to any of these questions, take a close look at a school food service management company.

The contract management company may provide a way of resolving the high labor cost, a possible way to avoid subsidizing the program, and a way of giving a face lift to school foodservice in some school districts. Management companies may be able to produce food in a central kitchen or, if the contract requires, provide needed equipment (which remains the property of the management company unless purchased with school foodservice funds). The need for replacement equipment is a rather common problem for school foodservices, because the equipment purchased with federal monies in the 1960s is wearing out and becoming antiquated.

When contracting out foodservice management, labor cost relief is possible only when the employees become the responsibility of the management company. In many situations, school boards are forced to keep employees on their present pay scales and to protect their retirement and insurance benefits. Thus, there may be two sets of employees— those employed by the school districts and those employed by the food management company (this arrangement often causes problems).

MANAGEMENT COMPANY SERVICES

Management companies are involved in school foodservice in three main ways: consulting, providing food only, and providing and serving food. The needs and financial situation of a particular school district will determine which type of service is most appropriate.

Consulting

If a school foodservice has good leadership but has financial problems and/or suffers from low productivity, the inability to supply the quantities of food needed, low participation, low sanitation standards, or labor problems, the expertise of a foodservice management company, a consulting company, or a successful foodservice director from another school district may be extremely beneficial. Frequently what the school foodservice needs is the objective outsider's overview or business advice that a consultant may be able to furnish. This seems to be an area where foodservice management companies and consultants can work effectively.

Providing Food Only

When facilities are not available or are inadequate for on-site preparation, a management company may be equipped to furnish good food at a cost per lunch that can be afforded. Some big city systems have turned their larger facilities into central kitchens or built central kitchens for preparing thousands of lunches for their own school districts but do not have the expertise to operate them effectively. Some districts do not want to make the large capital outlay necessary for such an operation or do not want to enter the food processing business. Food management companies or other school districts may be contracted to provide the food in such cases.

Providing and Serving Food

In the third type of arrangement, the food is procured, prepared, and served by a contractor. The preparation may take place in a commissary or on site. Some school districts require the food to be prepared on site; this limitation is costly and defeats some of the purposes for contracting out in the first place. On-site preparation will often reduce the levels of automation and efficiency that are the secret to reducing cost.

THE CONTRACT

Who Is Responsible?

As can be seen with the different types of services, it is important for the school district to spell out what they want to contract out.

Does contracting out the management (for both food and service) remove all responsibilities for school foodservice? This may be the hope of some administrators. According to Joseph Frey (Ganse 1988), chief of New York's Bureau of School Food Management and Nutrition Program,

> *A classically bad reason to hire a company is if a business manager thinks this relieves him of responsibility for an unglamorous or support function unrelated to education. . . . You will spend just as much time as if you had a self-management program.*

Frey recommends that every contract include a prevailing wage scale to allow hiring of a quality staff, and a successor clause requiring the new employer to pick up the employees' previous benefits. The state agency in New York inspects all bid specifications for management of foodservice. Each state has its own restrictions regarding contract management.

Responsibility for costs should be clearly spelled out in the bid specifications (Fig. 6-1). The school district is responsible for the free and reduced-price meal applications and carrying out the requirements of the program, as well as doing the paperwork to file a claim for federal reimbursement. The management company usually bills the school district for the service provided, with credit for all income received from sales. The school district is normally responsible for preparing the state report. Federal regulations require that all reimbursements are payable to the school districts. The management company contract may or may not require that the company pay for the labor and for the food and supplies used.

Competitive Bids

Federal regulations require that the school district contracting out its foodservice use a competitive bid system. The specifications need to be complete and carefully written. Many school administrators have experienced difficulty writing into the bid all that is needed for a satisfactory arrangement. It is difficult, for example, to write the "quality" desired into bid specification. Awarding to the lowest bidder is usually required. The contract needs to be monitored, which takes a staff member with expertise that includes knowing what the contract requires and familiarity with federal and state regulations.

When a school district contracts with a management company, the district is still the legal authority over the foodservice and is responsible for it; as far as federal and state authorities are concerned, the school district is responsible and is the food authority.

The cycle menu should be included in the bid specifications or it may be requested that the proposal from the bidding companies contain proposed menus (see Fig. 6-2). Additionally, an advisory board composed of parents, teachers, and students can be required. The purpose of such a board is to aid in planning menus and evaluating the services of the management company. When a school district includes several schools in

Category	School District	Contract Company
Food		
Purchasing of food		X
Processing invoices		X
Payment of invoices		X
Transportation and storage of USDA commodities	X	
Labor		
Payment of school district		
Employees' payroll	X	
Fringe benefits	X	
Payment contractor employees' payroll		X
Fringe benefits		X
Custodial services for		
Cleaning dining room	X	
Cleaning kitchen floors	X	
Clerical for preparing Monthly State Claim Report	X	
Additional Items		
Dishes/silverware/trays—		
Original inventory	X	
Replacement	X	
Telephone—local and long distance	X	
Removal of trash and garbage	X	
Replacement of small equipment (pots, pans, etc.)	X	
Replacement of large equipment	X	
Insurance—liability, fire, and theft	X	
Maintenance of equipment	X	
Vehicle for transporting USDA commodities	X	
Operating Expenses	X	
Supplies		
Detergent and cleaning supplies		X
Paper supplies		X
Menu paper and printing	X	
Free/reduced-price meal applications	X	
Meal tickets for free and reduced	X	
Postage	X	
Licenses	X	
Pest control	X	
Utilities	X	

FIGURE 6-1. Cost responsibility summary.

JANUARY

ELEMENTARY LUNCH MENU

MONDAY	TUESDAY	WEDNESDAY	THURSDAY	FRIDAY
	This is an equal opportunity program. If you believe you have been discriminated against because of race, color, national origin, age, sex, or handicap, write to the Secretary of Agriculture, Washington, D.C. 20250.	Milk Provided Daily		
No School 2	Corn Dog French Fries Orange Juice Bar Ketchup/Mustard 3	Cheeseboat Fresh Fruit Garden Salad Thousand Island Dressing 4	Bean & Cheese Burrito Peas & Carrots Fresh Fruit Taco Sauce 5	Hamburger Tater Tots Cherry Juicy Treat Hamburger Bun (2) Ketchup (2) 6
Golden Fried Chicken Hash Browns Grape Juicee Dinner Roll 9	Hot Ham & Cheese on English Muffin Fresh Fruit Carrot Sticks Condiment 10	Beef Enchilada w/Cheese & Sauce Seasoned Corn Cinnamon Apple Cup 11	Hot Dog Fresh Fruit French Fries Ketchup/Mustard Hot Dog Bun 12	Sausage & Cheese Pizza in a box 100% Apple Juice California Raisins 13
No School MARTIN LUTHER KING JR'S. BIRTHDAY OBSERVED 16	Beef & Bean Burrito Tater Tots Cherry Juice Bar Taco Sauce Ketchup 17	Cheeseburger Hamburger Bun Fresh Fruit Carrot Sticks Ketchup 18	Mexiboat Shredded Lettuce Fresh Fruit Taco Sauce 19	Meatballs Italiano Hash Browns Strawberry Ice Juicee Italian Bread Ketchup 20
Salisbury Steak w/Gravy French Fries Grape Juice Bar Dinner Roll Ketchup 23	Pepperoni Pizzaboat Fresh Fruit Garden Salad Thousand Island Dressing 24	Chick 'N Cheese Patty Tater Tots Frosty Fruit Cup Bun Ketchup 25	Chili Dog Fresh Fruit Seasoned Corn Hot Dog Bun 26	Ham & Cheese on a Sesame Seed Bun 100% Fruit Punch Juice Hash Browns Ketchup 27
Chicken Nuggets French Fries Strawberry Banana Twist Cup Hamburger Bun BBQ Sauce/Ketchup 30	Hamburger Fresh Fruit California Raisins Hamburger Bun Ketchup 31			

FIGURE 6-2. Sample school menu. (*Source:* Feeding Systems, Inc. 1988.)

97

the contract, there is a need for someone on the school district staff to oversee the contract and visit the schools' foodservices.

The financial arrangement with the management company may be on a flat-fee or fixed-fee basis or a fee based on quantity of service. Payment based on a percentage of the profits is not allowed under federal regulations. The flat or fixed fee provides little or no incentive to a management company to improve the program.

New York's state laws are probably the strictest on a management company. They require management companies to operate under a fixed-fee contract, and the school district has to take the lowest bid.

A fee based on the number of meals served is probably the most desirable, with all profits going back to the school district for use in the school foodservice program. In the fee charged by some of the major management companies in 1988, costs were between 7 and 10 cents per meal served plus administrative salaries.

Commodities may be an important consideration in the contract. It should specify that the management company use the commodities and be responsible to the school district if the commodities are allowed to spoil. The school district will be considered ultimately responsible for the commodities in any event.

Listed below are 11 personnel requirements to include in a contract compliance system, according to Zaccarelli and Ninemeier (1982).*

1. *Resumes of all key on-site management personnel provided to facility officials.*
2. *New management personnel approved in advance by facility officials.*
3. *All dietary staff passed required health examinations; certificates on file.*
4. *Training programs conducted for submanagement personnel; records of subjects, names of personnel attending, and training contract hours per month maintained.*
5. *Dietary staff (management and submanagement) considered objectionable by facility officials not retained.*
6. *Dietary staff paid on timely basis; fringe benefits paid according to plans in proposal.*
7. *Dietary staff policies, to the extent practical, same as those pertaining to nondietary staff retained by the facility.*
8. *On-site visit by management company regional and other staff specialists on the basis agreed upon in the contract.*
9. *Dietary staff in proper, required uniform.*
10. *Employees' wage rates paid as agreed upon in the proposal.*
11. *Employs registered dieticians and other professionally qualified staff as outlined in proposal.*

Contracts with management companies take many forms and vary greatly across the country. For example, a school district might maintain the employees on its payroll in order to continue the retirement and other fringe benefits and/or present salary scales. In this case, new employees hired would be put on the management company's pay scale. This does not relieve the school district of the immediate financial costs.

---

*Reprinted from *Cost Effective Contract Food Service: An Institutional Guide,* by H. E. Zaccarelli and J. D. Ninemeier, pp. 125-26, with permission of Aspen Publishers, Inc., © 1982.

School district-managed programs may have unfair disadvantages. The salary pay scales often are much higher than those of commercial foodservices. As health insurance rates continue to rise, the fringe benefits may be adding more than 30 to 35 percent to labor costs. At the same time, management companies generally pay lower wages and provide fewer benefits. Also, management companies do not have union employees or are not restricted to the laborious bid system for purchasing. They can react quickly and take advantage of "good prices."

The contract agreement should normally contain the answers to these questions:

- Will the foodservice be operated under federal regulations, continue to participate in the National School Lunch Program, and receive reimbursement and USDA-donated commodities?
    - If so, who files the claim with the state agency? Who furnishes the data? By what date each month?
    - Who is responsible for transporting and storage of USDA commodities? Who is responsible if commodities are stored improperly and are allowed to spoil?
- What quality and quantity (portion sizes) of food will be served? Will textured vegetable protein be used?
- What menus will be served? Will they be presented for approval on a regular basis? Will a la carte foods be sold? Will choices be offered on the menus?
- What type of service will be used? Will speed lines, vending machines, self-service, made-to-order service, and/or traditional cafeteria service be provided?
- Where will the food be prepared? Will it be prepared at a commissary or on site, and when?
- What are the nutritional standards of the food to be served?
- Which of the following costs are to be borne by each party?
    - Labor, payroll, personnel records, fringe benefits
    - Trash and garbage collection and disposal
    - Accounting system for federal and state claim forms
    - Invoices for food and supplies
    - Insurance—liability, worker's compensation, fire insurance, and theft
    - Maintenance and replacement of equipment
    - Utilities—electricity, water, gas, oil
    - Extermination service
    - Cleaning of the dining room; kitchen floors, tables, and chairs in the dining areas; floors and walls in the dining room
    - Sales tax
    - Telephone
    - Leftovers, overordering, meals not eaten because of emergency school dismissal

- Who is responsible for the following:
    - Setting lunch periods (how many and how long?)
    - Purchasing food and supplies
    - Cashiering, bank deposits, records, and reports
    - Sanitation standards, outbreaks of food poisoning
    - Labor negotiations

—Setting prices charged students for lunch
—Resolving student, parent, faculty, and community complaints
—Sale of lunch tickets and maintaining anonymity of students receiving free lunch
—Training new employees
—Selecting manager

Nonperformance and Discharge of Contractor

A 60-day cancellation clause should be written into any contract between a school district and foodservice management company. Such a clause can be exercised at the discretion of either party without the need for demonstrating nonperformance.

In addition, a management company and school district should each have a way out of their contractual obligations at any time during the term of the contract when one or more of the following can be shown to exist: (1) failure of the other party to perform a stipulated condition; (2) fraud and misrepresentation; (3) failure to perform because of actions of the other party; and (4) waiver of performance by the other party.

There are three situations in which the parties to a contract between a school district and management company are released from the duty to perform (Zaccarelli and Ninemeier 1982): Enactment of a new law makes performance illegal; property or material that is required to complete the contract is destroyed; an essential element that the contracting parties assumed to exist is missing (e.g., when a school is closed).

BIBLIOGRAPHY

Caton, Jay. 1988. "Sell Some Success for Lunch." *School Food Service Journal* 42(8): 17.
Crimmins, M. B. 1978. "We Belong in School Foodservice." *Food Management* 13(1): 31-32.
Eyster, J. 1980. *The Negotiation and Administration of Hotel Management Contracts.* 2d ed. Ithaca, N.Y.: Cornell University Press.
Ganse, Robin D. 1988. "How to Handle Food Management Company Contracts." *School Food Service Journal* 42(8): 31.
Public Law 91-248. [An amendment to the Child Nutrition Act of 1966.] 1970. 91st Cong., 2d sess. (84 Stat. 107). May 14.
VanEgmond-Pannell, Dorothy. 1985. "Table Arrangements: When Should a District Opt for Contract Management." *American School and University*, March, 64-66, 71.
White House Conference on Food, Nutrition and Health. 1970. *Final Report.* Washington, D.C.: U.S. Government Printing Office.
Zaccarelli, Brother Herman, and Jack D. Ninemeier. 1982. *Cost Effective Contract Food Service.* Gaithersburg, Md.: Aspen Systems Corporation.

7

Procuring and Controlling Inventory

OVERVIEW OF MARKET

School foodservice is a $14 billion business (in commercial-equivalent dollars), employing (according to USDA) 300,000 people, with purchases amounting to approximately $7 billion. The purchases are primarily food, which accounts for 30 to 50 percent of the revenue. Paper and disposable products and cleaning supplies will run between 3 and 12 percent of the revenue. Large and small equipment will generally take 2 to 4 percent of the revenue.

Some of the biggest changes that will affect procurement during the 1990s will be buyouts by giants like General Foods and the forming of four to five very large food companies. This will mean higher prices and less customization of products.

The use of technology will affect procurement in what is purchased and how specifications will read; for example, hydroponic growing of vegetables and fish farming will be more common. In the year 2000, it may be common for a school to have its own hydroponic garden and stocked pond. With the continuing advances in genetic engineering, even the shapes of foods may be modified; for example, flatter watermelons may be developed for easier storage.

Computerization will make the analysis of a bid much easier and the ordering of food simpler and faster. Schools will place their orders through the computer terminal network, and the order will be printed out in the distributor's office. At the same time, the order will be checked against the distributor's inventory to determine whether it will meet the demands of the order. The Universal Product Code (**UPC**) will become a standard requirement on products, and the use of computers and scanners will make inventory control and the checking in of products much easier and more accurate and complete.

Some major changes will be made in the processing of food. Irradiation of food, where a low dose of gamma rays is used, kills harmful bacteria, controls sprouting and germination of root vegetables, extends shelf life, and delays ripening and aging of fruits and vegetables. Another processing method that has been slow to catch on in the United States is aseptic packaging, which makes food shelf-stable. It will be widely used in the 1990s. Individual servings of juices were among the first products on the market. Shelf-stable "TV" dinners were introduced in this country five years ago but did not catch on. The "retort pouch" is being used for many items formerly sold only in the can (e.g., applesauce and catsup). The common can and glass jar may not be so common by the year 2000. Because these newer processes improve flavor over canned products and are more like the frozen product in flavor, the shelf-stable products will be preferred over canned and most frozen products. The advantages of shelf-stable products are numerous and usually mean financial savings.

DETERMINING WHAT TO PURCHASE

The food restrictions on federally subsidized school foodservice programs make it more difficult for sales representatives to sell food to schools than to hospitals. The seller needs to do his or her homework on regulations and understand the peculiarities of the child nutrition programs.

Purchasing is the process of procuring food, and to most of the school foodservice management it means more than merely ordering. "Purchasing" implies that planning has gone into the ordering. According to Kotschevar (1975), the challenge of purchasing is buying the "right product in the amounts needed at the time needed within the price that can be afforded."

The purchaser should have a knowledge of food and have contact with the customer in order to know what is needed, as well as the best sizes, cuts, and grades or quality desired. Specifications should be written by foodservice personnel describing what is desired.

Factors Influencing Purchasing

The factors that influence what is to be purchased are: menu and nutritional content, food budget, labor cost and skill of personnel, season and availability of food, storage, numbers of meals to be served, available equipment, customer likes and dislikes, USDA-donated foods, processing contracts, and federal regulations. These factors are discussed briefly below.

Menu and Nutritional Content
The menu is the blueprint for purchasing. A manager should buy for the menu rather than planning the menu around what has been purchased. The menu is planned to meet certain nutritional requirements; thus managers have to be concerned about the nutritional content of the products purchased. Specific nutrients such as sodium and fat will be of greater concern in the 1990s.

Food Budget
The food budget will determine to a large extent what is put on the menu and consequently what is purchased. On the average, 30 to 50 percent of the budget is spent on food. In school districts with unusually high labor costs, it will come closer to 30 percent, whereas nearer 50 percent is needed to provide a lot of variety.

Labor
The labor available and the skill of the employees should be considered by a foodservice manager or menu planner and purchaser when deciding if complicated recipes are to be followed, if raw ingredients will be used, or if convenience items will be purchased.

Season and Availability of Food

The price and quality of food are affected by the season and availability of food. Purchasing fresh green bell peppers in January will mean higher costs in most parts of the country than purchasing peppers in season. Drought and other factors may have an impact on prices. The drought of 1988 caused shortages in grain products that in turn caused food prices nearly to double for foods such as corn.

Storage

The type and quantity of storage needed and available should be carefully considered. Many products can be purchased in canned, fresh, and frozen states. The amount of freezer space available may determine if the product will be purchased frozen or canned, and storage capacity will affect the frequency of delivery.

Numbers of Meals to Be Served

The numbers of meals served and other food services offered will determine quantities needed.

Equipment

The types and amounts of equipment available also affect what foods should be purchased. In some cases, it may be more economical to purchase an item already prepared than to purchase a piece of equipment.

Customer Likes and Dislikes

Smart buyers realize that it does not matter what they like; it is what the customers like that really matters. Much can be learned about food preferences by talking with students and watching plate waste. (Methods of obtaining information on student opinions are discussed in chapter 11.)

USDA-Donated Foods

The commodities received by schools from the USDA will make a considerable difference in what is purchased. Donated foods, which account for 20 percent or more of the total food used, have to be worked into menus and in some cases immediately (when the product is fresh produce).

Processing Contracts

Using USDA-donated commodities as ingredients in processed foods has become very popular. Nearly 30 percent of the foods issued in 1988 by USDA went to companies for further processing. State processing contracts are used in most states. However, National Commodity Processing (**NCP**) is also available. It is operated by USDA and is limited to bonus commodities. The NCP is used particularly in states such as Kansas that do not have state processing contracts.

To participate in the NCP system, the school district must complete and submit an NCP System Post Card (Form FNS-516), which can be obtained from the Food and Nutrition Division of USDA.* The school district is assigned a nine-digit recipient agency code and a masterfile listing of food processors.

---

*Special Operations Branch, Nutrition and Technical Services Division, 3101 Park Center Drive, Alexandria, VA 22302; phone, 703/756-3888.

The buyer should be aware that some processing is no bargain. The value of the commodity should be considered money and added to the price charged to determine if it is a good deal. Receiving the value is usually through a "rebate" method, which is not easy. This means a claim form must be completed by the school or by the school district on each item. Some companies help by tracking the information and initiating the process.

Federal Regulations

The federal regulations that affect the school foodservice programs are many. The buyer needs to be very familiar with those regulations that come under the National School Lunch Act (see the appendix).

The school lunch and breakfast patterns influence portion sizes and ingredients that go into products for school foodservices. The USDA *Menu Planning Guide* (1983) provides a checklist of meal pattern-related factors to be considered when writing food specifications.

Procurement Standards

The Office of Management and Budget (1979) established procurement standards for purchasing for the child nutrition programs. These standards must be carried out for purchases of more than $10,000. The regulations require competitive bidding by school food authorities at the school district level. The major provisions of the procurement standards are as follows:

1. All procurement transactions must be conducted in such a way as to provide for maximum open and free competition.

2. Each school food authority must establish written procurement procedures that comply with procurement standards. These will include a system for contract administration to ensure the contractor's compliance.

3. Invitations for bids must be based on a clear and accurate description of the material, product, or services to be procured. "Brand name or equal" may be used, but the features of the brand name must be specified. This means that descriptive food specifications should be included in the invitations for bid.

4. Positive efforts should be made to utilize small businesses and minority-owned businesses.

5. School districts cannot use "cost-plus-a-percentage-of-cost" or "cost-plus-a-percentage-of-income" methods of contracting.

6. Awards are to be made only to responsible contractors that possess the potential ability to perform successfully under the terms and conditions of a proposed procurement agreement.

7. Each school district must maintain a code of conduct to govern the performance of its officers, employees, and agents in contracting for payment and expending program funds. This means that neither the officers, employees, nor agents will accept any gratuities, favors, or anything of monetary value from contractors. These codes of conduct carry penalties, sanctions, or disciplinary actions for violations.

8. Sufficient records must be maintained to detail the significant history of a procurement for 3 years.

9. All contracts awarded in excess of $10,000 must contain a provision requiring compliance with Executive Order 11246, entitled "Equal Employment Opportunity."

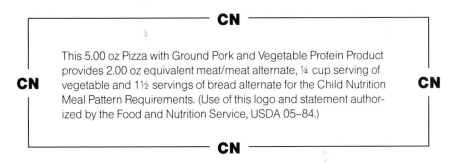

**PIZZA WITH GROUND PORK AND
VEGETABLE PROTEIN PRODUCT**

CN

This 5.00 oz Pizza with Ground Pork and Vegetable Protein Product provides 2.00 oz equivalent meat/meat alternate, ¼ cup serving of vegetable and 1½ servings of bread alternate for the Child Nutrition Meal Pattern Requirements. (Use of this logo and statement authorized by the Food and Nutrition Service, USDA 05–84.)

CN   **CN**

CN

FIGURE 7-1. Child nutrition label. (*Source:* USDA 1988.)

Child Nutrition (CN) Label

The Child Nutrition (CN) Labeling Program has existed since the early 1970s. It is administered by the Food and Nutrition Service (FNS) of USDA in conjunction with the Food Safety and Inspection Service and Agricultural Marketing Service of USDA, and the National Marine Fisheries Service of the United States Department of Commerce. Products that can be CN-labeled include: red meat, poultry, fish, seafood, cheese, eggs, dry beans, peanut butter, hot dogs, corn dogs, other similar sausage products, juice drinks, and juice drink products.

The advantages of purchasing a product with a CN label are (1) the contribution of the product toward meeting the meal patterns is known, (2) a warranty against audit claims is provided, and (3) the foodservices are protected from exaggerated claims about a product. The disadvantages are (1) the CN label adds cost to the product, and (2) there are some good products not being used because they do not have a CN label. In some cases the CN label creates a monopoly when the state requires the local district to purchase only products with CN labels.

The buyer or foodservice manager can identify products that are CN-labeled by the CN logo and statement, a six-digit product identification number, a statement of the product's contribution toward meal pattern, a statement that the use of the logo and CN label statement was authorized by Food and Nutrition Service of the USDA, and the month and year the label was approved. An example of a CN label is shown in Figure 7-1.

DETERMINING THE PURCHASING PROCESS TO USE

Bid Buying

Bid buying is the written process of requesting prices on products to be purchased. Good, detailed specifications that will describe each product to be purchased are needed. These help ensure that the product bid is the quality product wanted. Some very innovative systems of purchasing are being used today. The most common are (1) the open-market written bid; (2) open-market telephone quotes; (3) the blanket contract, with discounts off list prices; (4) the formal bid or requirement contract; and (5) cost plus fixed fee.

Open-Market Written Bid

The open-market written bid is like a formal bid and is a legal agreement between the school district and the vendor. In formal bid situations the purchasing agent should submit an invitation to bid to all approved vendors. The formal bid process requires written specifications and estimates of quantities to be purchased. The vendor who submits the lowest bid will be awarded the contract. The specification should convey clearly what the buyer wants.

Open-Market Telephone Quotes

The open-market telephone quote system of purchasing is used frequently when purchasing fresh produce, and is used by small school districts on other items as well. When the open market is used, prices should be compared among two or three companies, and more if time allows and the vendors are available. This obtaining of quotes and comparing of prices will encourage competition and will result in considerable savings.

Blanket Contract

The blanket contract with a discount off list price is used more often when purchasing office supplies, computers, and equipment than when purchasing food. This method can make the bid process easier and can extend over a large number of items. From studies of classroom supplies done by the Texas State Department of Education, however, it was found that the prices paid under the blanket contract were higher than when purchasing under a formal bid, listing exact quantities.

Formal Bid or Requirement Contract

With the formal bid or requirement contract, written specifications and quantities (or estimates of quantities) are needed. An invitation to bid is issued, and the bids are accepted at a designated time. The award is made as an aggregate or by line items to the low bidder who meets specifications. If food products are to be delivered to the schools, the aggregate will probably be necessary to have sufficient volume. Awarding a bid by line item may result in the best prices for large equipment and for truckload quantities of food and paper supplies. Distributors often prefer line-item bidding, rather than aggregate for large equipment and truckload quantities of food.

The bid may be for any period of time; however, the firm price can best be used for one year or less. The contract may contain the option to extend a bid contract and maintain the same prices if both parties agree (contractor and school district) for an equal length of time to the original contract or less time. An escalator clause is often used on milk and ice cream bids where price increases can be tied to the Federal Milk Market prices as published by the Federal Milk Market Administration in the *Market Administration Bulletin.*

Better prices are obtained in most cases with short-term contracts. Monthly contracts are ideal (in terms of price), but bidding monthly may not be feasible to manage. For most school districts, monthly bidding is too time-consuming. The best prices are obtained when quotes are given by telephone and for truckload quantities coming directly from processors; however, procurement standards may prevent public schools from using this method.

Cost Plus Fixed Price

This is a written contract system that is relatively new and has grown fast in popularity. Some refer to it as "formula pricing," "fee for service," "contract purchasing," and "one-stop shopping." The State Director for Mississippi, Marlene Gunn, R.D., and over 30 Mississippi school districts and Etha Bailey, the Indian River County, Florida School District Director in 1987 have been leaders in this method of purchasing.

This system is frequently used in commercial foodservices. It usually decreases the number of vendors, means fewer bids, prevents companies from having to take a risk of prices changing, allows bids to cover longer periods of time, and ensures to some degree that a school district will get a product even if the cost has increased. Product lines subject to frequent price changes (like produce and meats) are best bid on this more flexible basis. Table 7-1 provides an example of prices one school district paid for produce. The success of this system depends a great deal on the integrity of the company and how well the school district is kept informed. Purdue University's Restaurant, Hotel, and Institutional Management Department (Stix and Hiemstra 1989) has recently evaluated the cost-plus system in the state of Indiana. They found that the school districts using this method of

Table 7-1.   Cost-Plus-Fixed-Price[a] Ordering Form

Food Item	Fixed Price or Handling Cost
Apples, Red Delicious, packed: 125/case	$3.00/case
Bananas, petite, packed: 150/case	2.50/case
Broccoli, purchase unit: bunch	0.25/bunch
Cabbage, green and white, packed: 50-pound case	2.50/bag
Cabbage, red, purchase unit: head	0.40/head
Carrots, packed: 50-pound sack	2.50/sack
Cucumbers, packed: 5-pound bag	0.15/bag
Grapes, Thompson Green, purchase unit: pound	0.20/pound
Lettuce, iceberg, packed: 24/case	2.00/case
Melon, cantaloupes, packed: 36/crate	3.00/crate
Melon, cantaloupes, packed: each	0.20/each
Oranges, Valencia, packed: 125/case	2.50/case
Parsley, curly, packed: 4-ounce bunch	0.10/bunch
Peppers, green, bell, packed: 5-pound bag	0.15/bag
Pears, Anjou, packed: 120/case	3.00/case
Radishes, red, packed: 6-ounce bags	0.10/bag
Spinach, packed: 10-ounce bag	0.20/bag
Tomatoes, unworked, packed: 25-pound box	2.00/box
Tomatoes, cherry, packed: 12-pint/flat	2.00/flat
Watermelon (in season), packed: each	1.00/each

[a]Current market cost is added to the fixed price.

purchasing paid 4.2 percent less for their food during the period of study, August-December 1988.

The Indian River County School District's foodservice director in 1986-1988 found that they did better with cost-plus-fixed-price purchases on most items than with formal bid/requirement contract prices the year before. Their cost-plus-fixed-price contracts allowed the distributor to change item prices monthly (on a set day of the month, such as the first Monday) if the invoice price paid by the company was increased or decreased. The distributor was audited prior to the contract award and semiannually thereafter to ensure that items invoiced to the district were in fact distributor cost plus the delivery fee bid.

The Indian River County School District found that the prices changed on 78 of 107 items from November 1986 through May 1987. The changes averaged a 2 percent increase.

Centralized Purchasing

With centralized purchasing, one person or office purchases for a number of schools, whereas with decentralization, each manager meets with sales representatives from the companies and determines products that will be purchased. The advantages of centralized purchasing include the following: (1) time is saved; (2) buying power is greater, and prices are usually better; (3) the bidding process can be used; (4) the person handling purchasing can specialize; (5) the foodservices in the school district are standardized in terms of the products purchased; and (6) better budgetary control is achieved.

Cooperative Purchasing

Cooperative purchasing is a form of centralized purchasing in which several school districts within a geographical area combine their needs. Cooperative purchasing can improve buying power greatly. Small school districts in particular can profit from this method of purchasing. Many school districts in California, Michigan, Montana, and Colorado, for example, have saved considerably on food, paper goods, and supplies with cooperative purchasing. To arrive at specifications that all the directors/supervisors can agree upon may be the biggest challenge in the process. Cremers (1983) reported that in California generally each school district orders, receives, and is billed directly. In some instances, however, one district may buy for two or three districts and then deliver the orders to them or have the districts pick up the product.

State Contract

Many states have a purchasing agent who purchases foods for state institutions such as jails, hospitals, and universities. Some states (Virginia, for example) allow public schools to use the state purchasing service. The state may be purchasing in large enough quantities and have enough clout to obtain better prices than even a large school district can obtain, particularly on such items as sugars, flour, and detergents.

Most states also have contracts for uniforms and other supplies and equipment through which public schools can purchase.

CENTRALIZED WAREHOUSING

Centralized warehousing and delivery systems may or may not be the most cost-effective. In evaluating this option, several important questions need to be considered.

1. How much does it cost per case to warehouse and deliver? In determining what is a standard cost per case for warehousing and delivery, one could use the prices paid for warehousing and delivery of commodities less 5 to 10 percent (profit margin). (Most state commodity distribution agencies have in place bid prices for warehousing and delivering commodities.)
2. Is the price paid for the products delivered to the warehouse plus warehousing and delivery cost less or no more than that for purchasing the product delivered to the schools?
3. Can deliveries to each school by distributors be obtained?
4. Does central warehousing provide better quality control?

Another important concern is whether the volume of the school district's inventory is sufficient to warrant a centralized warehousing and distribution system. If not, it can cost four to five times more than having the product delivered by the commercial supplier. The Montgomery County, Maryland, Public Schools have a cost-effective warehouse system. The school district's volume warrants its operating a 22,000-square-foot foodservice warehouse. The warehouse, which stores 1.6 million pounds of food, is being utilized to its capacity through contracts with other school districts and with the county government for the storing of food and distributing of food to the needy.

SPECIFICATIONS

A specification is a precise description of the desired item. It should list particulars precisely and identify the product's characteristics in a manner mutually understandable to the buyer and potential sellers as shown below.

> Item name: Beans, green.
> Description: Canned, 1 to 1½ inch long school cut, dark green, Blue Lake variety, 3 sieve.
> Grade: Grade A.
> Pack size: 6/10 cans per case.
> Approved brands: Comstock, Code Red Label, or equal.
> Purchase unit: Case.

Depending on the products, a specification can include the following:

- *Name of the item:* If available, the official **Standard of Identity** should be listed for processed food products (such as mayonnaise, ketchup, and peanut butter).*
- *Ingredients of processed items* having no standard of identity.
- *Quality or official grade.*
- *Class, kind, style, and/or variety: Class* may refer to the sex of an animal. *Kind* may refer to types of foods such as flour (all purpose or whole grain). *Variety* refers to such foods

---

*Standards of identity, which are official descriptions of processed food products, can be obtained from the Superintendent of Documents (U.S. Government Printing Office, Washington, DC 20402).

as fruits and vegetables (Red Delicious, Jonathan, and Winesap apples). *Style* generally refers to how a product is processed (canned green beans may be cut, whole, or French style).

- *Size of the product:* Refers to weight (18- to 20-pound turkeys), number per container (125 per box), can size (number 10), and count (8 per pound). See USDA *Food Buying Guide for Child Nutrition Programs* (1984) for yield data to assist in determining sizes desired.
- *Origin:* Where the product was produced; domestic or imported. Congress encourages the purchasing of domestically grown and processed foods. (Public Law 100-237 [H.R. 1340] passed January 1988, states, "The Secretary [of Agriculture] shall require that recipient agencies [any school receiving commodities] purchase, whenever possible, only food products that are produced in the United States.") The law does not require purchasing domestic products, except for the food purchased by the commodity letter of credit sites using CLOCs (discussed in chapter 1).
- *Packaging unit:* Crate, carton, box, retort pouch, bag, barrel, or case.
- *Special instruction:* "Special instruction" may spell out other types of restrictions, for example: on processed canned foods, this year's pack may be required; and for frozen foods, the products must be delivered at 0°F or below. Also, many school districts are now requiring an ingredients list, nutritional analysis from a certified laboratory (Fig. 7-2) and restricting certain ingredients (such as artificial coloring and flavoring, MSG, sulfites, BHT, and BHL).
- *Labeling required:* Child Nutrition (CN) label, Institutional Meat Purchase Specifications (**IMPS**), low sodium, and in the case of equipment, National Sanitation Foundation (**NSF**), and so on. Some definitions of food label terms appear at the end of this section.
- *Special provisions:* Special provisions are usually listed in the preface of the invitation to bid. It is very important to the bidders to know what is expected of them and what they can expect of the school districts on the following:
    - —Quantity needed per delivery, number of delivery sites and locations
    - —Period of time, length of contract
    - —Conditions for payment, discounts accepted and considered in award of bid
    - —Frequency of deliveries (daily or weekly)
    - —Where to be delivered (inside the door, placed in ice cream cabinet, on dock, etc.)
    - —Time of delivery (date and hours)
    - —How the bid will be awarded—by line item or aggregate (aggregate means all or nothing)
    - —Conditions for adjusting and canceling orders due to changes in school schedule or other emergencies
    - —Display equipment, storage equipment* (such as ice cream cabinets), and promotional material required
    - —Samples and can cuttings (both are expensive to the company and should be limited to those needed to make decision on "equal" items when bid low)
    - —Penalty if contract is not complied with

---

*Including equipment for storage may exclude some companies from bidding and result in no competition in bidding process.

Sample B Pizza

ANALYSIS	RESULT AS RECEIVED		LIMIT OF QUANTITATION	LAB CODE
Moisture	41.9	% by wt.	0.01	010101000
Protein (N × 6.25)	12.0	% by wt.	0.1	010401800
Fat (Hydrolysis Method)	17.4	% by wt.	0.1	010802800
Fiber	0.7	% by wt.	0.1	011001700
Ash	2.79	% by wt.	0.01	011201300
Phosphorus	0.23	% by wt.	0.001	011301300
Est. Digestable Carbohydrate	25.9	% by wt.	0.1	011500000
Est. Caloric Value	308.	Cal/100g	0.1	011700000
Vitamin A (HPLC)	200.	IU/100g	20.	012407500
Thiamine	0.34	mg/100g	0.001	013104500
Riboflavin	0.29	mg/100g	0.002	013204500
Carotene	920.	mcg/100g	50.	013502500
Vitamin C	< 1.	mg/100g	1.	013704500
Fatty Acid Profile		attached		018909000
Cholesterol	0.047	% by wt.	0.006	019611000
Calcium	197.	mg/100g	0.05	039701300
Iron	1.61	mg/100g	0.05	040001300
Potassium	82.8	mg/100g	0.05	040701300
Sodium	736.	mg/100g	0.05	040801300
Sodium	736.	mg/100g	0.005	044000000
Sodium	209.	mg/oz.	0.001	044100000
Niacin	2.6	mg/100g	0.1	115904500
Saturated Fat	47.6	%		900100000
This result was calculated from the fatty acid profile for this sample.				
Total Sample Weight	See Below			900200500
Six slices of pizza weighed 813.7 grams.				
Monounsaturated Fat	34.1	%		900300000
This result was calculated from the fatty acid profile for this sample.				
Polyunsaturated Fat	18.2	%		900400000
This result was calculated from the fatty acid profile for this sample.				

FIGURE 7-2. Nutritional analysis. (*Source:* Lancaster Laboratories, Inc. 1989.)

Some product lines may be difficult to specify in such a way that more than one company can bid on the product. In the case of snack items such as cakes and pies, for example, each company may have its own special products. It may help to bid a product line, giving each company the opportunity to submit prices for a specific number of items that meet some general specifications. Student/adult taste panels can be used to determine acceptable product lines. Then the bid is awarded to the low bidder with an acceptable product line.

Accurate specifications are the secret to obtaining good quality, or the quality desired, in competitive bidding. A director or manager of a foodservice may blame poor quality on having to take a "low bid" when in fact low quality results from inadequately written specifications or a failure to enforce the bid.

When writing specifications, the following criteria should be considered:

1. Is the bid enforceable?
2. Is the product tailored to meet menu needs?
3. Is a customized product necessary? Will it add considerably to the cost?
4. Is the language used understandable to companies who may want to bid?

The prices charged in a bid for a school district will cover overhead influenced by (1) the cost to the distributor of delivering the product (including hidden costs such as taking directors/managers to dinner, gifts, and other "freebies"), (2) competition and how important the contract is to the company, and (3) the size of a minimum order. The hidden costs should be kept at a minimum, and local purchasing policies often address these issues.

Labeling Standards for Processed Foods

Food processors are expected to adhere to Food and Drug Administration ingredient standards in labeling their products. Some of the most current FDA nutritional standards are listed below.

> *Dietetic or Diet:* must either meet the requirements for low or reduced-calorie foods (defined below) or be for a special dietary purpose, such as "low-sodium diets."
> *Light or Lite:* describes a low- or reduced-calorie food. Syrup in canned fruit can be described as light, based on its density; the designation "light cream" indicates fat content.
> *Low Calorie:* must contain no more than 40 calories per serving or 11 calories per ounce.
> *Reduced Calorie:* must be at least one-third lower in calories than the product otherwise would be.
> *Sodium Free:* can contain no more than 5 milligrams of sodium per serving.
> *Very Low Sodium:* must contain no more than 35 milligrams of sodium in a serving.
> *Low Sodium:* must contain no more than 140 milligrams of sodium per serving.
> *Reduced Sodium:* sodium must be reduced by 75 percent of its usual sodium content.
> *Unsalted:* processed without the normally added salt.

ORDERING

The process of ordering just enough food and supplies, receiving them at the right time, storing them properly, issuing them, and accounting for them is quite complex. The process is even more challenging for the manager if the menu is to be strictly adhered to and a low inventory is desired. Orders should be geared to the menu: every item needed to produce the recipes that make up the menus should be listed, and those that are not in inventory need to be ordered.

The person preparing orders (usually the manager) will need (1) to have a list of all items needed to serve the planned menus, (2) to determine what is in inventory, and (3) to determine what will be used between the time the order is placed and the time the menu being ordered for will be served. Regrettably, many managers order by guess. Often they do not have all the ingredients needed and end up borrowing from other schools or changing menus at the last minute; or they overorder and carry a heavy inventory to avoid running short. Ordering just what is needed in the proper quantities is the "ideal" here and can best be done using a computerized system. Inventory changes are recorded at the point of sale, when the cashier keys into a programmed cash register what was selected—for example, a hamburger, sliced tomato and lettuce, potato sticks, and one-half pint of lowfat milk. Reordering is thus simplified and can be handled in a timely fashion (see chapter 14).

Orders need to be placed in sufficient quantity to make them cost-effective for the company to deliver. Delivery cost is figured into the price paid, and larger deliveries can mean better bid prices. "Emergency" ordering of one or two items can be very costly if it becomes habitual.

In central warehouses or large schools, particularly if a cycle menu is used, an *order point* and *maximum stock level* can be used very effectively. An order point is the minimum stock level needed until the next delivery. Maximum stock level or *par stock* is the maximum stock level for an item that should be carried in inventory in order to meet menu requirements. To determine how much to order using order point and par stock, the following formula should be used:

$$\text{Par stock} - \text{reorder point} + \text{normal usage} = \text{reorder quantity}$$

A list of ingredients and quantities from the recipe cards and the inventory is needed to determine what to order. The USDA *Food Buying Guide for Child Nutrition Programs* (1984) is an excellent source of information on yields and how much is needed.

INVENTORY MANAGEMENT

Though inventory management may not be considered by most managers as one of their hardest jobs, it is a very important one. Knowing the value of the inventory plays an important part in accurately determining the cost of goods sold and maintaining inventory control, which can make or break a foodservice. Proper storage is essential to safe, good-quality food and product turnover. In moving inventory, it is important to control aging of products by following the "first in first out" (FIFO) principle.

Managing inventory involves (1) proper receiving, (2) proper storing in an organized facility, (3) accountability for items in storage, and (4) proper removal from storage. These topics are discussed below.

Proper Receiving

The individual checking in deliveries needs to be knowledgeable about what has been ordered and the specifications of the products. Before the person receiving the order signs a delivery ticket, the following need to be verified: (1) the items ordered, (2) the quantity ordered, (3) the quality specified, (4) the correct prices and extensions, and (5) specifications of products. If it is determined that the correct quantity has been delivered and the specifications have been met, the receiving person can safely sign the delivery ticket. Determining all this may require opening cases, crates, and packages; weighing and counting to determine if the proper quantity has been delivered; and checking against a "short" version of the product specifications.

Before they are stored, the date received should be written on the cases or containers with a heavy magic marker.

Proper Storage in an Organized Facility

The dry storage area should be kept at 50° to 70°F with the lower temperature preferred. Shelving should provide good air circulation, and products should be kept off the floor. Refrigerated items should be stored at 32° to 40°F, with good air circulation and off the floor. Freezers should keep the food below 0°F.

Principles of good storeroom organization are as follows:

Arrange storeroom areas in assigned groupings.
Store heavy items at waist height or lower.
Store light items on the upper shelves.
Store detergents separately from food.
Store the least-used items in the less accessible areas.
Label areas with group names and shelves with item names.
Date all cases before placing them on shelves.
Store goods in cases with identifiable labels visible.
Do not store items on the floor.
Empty cases as they are opened.
Schedule cleaning of storage areas.
Assign one employee the duties of storekeeper.
Limit the hours during which items can be obtained from the storeroom.

Accountability for Items in Storage

For an accurate count of items in inventory and accurate payment for what was received, invoices or delivery tickets must be correct when signed, verifying that the items were received. When items are removed from the storeroom in a large operation, an in-house requisition records what is removed.

Perpetual Inventory
A perpetual inventory system is an up-to-date, running record of each item on hand in the storeroom. It provides ready information to a manager for placing orders. Many managers discontinued this control measure in the mid-1970s because they could no longer justify the cost. Small school foodservices may still find it not feasible to keep a perpetual inventory. It is time consuming; however, with the use of computers, scanners, and Universal Codes, it can easily be maintained. Perpetual inventory is desirable and recommended when automated for keeping track of food and supplies.

Physical Inventory
A physical inventory is an actual count of goods in stock. If a perpetual inventory is not being kept, a "mini" physical inventory will have to be taken before placing orders. An

accurate physical inventory should be taken monthly, at the end of the month. The state reports for federal reimbursement require that the value of inventory (purchased and donated-commodity) be provided. If a perpetual inventory is maintained, the physical inventory should be compared and reconciled. Any difference should be evaluated by management.

The following are some general rules for taking inventory:

1. Inventory is taken by two people, one to count and the other to record. It should not be taken by the storekeeper, since it is a check on what is in inventory.

2. Items should be inventoried by location, in the order that they are stored. Jumping around may cause an item to be overlooked.

3. Cans should be left in cases or boxes until needed and removed from the case once it has been opened.

4. Consistency should be observed. If broken cases, opened containers, or parts of containers are counted, this should always be done. If food in process is counted, this should be done consistently (particularly in large production sites).

Value of Inventory

To obtain the value of inventory, the current price paid per purchased unit should be multiplied by the quantity on hand. Some in the profession will argue that the value is the price paid, others use the price of the item at the time inventory is taken, and still others use an average. There is an argument for each approach. The main thing in obtaining a meaningful cost of goods sold is consistency in how inventory is figured. Management needs to determine its policy and stick with it.

The process of determining the cost of food and supplies used for a period of time is as follows:

$$
\begin{array}{l}
\quad \text{Value of (beginning) inventory} \\
+ \text{ Cost of goods received} \\
\hline
= \text{ Total goods available} \\
- \text{ Value of ending inventory} \\
\hline
= \text{ Cost of goods used}
\end{array}
$$

Inventory Turnover

What is a reasonable inventory? How much should a manager have on hand at any one time? No more should be on hand than can be used between one delivery and the next. For fear a delivery will be late or participation will increase, no one keeps "just enough."

A good gauge is to have inventory turnover once every 2 weeks. The method for determining inventory turnover is shown below:

$$
\text{Average inventory} = \frac{\text{Beginning inventory} + \text{Ending inventory}}{2}
$$

$$
\text{Inventory turnover} = \frac{\text{Food cost for the month}}{\text{Average food inventory}}
$$

For example, if

$$\text{Beginning inventory} = \$2,250$$
$$\text{Ending inventory} = \$2,900$$
$$\text{Food cost for the month} = \$5,200$$

$$\text{then } \frac{\$2,250 + \$2,900}{2} = \$2,575 \text{ Average inventory}$$

$$\text{and } \$5,200 = 2.0 \text{ Inventory turnover rate per month}$$

BIBLIOGRAPHY

Blake, K. 1987. "Centered in Diversity." *Food Management* 22(6): 132-37, 192-99.

Cremers, Eve, et al. 1983. *School Food Service "Cooperative Purchasing. . . . It Can Be Done!"* California Association of School Business Officials (address changes yearly).

Dittmer, Paul R., and Gerald G. Griffin. 1984. *Principles of Food, Beverage, and Labor Cost Controls for Hotels and Restaurants.* 3d ed. New York: Van Nostrand Reinhold.

Kotschevar, L. 1975. *Standards, Principles, and Techniques in Quantity Food Production.* 3d ed. New York: CBI and Van Nostrand Reinhold.

Ninemeier, Jack D. 1983. *Purchasing, Receiving, and Storage: A System Manual for Restaurants, Hotels, and Clubs.* New York: CBI and Van Nostrand Reinhold.

North Carolina. n.d. *Administrators' Procurement Manual: A Guide to More Effective Buying.* Raleigh: North Carolina Department of Public Instruction and North Carolina Foodservice Distributors and Suppliers Association.

Office of Management and Budget. 1979. *Standards Governing State and Local Grantee Procurement.* Attachment O of OMB Circular A-102. Washington, D.C.: U.S. Government Printing Office.

Peddersen, R. B. 1977. *Specs: The Comprehensive Foodservice Purchasing and Specifications Manual.* New York: CBI and Van Nostrand Reinhold.

Stefanelli, J. M. 1981. *Purchasing: Selection and Procurement for the Hospitality Industry.* New York: John Wiley & Sons.

Stix, Carl Louis, and Stephen J. Hiemstra. 1989. *Analysis of the Cost Plus Fixed Fee Purchasing System in Indiana Schools.* West Lafayette, Ind.: Purdue University, Restaurant, Hotel and Institutional Management Department.

U.S. Department of Agriculture (USDA). 1983. *Menu Planning Guide for Child Nutrition Programs.* PA 1260. Washington, D.C.: U.S. Government Printing Office.

―――. 1984. *Food Buying Guide for Child Nutrition Programs.* Washington, D.C.: Government Printing Office.

―――. Food and Nutrition Service, Food Distribution Division. 1985a. *Catalog of Specifications for School Foodservice,* vol. 1. Worthington, Ohio: Ed Hill & Associates.

―――. 1985b. *Contract Food Purchasing Manual for School Food Service Supervisors,* vol. 2. Worthington, Ohio: Ed Hill & Associates.

―――. 1985c. *Directory of Information Sources for School Food Service Supervisors,* vol. 4. Worthington, Ohio: Ed Hill & Associates.

————. 1985d. *Food Fact Sheets,* vol. 3. Worthington, Ohio: Ed Hill & Associates.

————. 1985e. *Storage and Care.* Washington, D.C.: U.S. Government Printing Office.

————. Food and Nutrition Service. 1988. *Child Nutrition Label.* Washington, D.C.: U.S. Government Printing Office.

VanEgmond-Pannell, Dorothy, and School Food and Nutrition Management Research Committee. 1987. *The School Foodservice Handbook: A Guide for School Administrators.* Reston, Va.: Association of School Business Officials International.

West, B. B., G. S. Shugart, and M. F. Wilson. 1978. *Food for Fifty.* 6th ed. New York: John Wiley & Sons.

World Health Organization. 1988. *Food Irradiation: A Technique for Preserving and Improving the Safety of Food.* Geneva, Switzerland: World Health Organization.

8

Managing Production and Service

PREPARATION

The preparation of food in school foodservices, as in many other food industries, no longer requires a "chef" or "good cook" per se. It is with this in mind that this chapter is written. Even when food is prepared from raw ingredients, the standardized recipes and controlled equipment available today make it possible—even easy—for the novice to turn out good products. The cook must be able to read and understand directions; the manager must be skilled in scheduling the cooking; and the person portioning must be creative enough to present the food in an attractive, appetizing, and interesting way.

Food preparation has changed greatly in the last 10 years as convenience foods have improved and become more commonly used, better accepted, and more reasonably priced. As labor costs increased in the 1980s, it became less practical to prepare certain foods from raw ingredients. In the 1970s pizza took days to prepare. Today most school districts purchase prepared, frozen pizza that requires only 10 to 12 minutes in the oven before serving. A school-made cinnamon roll may cost 15 to 20 cents per roll to make, whereas the purchased roll costs 12 to 13 cents. Students may prefer the purchased product, whereas the adults (principal, teachers, and manager) may prefer the school-made roll. Many school districts have failed to check the costs of producing from raw ingredients, having convinced themselves that such foods are always better and less expensive. The important questions to consider are what the customer prefers, whether the cost is affordable, and whether the item is priced correctly a la carte.

Whether the foodservice is using raw ingredients or convenience foods, its primary functions are to (1) improve the digestibility of the food, (2) conserve its nutritive value, (3) improve its flavor and appearance, (4) provide the quality food the customer wants, and (5) make the food safe for consumption. All of these goals can be achieved only when preparation starts with a good-quality food product.

Standardized Recipes

One of the most important tools in preparing food in large quantities is a standardized recipe. A standardized recipe is one that has been tested for quality and yield. Using standardized recipes and standard weights and measures in following recipes

Ensures uniform quality and eliminates "trial and error"
Helps to ensure planned yields and prevent waste
Saves time and money
Facilitates more accurate precosting of menus
Simplifies the job for employees
Helps in determining what to order and how much
Helps ensure compliance with meal requirements

Numerous published sources of standardized recipes are available. The 150 standardized school lunch recipes published by the USDA (1988) in *Quantity Recipes for School Food Service* have the advantage of calculating the contribution of each recipe to the school lunch and breakfast patterns. When using recipes from other sources, it is necessary to use the USDA *Food Buying Guide for Child Nutrition Programs* (1984) to determine the contribution the recipe makes toward these patterns.

The biggest challenge may not be the recipe itself but ensuring that the staff follows it. Unfortunately, the directions on convenience foods are not always followed. Cooks often will not check recipes or directions on the container, but rather cook everything at the same temperature (high). A chart summarizing cooking and serving instructions (see Table 8-1) can make such information more accessible. Posted in the cooking area, it encourages the cook to check temperatures and cooking time.

Adjusting Recipes

When increasing or decreasing a recipe, the factor method can be used. It is explained in detail in the information section of the USDA *Quantity Recipes for School Food Service* (1988). Simply stated, it is done by dividing the number of servings needed by the yield amount of the recipe (using decimals). This will determine the factor. The quantity of each ingredient is multiplied by the factor. The factor will be greater than 1.0 when increasing the number of servings and less than 1.0 when decreasing the yield. For example: If 475 portions are needed (1) divide 475 by the yield of recipe (50 portions); $475 \div 50 = 9.5$ factor; (2) convert measures to weight (see Kotschevar 1974 or the USDA *Food Buying Guide* for conversion tables); (3) multiply the weight of each ingredient by the factor to obtain the amount to be used for the number of servings desired.

A computer system like CBORD's Menu Management provides for enlarging of recipes. The advantages are more accurate extension of quantities, the convenience of determining exact quantities (the number of portions) in seconds, and the conversion of quantities to the largest measurable units.

Quality Control

Quality control starts with the quality of the product or the ingredients that make up the product, storage and handling in the process of delivery, and storage and handling on site up to point of service. A standardized recipe, standard measures, and following the directions in the recipe or on the package are necessary to obtain a good-quality product. Regrettably, the quality of the product is often damaged after the cooking or heating, while it is being kept hot. For fear the food will not be ready on time or because the employees

Table 8-1. Chart of Cooking and Serving Instructions

Item	Rec # Fx	Rec # Mmgt	Pan	Cooking Method	Oven Temp °F	Cooking Time	Portion Size
Chix nuggets*	D-23	247	Sheet pan	Oven	350	15 min.	(K-3) 4 (4-6) 5
Steak sub	G-16	39	Sheet pan	Oven	325	15 min.	2 oz.
Steak/cheese	G-17	56	Sheet pan	Oven	325	15 min.	1 oz. 1 oz.
Hot dog	G-22	51	Perf pan Sheet pan	Steamer Oven	— 325	5-10 min. 10-15 min.	1
Cheese pizza	D-10	31	Sheet pan	Oven	375	8-12 min.	1
Meat pizza	D-10	32	Sheet pan	Oven	375	8-12 min.	1
Pepperoni pizza	D-10A	93	Sheet pan	Oven	375	8-12 min.	1
Chicken*	D-5	53	Sheet pan	Oven	375	25-30 min.	2 pcs
Hamburger*	G-3	13	Sheet pan	Oven	325	5-10 min.	2.4 oz
Cheeseburger*	G-4	42	Sheet pan	Oven	325	5-10 min.	2 oz. ½ oz. cheese
Burrito	D-22B	298	Sheet pan	Oven	325	15-20 min.	1
Taco	D-16	291	Solid pan	Steamer Oven	— 325	Internal temp 170°	#8 Disher
Chili/nachos, cheese sauce	D-17A	135	Solid pan	Steamer Oven	— 325	Internal temp 170°	#8 Disher #16 Disher
Spaghetti sauce	D-15	25	Solid pan	Steamer Oven	— 325	Internal temp 170°	#8 Disher
Spaghetti noodle	B-15	26	Solid pan Kettle	Steamer Boil	— —	15 min.	#6 Disher
Chili/taco bar	D-17A	280	Solid pan	Steamer Oven	— 325	Internal temp 170°	#12 Disher

Source: Fairfax County, Virginia, Public Schools
*Pre-cooked items

want to eat together before lunch is served, rather than in shifts, food is often cooked too long before it is to be served.

A quality assurance program is needed for determining quality aspects of food receiving, for checking food-handling practices at the school level, and for determining if the customer is satisfied with the quality served.

MANAGING PRODUCTION

Production Records

Production records are required by federal regulations. The records should provide an **audit trail** to determine whether enough food was planned and prepared to serve the appropriate portion size. With the introduction of "offer versus serve" into the school lunch program, it became very difficult, indeed nearly impossible, to determine by auditing production records if enough food was available for each student to be served all components of the meal pattern, if so desired.

The information on a production record, such as the one shown in Figure 8-1, not only meets federal requirements but also provides very useful information. This information can be a valuable guide the next time that menu is served.

Scheduling Batch Cooking

Most foods deteriorate in quality with holding at hot or cold temperatures for long periods of time. Hot foods in particular need to be cooked by batch (in quantities needed for a short period of time) as close to serving time as possible. Most student complaints about quality will be due to cooking too far ahead, not about the quality of the ingredients that go into the product.

To schedule cooking close to service, the cook needs to know how long it will take for the product to cook and be prepared for service. Regrettably, there are very few time studies for one to use and many recipes do not provide information on preparation time. There may be variables to consider; therefore, it may be necessary for standards to be set locally or within the state. (A model for a time study is shown in Fig. 8-2.) All recipes should indicate how many minutes preparation will take. If work scheduling is to be done by computer, the time required must be calculated.

PRESENTATION AND SERVICE

Major parts of planning menus and preparing food are the presentation and service. How will the food be served, in what dish, and with what garnish? The service should be such that the food can be served at the proper temperature—hot foods hot and cold foods cold. The service also determines if the federal regulations are met: Will portions served meet the meal pattern? Is "offer versus serve" carried out?

A.C. 020 8/88

VIRGINIA DEPARTMENT OF EDUCATION
SCHOOL FOOD SERVICE
FOOD PRODUCTION RECORD

(1) School _____

(2) DATE _____

(3) DAY (CIRCLE)   M   T   W   TH   F

(4) MEAL (CHECK) Breakfast ☐   Lunch ☐

(5) Menu _____

(6) NUMBER MEALS SERVED   Student: _____   Adult: _____

Food Used to Meet Requirements	(12) Recipe No	PORTION			Number Planned		(17) Allowable Servings Per Purchase Unit	(18) Quantity of Food Used	PORTIONS			(22) Comments
		(13) Size	(14) Serving Utensil		(15) Meals	(16) A la carte			(19) Number Prepared	(20) Number Leftover	(21) Number Used	
(7) Meat/Meat Alternate*												
(8) Vegetable/Fruit*												
(9) Bread/Alternate*												
(10) Milk As Beverage												
(11) Other Foods												

*If pre-cooked, put "PC" by food item.
If USDA donated food, put "D" by food item.

I verify that the above information is correct

(23) _____
(Manager or Designated Person)

FIGURE 8-1. Sample production record and instructions. (*Source:* Reprinted with permission of Commonwealth of Virginia. All rights reserved.)

FOOD PRODUCTION RECORD INSTRUCTIONS (AC020)

GENERAL: To be completed daily and maintained as a record of food used.

HEADING

(1) Fill in school name *and* grade levels.

(2) Write the calendar date this menu is served.

(3) Circle the day of the week this menu is served.

(4) Check if it is breakfast or lunch.

(5) List all the menu items offered. For example: cheeseburger/bun, fish square and cheese/bun, green beans, mexican corn, carrot and celery sticks, apple, milk, cookie, lowfat milk, and whole milk.

(6) Complete the number meals served when recording SL 12 totals. (Write in number of paid and number of non-paid meals).

FOOD USED TO MEET REQUIREMENTS

(7) (8) Record the food (ingredients) used to meet meal requirements under the appropriate food category (For Example: Cheeseburger on a bun is listed under the menu as a

(9) (10) menu item; hamburger, raw would be listed as a food under the meat/meat alternate category; hamburger buns would be listed as a food under the bread/bread alternate category). If the food item is pre-cooked and/or pre-portioned (For example: fish square), identify this by placing "PC" by the food item. If the food item is cheese, American, "USDA Donated Food," identify this by placing "D" by the food item.

(11) List other foods served that do not count in meeting meal requirements (for example: oatmeal raisin cookie).

RECIPE

(12) List USDA recipe number of local school division and recipe number of each menu item. If a food does not have a recipe a number is not required (for example: chicken nuggets).

PORTION

(13) Portion Size—List the size of the serving: ½ cup, ¼ cup or count (For example: six nuggets ½ oz). When portion size varies for different age group, list the different size portions to be used.

(14) Size Utensil—List size of serving utensil: No. 10 Scoop, ½ ladle, etc. When an item is served such as patties or nuggets, no utensil size is needed (glove may be used).

(15) Number Planned Meals—Record by each menu item the number planned (forecast).

(16) Number Planned a la Carte—Record by each menu item the number planned (forecast for a la carte items available).

ALLOWABLE SERVINGS

(17) Record allowable servings per unit for food item. This information is obtained from the *Food Buying Guide for Child Nutrition Programs* (PA 133) and from USDA approved Child Nutrition labels on products.

QUANTITY OF FOOD USED

(18) Record the quality of each food used to meet meal requirements and for service for a la carte items. Record amounts by weight, measures or number of cans used (For example: 39 pounds ground beef, 5 number 10 cans green beans.)

NUMBER OF PORTIONS

(19) Record number of portions prepared. (Allowable Servings Purchase Unit multiplied by Quantity of Food Used equals Number of Portions Prepared). If this varied due to yield discrepancy, note reasons for change in comment section (#22).

(20) Record number of portions left over. Estimate as accurately as possible. Be sure to account for all portions prepared.

(21) Record number of portions used. (Number of portions prepared minus number of portions leftover equals number of portions used.)

COMMENTS

(22) Record any information you might need. (For example: amount discarded, cost per serving, change in participation, recipe acceptance/yield discrepancy, etc.)

SIGNATURE

(23) Manager or designated person must sign verifying that the information is correct.

FIGURE 8-1. *Continued.*

123

1. Pan 100 pieces of pizza when packed on pan liner:
   Pan 100 pieces of pizza when not packed on pan liner:
2. Make 100 peanut butter and jelly sandwiches:
   Make 100 ham and cheese sandwiches on croissants:
3. Slice 10 pounds of cheese in 1-ounce portions:
   Slice 10 pounds of ham in 1-ounce portions:
4. Make 400 servings of spaghetti sauce:
   Make 400 servings of lasagna casserole:
   Make 100 servings of vegetable soup:
5. Make 100 portions of tuna salad:
   Make 100 portions of coleslaw:
6. Set up a serving line ready for service:
   Set up a dish machine ready for dish washing:
7. Portion into ½ cups a tray (18" × 26") of fresh fruits and vegetables:
   Portion French bread loaves into 100 slices:
8. Assemble and wrap 100 hamburgers ready for serving:
   Make 300 dinner rolls (starting with raw ingredients):
   Make 300 sugar cookies (starting with raw ingredients):
9. Prepare salad greens and other ingredients for salad bar:
   Set up a salad bar:
10. Prepare 100 portions of salad dressing (using dry mix):
    Portion 100 servings of honey (1 to 2 ounce):

FIGURE 8-2. Time study on how long different jobs take (in minutes).

Portion Control

Portion control means giving a definite quantity of food for a definite price and obtaining the number of servings planned from a given recipe. Portion control plays an important part in food cost control.

Some of the essential tools needed to achieve portion control are slicers, scales, scoops or dishers, ladles, and other measures. Scoops or dishers and ladles come in different sizes. A chart like the one shown in Table 8-1 can be posted near the serving line. It will save time and may mean the difference in whether the correct portion size is served.

According to West et al. (1984), portion control can be accomplished in four ways:

1. *By purchasing foods prepackaged in portion sizes desired*
2. *By developing standard recipes with yield calculations in portion sizes. A recipe can give the stated number of portions only if the servings are of uniform size.*
3. *By using standard-size containers and tools for serving*
4. *By establishing the number of servings to be obtained from canned foods*

Food Presentation and Garnishing

Garnishing refers to the serving and decorating of food in such a way as to make the food more appealing. People tend to select food based on its appearance. A meal of excellent quality may be perceived as dull and uninteresting as a result of presentation.

Does the food have that "cafeteria look"? Does it look so good that customers can't resist it? Eye appeal is influenced by the color and shape of food, the dishes on which it is served, portion size, the neatness with which it is served, the expectations its appearance arouses in customers, and the colors around or in the setting.

Garnishing is the finishing touch that makes food look better and increases its eye appeal. Garnishes can be as simple as a sprinkle of paprika or as elaborate as a radish rose. The following guidelines to garnishing and the use of color in presentation come from the filmstrip "The Art of Getting Kids to Eat," produced by Chiquita Brands:

- *Choose garnishes that fit the budget.*
- *Make sure the garnishes can be accomplished by the average worker (not everyone is an artist).*
- *Make sure garnishes do not require too much time-consuming hand work.*
- *Use seasonal garnishes and decorations when appropriate.*
- *Use garnishes that are natural.*
- *Add color to fruit dishes, salads, etc., with red apples. Leave the peel on; it adds texture, color, and freshness.*
- *Use raw carrots chopped, grated, or cut into sticks or circles.*
- *Use a small amount of fresh spinach to bring an Iceberg lettuce salad to life with color and texture. Spinach also adds nutritional value.*
- *Use onions (green, white, or red) for color, flavor contrast, and crispness. Chop them, or cut them into rings or strips.*
- *Use small amounts of beets, though they are not usually a favorite vegetable, as an effective garnish, particularly cut in julienne strips.*
- *Add cabbage, grated or shredded, in all its varieties (red, green, or white) for color and chewiness.*
- *Make beautiful garnishes with oranges, lemons, limes, and kiwi fruit. Cut them into wedges or thin slices, or—if time permits—shape them into a twist.*
- *Add snap and interest with cucumbers sliced thinly—unpeeled or peeled. Run the tines of a fork down the side of an unpeeled cucumber for an interesting fluted effect.*

A pastry bag with tips is a useful garnishing tool. Whipped topping, for example, is much more attractive when dispensed from a pastry bag than when dropped by the spoonful. A twig of parsley or a mint leaf can add the fresh look desired. The addition of red and green bell peppers to corn can create a colorful Mexican-type dish. Cutting French bread on an angle not only makes it look like a larger piece, but makes it look good. The extra touch is what food presentation and effective merchandising are all about. The Mississippi State Department of Education *School Recipe Portfolio: A Merchandising Manual* (1984) and the USDA *Menu Planning Guide for School Food Service* (1983) provide excellent ideas on food presentation.

MANAGING SERVICE

Generally food in schools is served cafeteria style; however, self-service bars became very popular in the later half of the 1980s. Family style is used in a few instances. Setting up the serving line or the self-service bar correctly is an important part of efficient service.

Time Required to Serve

Ordinarily, high school students are not willing to stand in line more than 10 minutes. If the rate of service is ten meals per minute, then a line of more than 100 students will cause discontent. Running out of food, not having the advertised menu, and having to make students wait while more food is prepared all make for unhappy customers. They are forgiving the first time (usually), but not after repeated occurrences.

Attitude of Employees

The attitude of employees makes a lot of difference in how customers feel about the school's food. Too often when students are questioned about their school foodservice, they complain that those serving are "mean," "always grumpy," or "always yelling."

Temperature of Food

It does not matter how pretty food looks if it is not good or if hot food is served cold. The serving temperature should be appropriate to each food. Hot food should be served

Menu: Salad Greens
      Broccoli Florets, Celery Slices, Tomato Wedges, Radish Roses
      Chunk Tuna
      Applesauce with Maraschino Cherries
      Choice of Dressing
      French Bread and Butter
      Half-pint of Milk

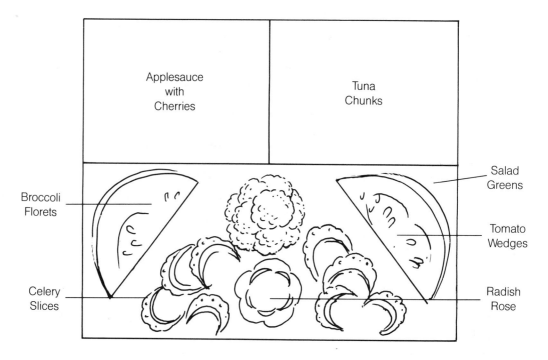

FIGURE 8-3. Presentation of a chef salad lunch.

hot—150°F. Cold food should be served cold. Most food does not get better with holding for long periods of time, even at the proper temperature of 150°F. There is very little written on how best to hold cooked foods at the appropriate temperature; however, more damage occurs to quality during the holding period, after the food is cooked, than at any other stage of the process.

Batch cooking should be encouraged during service, to prevent food from having to be held for long periods of time (discussed above). Hot- and cold-holding equipment placed near the serving line can help provide proper temperatures, which are necessary to safe and good-quality food.

How Food Is Served

How the food is served and on what it is served can make a difference. For example, serving hamburgers and other sandwiches in the aluminum or paper wraps used by fast-food restaurants has been found to increase customer satisfaction and to keep sandwiches warm longer. However, the cost has to be considered. Serving French fries in bags makes portion control easier, and the students feel content with the serving size because it is the same as that served in fast-food restaurants. For some, this makes the portion look much like fast food, which may or may not be desirable.

Novel ways of serving food will spark interest. Serving lunch on a frisbee in the spring, in a bag on a nice day, or in a basket for a picnic or field trip adds interest to eating in the school's cafeteria. For example, serving a sandwich lunch at Halloween in a "trick or treat" bag, imprinted with safety tips, can make a hit with students (and parents).

Some school districts give detailed instructions to achieve the desired presentation. The example shown in Figure 8-3 gives exact directions for assembling a chef salad lunch.

BIBLIOGRAPHY

Barker, Lewis M. 1982. *The Psychobiology of Human Food Selection.* New York: Van Nostrand Reinhold.

Freeland-Graves, Jeanne, and Gladys Peckham. 1987. *Foundations of Food Preparation.* 5th ed. New York: Macmillan Publishing Co.

London, Roberta A., and Sarah F. Stallings. 1986. *Food Preparation and Service.* Columbia, S.C.: State Department of Education.

Mississippi State Department of Education. 1984. *School Recipe Portfolio: A Merchandising Manual.* Jackson: State Department of Education.

U.S. Department of Agriculture. 1983. *Menu Planning Guide for School Food Service.* Washington, D.C.: U.S. Government Printing Office.

———. 1984. *Food Buying Guide for Child Nutrition Programs.* Washington, D.C.: U.S. Government Printing Office.

———. 1988. *Quantity Recipes for School Food Service.* Washington, D.C.: U.S. Government Printing Office.

West, Bessie B., and LeVelle Wood. 1988. *Foodservice in Institutions.* Revised 6th edition. Revised by Virginia F. Harger, Grace S. Shugart, and June Payne-Palacio. New York: Macmillan Publishing Co.

West, Patricia H., Kathryn M. Kolasa, and Eugenia M. Zallen. 1984. *School Food Service Training Manual: Quantity Production.* Raleigh, N.C.: State Department of Education.

9

Sanitation and Safety Management

FOODBORNE ILLNESSES

One of the greatest fears of most foodservice managers is an outbreak of food poisoning resulting from food served in their facility. The symptoms of foodborne illnesses include abdominal pain, nausea, vomiting, and/or diarrhea. Death can result from foodborne illness. (Chapter 11 addresses responses to the media in case of such emergencies.)

During the 1980s, the overall public health risk from foodborne organisms rose. Bacterial organisms in meat and poultry are frequently the cause of the increased number of foodborne illnesses. For example, food poisoning cases in California caused by salmonella bacteria increased from 203 in 1984 to 756 in 1985. According to the Center for Food Safety and Applied Nutrition in the FDA, more than 81 million cases of diarrhea of foodborne origin occur in the United States each year. Young children less than five years of age and elderly people are more susceptible.

An outbreak of typhoid in suburban Washington, D.C. in 1988 was traced to a local McDonald's. Shrimp salad contaminated by an infected employee was the vehicle for transmitting typhoid to the customers. The disease is normally rare in the United States.

Salmonella and campylobacter organisms are responsible for many of the outbreaks of food poisoning. They cause a "flu" type illness. *Campylobacter jejuni*, a recently identified pathogen, is an organism that is responsive to antibiotic drugs. It is most common in poultry and is transmitted when poultry is served raw or insufficiently cooked. The FDA and USDA have begun a nationwide voluntary program of testing poultry to track down sources of salmonella contamination. It is believed that the bacteria enters the eggs during ovulation. Eggs are an unusually high source of salmonella poisoning. Originally, it was thought that only cracked and uncooked eggs transmitted salmonella, but research has shown that this is not the case.

It is important in food preparation to cook poultry and pork until done. Meats like deli turkey and chicken meats for sandwiches should be purchased only from processing plants with good quality control measures and high sanitation standards.

The FDA has a comprehensive unicode which calls for lowering the required refrigeration temperature for potentially hazardous food from 45° to 40°F. Fast food chains are requiring processors and suppliers to provide hamburger, poultry, and other fresh or frozen protein foods with low pathogen levels, essentially free of bacterial contamination. School foodservice managers may wish to add these requirements to meat, poultry, and fish specifications.

There have been a few instances when USDA-donated commodities were contaminated. For example, a meat processing company in Minnesota produced precooked beef patties that were not totally cooked and carried bacteria that caused illness. The USDA has taken corrective action and stepped up its inspection of plants. The department has also tightened up regulations on the storage of raw ingredients and the processing of pre-cooked foods, time and temperature requirements. The labels on precooked foods now warn the users: "For Safety, Cook Until Well Done (Internal Meat Temperature of 160 Degrees Fahrenheit)."

The Food Safety and Inspection Service of the Department of Agriculture has been pressured to force the poultry industry to clean up its products. Poultry was the largest single source of salmonella and other foodborne organisms that cause food poisoning in the 1980s. The Food Safety and Inspection Service has developed an excellent training package, which contains a videotape, posters, and a trainer's guide, called "Food Safety Is No Mystery." This training package can be obtained at a nominal sum from the Food Safety and Inspection Services of the USDA. This department has also established a Meat and Poultry Hotline (1-800-535-4555) in Washington, D.C., to answer questions about meat and poultry safety.

The three basic rules for keeping food safe and preventing food-related diseases are (1) buy safe food; (2) keep food safe; and (3) when in doubt, throw it out.

PURCHASING SAFE FOOD

There are ten or more major federal laws protecting the public against contaminated foods. Public awareness and increased sensitivity to certain chemicals in foods have brought attention to the various chemicals found in processed foods.

The **Delaney clause** is a provision of the U.S Food, Drug, and Cosmetic Act that prohibits the use of additives that have been shown to be carcinogenic in animals or humans. Color additives amendments mandate that public safety be the primary consideration in the regulation of color additives.

The Food, Drug, and Cosmetic Act defines a *food additive* as a substance the intended use of which results in its becoming a component or otherwise affecting the characteristics of any food. There are more than 2,000 chemicals used as direct additives to food. These have to be designated as "generally recognized as safe" (**GRAS**) under the Food, Drug, and Cosmetic Act.

Concerns about Ingredients

Artificial coloring, such as yellow dye, number 5, is associated with allergic reactions. Feingold (1974) has brought attention to this substance.

BHA and *BHT* are chemicals that are added to fat-containing foods to prevent oxidation and to delay rancidity. Butylated hydroxyanisole (BHA) is in processed foods such as potato chips, presweetened cereals, and bouillon cubes. Butylated hydroxytoluene (BHT) is used in frying oils.

Monosodium glutamate (MSG) enhances the flavor primarily of protein-containing foods, but is used in everything from soup to nuts. Some people are allergic to it and experience headaches, tightness in the chest, and a burning sensation in the forearms and back of neck sometimes referred to as the "Chinese Restaurant Syndrome."

Sodium nitrite and *sodium nitrate* are used to preserve meat, maintain red colors, contribute to flavor, and prevent the growth of bacteria. The levels used have been lower in recent years, and these chemicals have been eliminated in some foods where previously used. Whenever they are eliminated, however, the products become very perishable, particularly in the case of pork.

Sulfite is used to prolong the shelf life of fresh fruits and vegetables. Because of the chemical reactions some people experience, particularly asthmatic children, the federal government banned sulfites in July 1986 in most fresh fruits and vegetables. This ban did not cover processed potatoes. The FDA requires that the ingredient label indicate if sulfites have been used in the products.

Alar, a trade name for the chemical daminozide, is used on fruits and vegetables to increase firmness, enhance color, and extend storage life. It is currently thought to be used on as much as 20 to 30 percent of the apple crop. The Environmental Protection Agency (EPA) says it is used on as little as 5 percent of the crop. As a result of animal studies showing the potential carcinogencity of Alar, the EPA recently announced that it would halt the use of the product. (*Consumer Reports*, 1989).

The EPA tolerance for daminozide is 20 ppm for apples and apple products and 55 ppm for canned cherries. *Tolerance* means the maximum safe level of pesticide, and that anything over the tolerance is not safe (*FDA Consumer Report*, 1988).

Washing or peeling an apple will not remove daminozide if it has been used on the crop. School districts have been concerned about the possibility that the products they are purchasing are unsafe to use. To prevent the risk, many school districts are requiring of the distributor lists of pesticides used, lab analyses, and/or a certificate from the food processor or orchard that Alar and other unsafe pesticides have not been used on the product.

Insecticides, depending on the amount ingested, can cause a person to experience the following symptoms within five minutes if particularly allergic: headache, nausea, vomiting, diarrhea, salivation, blurred vision, cyanosis, nervousness, sweating, and chest and abdominal pains (Tartakow and Vorperian 1981). One way of preventing harm from most insecticides is to wash all fresh fruit and vegetables carefully before using or serving. However, some residues cannot be removed by washing.

It is nearly impossible to eliminate all chemicals from foods. Even processed American cheese has artificial coloring added. Ben Feingold's book, *Why Your Child Is Hyperactive*, led to the organization of many Feingold parent groups in the late 1970s. These groups brought pressure on school foodservice directors in several different parts of the country. From a one-year study done by the Fairfax County, Virginia, School Food Service Office, it was determined that it was possible to eliminate some of the additives, preservatives, and artificial flavorings and colorings; however, the costs of the food products were higher.

Foreign Substances

Foodservice managers have to be alert to foreign substances that might find their way into foods—before reaching the kitchen as well as during preparation and service. The most common substance is hair, which can turn a customer off and also carry bacteria. Other substances that occasionally make their way into food are nuts or bolts from equipment, wire ties, metal shavings, and broken glass. If consumed, these substances may damage teeth or the intestinal tract. Manufacturers carry liability insurance that will pay for damage or injury.

Pests, such as rats, mice, flies, and roaches, may sometimes be found in any foodservice. When they are present all the time, however, it is a sign of poor sanitation standards. These insects and rodents can spread disease organisms and filth.

Periodic visits by an exterminator can help control pests in a foodservice, but good housekeeping practices, described below, are the basic means of controlling pests:

- Inspect food supplies before storing for signs of insects and rodents.
- Keep stocks of food as fresh as possible by rotating stock.
- Store foods in containers with tight-fitting lids.
- Store foods in a dry place at the correct temperature.
- Do not store food or supplies directly on the floor.
- Remove and destroy infested food.
- Clean up spillage immediately.
- Do not use shelf paper.
- Screen all windows, doors, and outer openings.
- Make sure that all doors are self-closing and open outward.
- Keep all food covered.
- Place all garbage promptly into nonabsorbent, easily cleaned garbage cans with tight-fitting lids.
- Scald and air garbage cans daily.
- Clean up all piles of rubbish, boxes, rags, and so on.
- Seal all openings around pipes.

PREVENTING BACTERIAL GROWTH

Foodborne illnesses are a major health problem in the United States today. There are four major types of food poisoning, which are shown in Table 9-1. Foodservice management can prevent bacterial growth by eliminating the conditions under which bacteria reproduce. Bacteria need a suitable temperature, food, moisture, pH, and in some cases, oxygen. Temperature and pH are discussed below.

Temperature

There are many critical points in preventing food poisoning. A very important step in preventing bacterial growth is to keep food cold or hot. (See Fig. 9-1 for guidelines on safe temperatures for foods.)

A food thermometer should be used by the manager and cook several times a day to determine if the food is at the correct temperature. Harmful bacteria multiply extremely rapidly when the temperature is between 40° and 140°F. When most perishable foods are refrigerated, most harmful bacteria will be in a dormant stage. Cooking at temperatures above 140°F kills most bacteria.

Once food is cooked, the cooling-down period is crucial. Improper cooling can be the reason for food poisoning outbreaks. Food should not be left at room temperature for long.

Table 9-1.   Four Major Types of Food Poisoning

Type of Food Poisoning	Description and Characteristics
Salmonellosis	Grows in intestinal tracts of humans and animals *Transmitted by:* poultry, raw eggs, red meats, dairy products, and infected persons *Symptoms:* severe headache, vomiting, diarrhea, abdominal cramps, and fever *Characteristics:* onset 6-36 hours; lasts 2-7 days. *Preventive measures:* heat food to 140°F for 10 minutes
Perfringens poisoning	The spore-forming bacteria, *Clostridium perfringens,* can grow without oxygen *Transmitted by:* eating foods containing the toxin *Symptoms:* nausea, diarrhea, and acute inflammation of stomach and intestines *Characteristics:* onset 8-20 hours; lasts 24 hours *Preventive measures:* cooked meats, gravies, and meat casseroles that are to be stored should be cooled rapidly and refrigerated at 40°F or below
Staphylococcal poisoning (staph)	This bacterium produces a toxin that is very difficult to destroy even with heat *Transmitted by:* food handler to foods; usually high-protein foods, e.g., egg custard, egg salad, casseroles *Symptoms:* vomiting, diarrhea, and abdominal cramps *Characteristics:* onset 3-8 hours, sometimes within 30 minutes; lasts 1-2 days *Preventive measures:* control growth by keeping hot foods hot and cold foods cold
Botulism	Caused by a spore-forming organism and produces toxin; fatality rate is high (about 65 percent) *Transmitted by:* canned, low-acid foods, and smoked fish *Symptoms:* double vision, difficulty swallowing, speech difficulty *Characteristics:* onset 6-36 hours; lasts 3-6 days *Preventive measures:* proper canning procedures; the toxin is destroyed by boiling for 10-20 minutes

Source: Chenault 1984.

Warm or hot foods should be stored in shallow pans. If stored in deep pans, it may take five to six hours to reach a safe temperature; during that time bacteria can grow rapidly.

The pH of Food

The pH is a measure of the acidity or alkalinity of a medium. A pH of 7 is neutral, neither acidic nor alkaline. A food with a pH below 7 is acid, and above 7 is alkaline. The pH range of a food will determine to some degree if food poisoning can be transmitted very readily. The normal pH range of food is from 0-14, 0 being the level of high-acid foods. The lower the pH, the less likely bacteria will grow: a pH of 4.5 or lower inhibits growth.

The effect of pH on bacterial growth is shown in Figure 9-2. Bacteria grow best in foods that have a neutral pH or are slightly acidic or slightly alkaline (a range between 5 and 9). The growth of bacteria is greatly inhibited by a very acidic medium. Table 9-2 shows the approximate pH of selected foods.

Next to pH, the temperature of food is most important to the growth of bacteria.

Temperatures for Food Safeness

TABLEWARE AND UTENSIL SANITATION		F.	C.	FOOD HANDLING AND STORAGE
Maximum temperature for mechanical rinse		195°	91°	Food cooked to this temperature – harmful bacteria killed
Mechanical rinse at nozzle		180°	82°	
Minimum rinse temperature at dish (mechanical or dip rinse)		170°	77°	
		165°	74°	Minimum safe temperature of cooked food Store or display hot cooked foods above this temperature (after cooking)
Temperature for mechanical dishwashing		150°	66°	
		140°	60°	
Water temperature for hand dishwashing		130° TO 120°	54° TO 49°	Rapid Bacterial Growth DANGER ZONE FOR FOOD SAFENESS
Temperature for scraping dishes		110° TO 100°	43° TO 38°	
		90° TO 65°	32° TO 18°	Normal room temperature
		50°	10°	
		40° TO 32°	4° TO 0°	Cold or chill food storage (slow bacterial growth)
		0° TO -10°	-18° TO -23°	Frozen food storage

FIGURE 9-1. Food safeness temperature chart. (*Source:* Hatco Corporation 1988.)

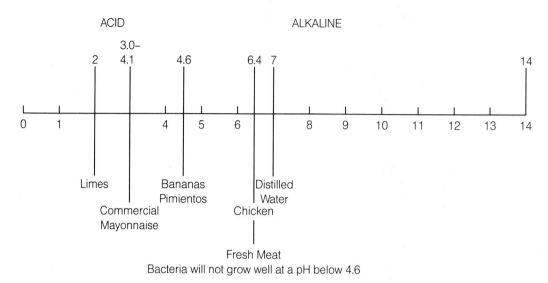

FIGURE 9-2. Effect of pH on bacterial growth. (*Source:* National Institute for the Foodservice Industry 1985.)

Table 9-2. Approximate pH of Selected Foods

Food	pH Range	Food	pH Range	Food	pH Range
Egg white	7.6-9.5	Celery	5.7-6.0	Dry sausages	4.4-5.6
Shrimp	6.8-8.2	Peas	5.6-6.8	Pimientos	4.3-5.2
Crab	6.8-8.0	Turkey	5.6-6.0	Tomato juice	3.9-4.7
Scallops	6.8-7.1	Chicken	5.5-6.4	Mayonnaise	3.8-4.0
Cod, small	6.7-7.1	Halibut	5.5-5.8	Tomatoes	3.7-4.9
Cod, large	6.5-6.9	Beans, lima	5.4-6.5	Jams	3.5-4.0
Catfish	6.6-7.0	Potatoes, Irish	5.4-6.3	Apricots	3.5-4.0
Soda crackers	6.5-8.5	Walnuts	5.4-5.5	Applesauce	3.4-3.5
Maple syrup	6.5-7.0	Pork	5.3-6.4	Pears	3.4-4.7
Milk	6.3-6.8	Beef	5.3-6.2	Grapes	3.3-4.5
Brussels sprouts	6.3-6.6	Onions	5.3-5.8	Cherries	3.2-4.7
Whiting	6.2-7.1	Sweet potatoes	5.3-5.6	Pineapple	3.2-4.1
Haddock	6.2-6.7	Cabbage	5.2-6.3	Peaches	3.1-4.2
Cantaloupe	6.2-6.5	Turnip	5.2-5.6	Rhubarb	3.1-3.2
Dates	6.2-6.4	Spinach	5.1-6.8	Strawberries	3.0-4.2
Herring	6.1-6.6	Asparagus	5.0-6.1	Grapefruit	2.9-4.0
Butter	6.1-6.4	Cheeses, most	5.0-6.1	Raspberries	2.9-3.7
Honey	6.0-6.8	Camembert	6.1-7.0	Apples	2.9-3.5
Mushrooms	6.0-6.5	Cottage	4.1-5.4	Plums	2.8-4.6
Cauliflower	6.0-6.7	Gouda	4.7	Oranges	2.8-4.0
Lettuce	6.0-6.4	Bread	5.0-6.0	Cranberries	2.5-2.8
Egg yolk	6.0-6.3	Carrots	4.9-6.3	Lemons	2.2-2.4
Corn, sweet	5.9-6.5	Beets	4.9-5.8	Limes	1.8-2.0
Oysters	5.9-6.6	Bananas	4.5-5.2		

Source: Banwart 1981.

134

STORING FOOD SAFELY

Food should be checked for spoilage. Canned food should be checked for containers swollen at the top and bottom, dents along the side seam, and foam or "off" odors when the can is opened. Fresh fish and seafood are usually spoiled if there is an off odor similar to ammonia and the eyes are sunken and off color around gills. Meat will usually have an off odor if spoiled. Regrettably, many prepared salads do not show telltale signs until the foods are totally spoiled. Purchasing prepared chicken salad, tuna and other fish salad, nonacid potato salad (made without vinegar), and all types of custard-filled pastries is risky. It is important to purchase only from a reputable processor and distributor.

FOOD HANDLERS

Many of the bacteria that cause food poisoning are transmitted to the food by the food handler. Many of these diseases are caused by human respiratory bacteria. Respiratory illnesses are often transmitted through (1) discharges from the mouth and nose, (2) spoons used for tasting more than once without cleaning, and (3) sneezing and coughing on displayed food. The other main source of bacteria causing foodborne illness is the intestinal tract. These bacteria are transmitted to food by the food handler who does not thoroughly wash his or her hands after visiting the toilet. Hand washing cannot be overemphasized in the kitchen.

Some undesirable hand habits that should be avoided are:

- Scratching one's head
- Arranging one's hair
- Touching the mouth or nose
- Protecting a sneeze or blowing one's nose without afterward washing the hands
- Touching one's moustache or beard
- Touching pimples or infected cuts or burns

SANITARY PREPARATION AND SERVING CONDITIONS

Keeping food at a safe temperature at all times is the most crucial and the most controllable aspect of handling food. The cook can assume that most foods have the potential to become contaminated with sufficient bacteria to cause foodborne illnesses. To prevent bacterial growth, food should be held below 45°F or above 140°F at all times. To ensure bacterial destruction in the cooking process, foods should be cooked above 165°F.

Potentially Hazardous Foods

Moist, nonacid, protein foods are the most hazardous. These include most meats, poultry, seafood, eggs, milk and other dairy products, and to a lesser extent cooked cereal grains and vegetables, sauces, and gravies. The "safe flow chart for beef stew," shown in Table 9-3, illustrates how foods can become contaminated in the cooking process.

Table 9-3.   Potential of Contamination During Cooking Process: Safe Flow Chart for Beef Stew

Preparation Step[a]	Hazards	Controls and Alternatives
A. Cube and sear beef (1:00 P.M.)	Cross-contamination to other foods	Clean and sanitize utensils; wash hands; handle separately from other foods
B. Wash, peel, and cut vegetables (1:10 P.M.)	Natural and cross-contamination	Wash vegetables thoroughly and handle separately from other foods. Use clean/sanitized utensils. Wash hands
C. Combine ingredients and seasonings (1:30 P.M.)	Chemical contamination; if "seasoned to taste," bacterial contamination	Read labels. Store and use chemicals away from foods. Measure seasonings in advance or use clean tasting spoon each time
D. Simmer, cook (4:30 P.M.)	Survival of bacteria	Cook until parts reach an internal temperature of 165°F
E. Hot table holding (7:30 P.M.)	Recontamination, growth of bacteria	Use clean/sanitized utensils. Keep covered. Keep internal temperature above 140°F. If temperature falls below 140°F, reheat to 165°F
F. Cool for storage (11:30 P.M.)	Growth of bacteria (extremely critical)	Cool rapidly to 45°F within 4 hours. Use shallow pans 4″ deep or less and ice baths and stir food to facilitate cooling. Check temperature every 30 to 60 minutes. If food has not reached 45°F, within four hours, reheat to 165°F and cool again
G. Storage	Recontamination	Keep covered. Store away from contaminants
H. Reheat for service (4:00 P.M., following day)	Recontamination, bacterial growth	Use clean, sanitized utensils. Do not "top off" with new product. Heat rapidly on stove to 165°F. Do not hold. Serve immediately

Source: Harrington 1986.
[a]Times indicate when the step is completed.

Thermometers

All cooks and managers should have a food thermometer accessible at all times when cooking and serving food. Thermometers need to be calibrated frequently to ensure accurate readings. The better-quality food thermometers have a calibration nut near the dial that allows for adjustment. Boiling (200°-212°F) and beginning-to-freeze (32°F) temperatures should be used as reference points in making the adjustment or in checking the reliability of the thermometer.

Sterilization of Work Surfaces and Utensils

Two basic sanitizing techniques should be taught all employees:

1. *How to prepare a sanitizing solution.* Use enough bleach in water to reach 100-200 ppm. Test this with a chlorine test kit to make sure this is at the correct strength, or add 1

tablespoon of bleach per gallon of water. Use this solution for sanitizing tables and serving counter areas.

2. *How to set up three-compartment sinks correctly for washing pots and pans.* Establish the first compartment for hot soapy water, the second for rinsing, and the third for sterilization. Sterilization can be done by two means: water at 180°F or sanitizing solution (1 tablespoon of bleach per gallon of water).

EMPLOYEE AND CUSTOMER SAFETY

AIDS Risk

The chance of a school foodservice employee who has AIDS spreading it through casual contact or food is almost nonexistent. AIDS is transferable through sexual contact, shared needles, and blood transfusions, or possibly from an infected mother to her child at birth.

To minimize the risk of spreading any infectious disease, it should be the policy to wash hands routinely and wear gloves to clean up with a household bleach, especially if there is a cut and bleeding.

Employees who have AIDS cannot be discriminated against or fired for that reason. Legally, a supervisor cannot violate the confidentiality of an employee with AIDS by telling other employees. People who have infectious diseases, including AIDS, are considered to have a handicap and legally cannot be dismissed any more than any other person with any other handicap.

Hazardous Substances

The concern surrounding hazardous substances relates to their potential effects on both the employee and the customer. The employer has an obligation to provide a safe place for people to work as well as for people to be served. (This is discussed further in chapter 10.)

In 1971, the Occupational Safety and Health Administration (**OSHA**) adopted regulations regarding hazardous chemicals or substances and the employer's responsibilities in the work location. These regulations are referred to as the **Federal Hazard Communication Standard.** Many states have acted further in this area, probably more because of the hazardous substances used in school chemistry laboratories than because of the employees at risk.

A *hazardous substance* is defined as any substance which is capable of producing adverse effects on the health and safety of human beings. Any product that has a health or safety warning on its label is considered hazardous. Labeling secondary containers (if the product has been removed from the original containers to other containers) is very essential to safety.

The Federal Hazard Communication Standard, sometimes referred to as the "Right-to-Know Law," requires that employees be protected against harm, requires in-service training for all employees who handle or use potentially hazardous chemicals, and requires that the employer have a "material safety data sheet" (**MSDS**) on each hazardous chemical known to be used by that particular group of employees in the workplace. The MSDS is provided by the manufacturer (an example is shown in Fig. 9-3) and must contain the following information:

- Product identity (used on the container label)
- Physical and chemical characteristics of the hazardous chemical or chemicals

Section 1—Product Name:

Manufacturer's Name: Address: Emergency Telephone No.:

Section 2—Hazardous Information:

Components	C.A.S. Number	CERCLA RQ Spill lbs.	RCRA Waste	AGGIH TLV	OSHA TWA	%, Wt.

Carcinogens (As defined in 29CFR 1910–1200)	NTP	IARC	OSHA

Proper Shipping Name:	Hazard Class:	Hazard I.D. No.:

Section 3—Physical Data:

Boiling Point, °F:	Specific Gravity:
Vapor Pressure (mmHc):	Volatile, % by vol.:
Vapor Density (air = 1):	Evaporation Rate (Bu. Ac. = 1):
Appearance and Odor:	Solubility in Water: pH (Cont.):

Section 4—Fire and Explosion Hazards:

Flash Point and Method Used:
Extinguishing Media:
Special Fire Fighting Procedure and Precautions:
Unusual Fire and Explosion Hazards:

Section 5—Health, Emergency, and First Aid Information:

Effects of Over Exposure: Eyes:
Skin:
Inhalation:
Ingestion:
Medical Conditions Which May Be Aggravated:

FIGURE 9-3. Sample material safety data sheet.

First Aid: Eyes:
Skin:
Inhalation:
Ingestion:
Primary Routes of Entry: Inhalation ____ Skin Contact ____ Other ____

Section 6—Reactivity Date:

Stability: Stable ____ Unstable ____
Conditions to Avoid:
Hazardous Decomposition Products:

Section 7—Spill, Leak, and Disposal Procedure:

Spill or Release Procedure: Concentrate: Use Solution:
Disposal Information: Concentrate: Spent Solution and Rinses:

Section 8—Special Protection Information:

Respiratory Protection:
Ventilation:
Protective Equipment: Chemical Face Shield or Goggles: ____ Gloves ____ Boots ____ Apron ____ Protective Suit ____ Gloves, Boots, Apron, and Suit Made From:
Recommended Personal Hygiene:

Section 9—Other Information:

Special Precautions—Storage and Handling:
Mixing:
Repair and Maintenance of Contaminated Equipment:
Date Prepared: Date Reviewed: Approved:

FIGURE 9-3. *Continued.*

- Physical hazards (potential for explosion, fire, and so on)
- Known acute and chronic health effects and related health information
- Primary routes of entry into the body
- Information on exposure limits
- Whether the chemical is considered a carcinogen by OSHA, the International Agency for Research on Cancer, or the National Toxicology Program
- Precautions for safe handling
- Generally acceptable control measures (engineering controls, work practices, and personal protective equipment)
- Emergency and first aid procedures
- Date of MSDS preparation or last revision
- Name, address, and phone number of party responsible for preparing and distributing the MSDS

Some of the hazardous substances found in most school kitchens are household ammonia and bleach, institutional cleansers with bleach, detergents, oven and grill cleaners, rinse agents used in dishwashing machines, lime-cutting agents, and stainless steel cleaners.

Managers should ensure that all of these chemicals are in the original labeled container or in a secondary container that has been properly labeled. If the employees do not read and understand English, the labeling should be in their languages or at least bear a danger sign on the label.

1. Is an OSHA poster posted in a prominent place where employees report to work? _____
2. Is a properly filled first-aid kit readily accessible to employees? _____
3. Is there ongoing safety training? _____
4. Are aisle ways clear of obstructions? _____
5. Are there hand rails or railings on stairways? _____
6. Do employees know where the nearest fire extinguisher is? _____
7. Are fire extinguishers tested (hydrostatic test every five years)? _____
8. Have foodservice employees participated in fire drills and do they know procedures? _____
9. Are emergency exits marked and illuminated? _____
10. Is the electrical wiring system grounded? _____
11. Are food mixers, grinders, slicers, dish machines, and other pieces of electrical equipment grounded? _____
12. Is cutting, chopping, and grinding equipment guarded? _____
13. Are all hazardous chemicals (substances), e.g., bleach, detergents, labeled properly? _____
14. Are all hazardous chemicals stored in places separate from food? _____
15. Are ventilation and illumination adequate in the kitchen and storage areas? _____
16. Is instruction given on the proper use of steam equipment? _____
17. Is there a safety latch on walk-in freezer and refrigerator doors? _____
18. Are all fixed machines securely anchored to prevent "walking" or moving? _____
19. Is someone on duty within the school (and readily available to the foodservice area) who knows basic first aid? _____

FIGURE 9-4. Safety checklist.

Emergency Situations

The foodservice manager should have training in basic first aid. There are many pieces of potentially hazardous equipment in an institutional kitchen. Also, a person choking on food and an employee having a heart attack on the job are emergencies that may occur that have to be reacted to within minutes for the victim to survive. Figure 9-4 provides a safety checklist to be used in the work location.

Choking

It is not uncommon in a foodservice dining room for a customer to choke on food. The most acceptable technique to use in these cases is the abdominal thrust maneuver. Minutes count in this emergency situation, but it is important that the person performing emergency treatment be trained in proper procedures. The American Red Cross teaches first aid courses that include the abdominal thrust maneuver.

Heart Attack

If a person's heart stops beating, action is needed immediately. Cardiopulmonary resuscitation (CPR) is the technique used to keep the person alive until medical help can be obtained.

BIBLIOGRAPHY

"Bad Apples." 1989. *Consumer Reports* May: 288-291.

Banwart, G. J. 1981. *Basic Food Microbiology.* New York: Van Nostrand Reinhold.

Chenault, Alice A. 1984. *Nutrition and Health.* New York: Holt, Rinehart & Winston.

Fairfax County (Virginia) Public Schools. 1989. *Material Safety Data Sheets.* Fairfax: Fairfax County Public Schools, General Services Department.

Feingold, B. F. 1974. *Why Your Child Is Hyperactive.* New York: Random House.

Guthrie, Rufus K. 1980. *Food Sanitation.* 2d ed. New York: AVI and Van Nostrand Reinhold.

Harrington, Robert E. 1986. "How to Implement a SAFE Program." *Restaurant USA* 6(7): 31-33. Washington, D.C.: National Restaurant Association.

Longree, Karla, and Gertrude Armbruster. 1987. *Sanitary Techniques in Foodservice.* 4th ed. New York: John Wiley & Sons.

Minor, Lewis J. 1983. *Sanitation, Safety & Environmental Standards.* The L. J. Minor Foodservice Standards Series, vol. 2. New York: Van Nostrand Reinhold.

Nash, George E. 1987. "Applied Food Sanitation Course Offered to Members." *School Food Service Journal* 41(4): 117.

National Institute for the Foodservice Industry. 1985. *Applied Foodservice Sanitation.* 3d Ed. Chicago: William C. Brown Publishers.

"New Bacteria in the News: A Special Symposium." 1986. *Food Technology* 40(8): 16-26.

"Setting Safe Limits on Pesticide Residues." 1988. *Food and Drug Consumer Report*: 41-45.

Tartakow, I. Jackson, and John H. Vorperian. 1981. *Foodborne and Waterborne Diseases.* New York: Van Nostrand Reinhold.

United States Department of Agriculture. 1987. "Food Safety Is No Mystery." A training package in VHS and BETA. Washington, D.C.: Food Safety and Inspection Service, USDA.

World Health Organization. 1988. *Food Irradiation: A Technique for Preserving and Improving the Safety of Food.* Geneva, Switzerland: WHO.

10

Managing Human Resources

OVERVIEW OF THE LABOR MARKET

In the 1950s this chapter would have been called "Personnel Management," for during that period personnel management was little more than seeing that there were sufficient people to do the work and that the paperwork was done whereby the employees got paid. The 1970s and 1980s were known as "employees' rights" years. The federal government performed the role of protector of the employee. Even if an employee did not perform his or her job especially well, the paychecks continued. School districts seemed to be more susceptible to this situation and required management to have "just reasons" for any action, which intimidated some. In the 1990s there will be more emphasis on the employee doing the job effectively, and the rights of both the employee and the employer will be considered.

The 1990s will see three very different generations in the workplace, with different goals and characteristics. The differences in values of these three generations might cause conflicts if a team approach is not successfully used. The attitudes and values of these generations will be a challenge to management. The older employees may want to contribute to the school foodservice program and to feel that what they are doing is a contribution to society. The middle-aged employees will want more meaningful work and will want group involvement and participation. The younger employees may want to move up the ladder of success and be willing to work hard to do so. However, some of the youngest of the group may seem demanding and plugged into their own worlds—wanting to work when they want to work, to do what they want to do, and to do no more than they have to. It has been said that the older worker "lives to work" and the younger worker "works to live."

During this period, employees will want to be appreciated for the job they do. Most managers will agree that employees basically want to do a good job. They want to take pride in what they do and in the school district for which they work. The "overnight" and continued success of companies like Federal Express and Apple Computer has been based on employee pride. Employees want to know that they are contributing something good to the community in general or that they are growing. When this happens, the results are happy, motivated employees with good morale and a positive attitude.

Another factor will be the increase in minorities in the workplace. According to 1987

Table 10-1.   Labor Force Change (in millions)

	1986	2000	Annual Growth Rate %
White	101.8	116.7	1.0
Black	12.7	16.3	1.8
Hispanic	8.1	14.1	4.1
Asian and other	3.4	5.7	3.9

Source: U.S. Bureau of the Census 1987.

U.S. Census data, there will be an annual increase of approximately 4 percent in Hispanics and Asians in the labor force (see Table 10-1). According to Deutsch (1985) in *The Futurist* magazine, "The manager's ability to recognize individual lifestyles and preferences will become even more crucial as the next new wave of employees, weaned on choice, sweeps into the work place."

Labor shortages will be a leading personnel problem as the need for service employees continues to increase in the 1990s. These shortages of labor have already been felt in some parts of the country and recruiting has become necessary to fill the positions. *Recruitment* is a new word to some in school foodservice; however, it may become more familiar since these shortages are expected to continue through 1995.

LABOR-RELATED LAWS

The following sections will rely heavily on a training manual titled *Focus: Management Skills for School Foodservice Managers,* published by the Mississippi State Department of Education (VanEgmond-Pannell 1987) and on *The Legal Problem Solver for Foodservice Operators* (Griffith, Johnson, and Palmer 1987).

Anyone who works with recruiting, interviewing, hiring, and, particularly, managing employees needs to be familiar with the **Fair Labor laws.** Employees have rights by law, and ignorance of the law is not an acceptable excuse in a discrimination suit.

The Fair Labor laws are especially concerned with equality and the rights of the person. These concerns apply not only in the selection process but in the treatment of the person on the job. Lack of knowledge about these laws could result in discrimination charges being brought against the manager/supervisor or school district. Some of the Fair Labor laws that school foodservice management need to know are discussed below.

The Civil Rights Act of 1964 (Title VII) provides for equal employment opportunities. It became effective in 1965 and was revised in 1972 as the Equal Employment Opportunity Act. This law makes it unlawful for employers to refuse to hire, to discharge, or to discriminate with respect to compensation or terms and conditions on the basis of race, color, religion, sex, or national origin. It applies to all employers having 15 or more employees and to public school systems, regardless of how many people are employed.

The Civil Rights Act is concerned with more than discrimination. It requires that (1) certain safety regulations be followed, (2) equal rights in selection and transfer of employees be followed, (3) minimum hourly rates be paid, and (4) suitable jobs be found for unemployed minority people who have the skills and meet the qualifications. The Equal Employment Opportunity Commission investigates complaints by applicants and employees that this act has not been carried out.

The Equal Pay Act requires employers to provide equal pay for men and women performing similar work.

The Age Discrimination in Employment Act of 1967 and the amendment of 1978 promote the employment of older persons (40-70 years of age) based on ability, not on age. This law prohibits discrimination against people between these ages. It makes it illegal to ask the age or age group of applicants, or to request proof of their ages before hiring. After employing, it is legal to require proof of age, if it is needed. For example, if the position requirement is that the person be eighteen years old and the person does not look eighteen years old, the employer could ask the person to provide his or her age after the person has been employed. Also, retirement plans will require verification of age.

Handicap Discrimination Guidelines of the Revised Code, Chapter 4112, and *Section 504 of the Rehabilitation Act of 1973* make it illegal to exclude handicapped applicants as a group on the basis of their types of handicaps. If the handicap would prevent the person from performing the job, the employer does not have to employ the person; however, the employer could have to defend that decision.

Title IX of the Educational Amendments of 1972 and the amendments of 1978 ban discrimination on the basis of sex in all federally assisted education programs. It is illegal to ask in an interview about marital status, number and ages of children, who takes care of the children while the mother works, and similar matters. Further, it is illegal to ask if a woman is a "Miss," "Mrs.," or "Ms." or to ask the maiden name or previous name used.

The purpose of these laws is to prevent discriminatory practices. The Equal Employment Opportunity Office is the watchdog and will investigate employers reported as discriminating.

Affirmative Action, which is required nationwide by executive orders, requires that an employer make efforts to hire and promote minority groups.

The *overtime pay requirement* became effective in 1986 for public school employees. The employer is required to provide overtime compensation to nonexempt employees who work more than 40 hours in a week. Compensation can be in either of two forms: (1) *overtime pay* at the rate of 1½ times the regular rate of pay for all hours worked over 40 hours in a regular work week, or (2) *compensatory time off* at a rate of 1½ hours for each hour worked over 40 hours in a regular work week.

The school district needs to identify those who are nonexempt and exempt. The foodservice manager may or may not be exempt, depending on whether the person is employed to do a job within a certain period of time, as in the case of a principal. If the person is employed to do a job, then the person is exempt and does not qualify for overtime pay.

It is the management's responsibility to see that an employee who is nonexempt does not continue to work past the 40 hours, unless the overtime rate is to be paid. An employee of the school may volunteer. However, to provide services to the school or school district without the hours worked as a volunteer counting toward overtime compensation, the volunteer services provided should not be "the same type services which the individual is employed to perform." For example, the foodservice cook who volunteers to work at the PTA fund raiser should not be assigned to cook, but instead to do something unlike the paid job, like taking tickets.

The *Immigration Reform and Control Act of 1986* requires that employers verify employees' eligibility to work if hired after November 6, 1986. To be eligible, a person must be (1) a citizen or national of the United States, (2) an alien lawfully admitted for permanent residence, or (3) an alien with a work permit authorized by the Immigration and Naturalization Service to work in the United States. A form referred to as I-9 is provided by the U.S. Department of Justice, Immigration and Naturalization Service. The form requires that the employer review acceptable documents as verification of eligibility and complete and sign the form stating that the documents have been verified.

The *Occupational Safety and Health Act (OSHA) of 1970* has the mission "to assure so far as possible every working man and woman in the Nation safe and healthful working conditions and to preserve our human resources." It is important to provide a safe place for people to work, not only for morale and human considerations but also because of OSHA law. If an employee is injured on the job, the employer can be sued if the injury was due to negligence or unsafe working conditions.

Many questions management may need answers to are answered in *The Legal Problem Solver for Foodservice Operators* (Griffith et al) Among these are the following: Does training time have to be considered work time? Can an English language proficiency be required and tested? Can an employee be required to wear a uniform?

UNIONS

Many school district foodservice employees belong to unions. In these districts, employees use collective bargaining as a means of acting as a single unit when dealing with management. The areas of common concern are wages, hours and scheduling, layoffs and firing, days off, and paid holidays.

An important element of good labor-management relations is the bargaining group. Does the group really represent the labor force? The U.S. Office of Personnel Management (see Biasatti and Martin 1979) has identified the elements essential for effective union-management relations:

1. Acceptance of collective bargaining
2. Balance of power between the union and management
3. Respect for each other's goals
4. Recognition of common goals
5. Well-organized labor relations programs set up by management
6. High level of communication
7. Sincere negotiations
8. Effective administration of the labor contract
9. Comprehensive grievance processes
10. Evaluation by both parties of their relationship
11. Sense of participation in their own welfare on the part of employees

ORIENTATION AND TRAINING

Orientation

Orientation should be a rule for all new employees. Most employees new to school foodservices need training. They may or may not have any experience or knowledge of food, particularly preparation of large quantities. Training is necessary when the job the person is to do is different from any job he or she has done before, or if the manager wants the job performed in a specific way.

How an employee is oriented can have an impact on how long it takes him or her to learn the job, how well the new employee likes the job, the attitudes of fellow staff members toward the new employee, and job turnover. As soon as a person is employed, that person begins to share in forming group morale or group spirit.

An orientation checklist such as that shown in Figure 10-1 can be used for the new employee. A checklist will help ensure that the orientation is complete and includes all the areas that were intended.

_____ **Basic Information:** School name, grades in the school, principal's name, manager's name, and general information about the foodservice program, including objectives.

_____ **Welcome:** Greetings to make the employee feel at ease.

_____ **Introduction:** Introduction to the other employees in the kitchen. Tell the new employee something about what each one does.

_____ **Uniform:** Dress code. If uniforms are furnished, make arrangements for the employee to obtain them as soon as possible. Discuss good grooming standards, basic cleanliness, handwashing, hair restraints, and policy on jewelry, shoes, stockings, and aprons.

_____ **Payroll:** Payday, length of pay periods, how pay checks are delivered, and how overtime is calculated.

_____ **Requirement:** Social security number, completion of federal and state tax forms, sanitation certification (if applicable) requirements, and verification of eligibility to work.

_____ **Expectations:** What the duties are and what is expected of the employee—"a day's work for a day's pay."

_____ **Policies:** Breaks and mealtimes. Whether the meal is a fringe benefit or the employee must pay for it. Vacation days, personal leave, sick leave, and other types of leave, and when they can be taken. What to do in case the person is sick or for some other reason cannot be at work.

_____ **Performance Review:** When the employee will be reviewed, by what criteria, and the importance of the performance review.

_____ **Sanitation and Food Safety:** The importance of good personal habits, hand washing, and how the food should be handled.

_____ **Tour of the Kitchen:** Where to park and school facilities. Where things are located, such as dry storage, detergent closet, locker (or place to store purse, coat, etc.), and rest rooms.

_____ **Training:** Determination of training needed and provision of training for the job to be done.

_____ **Professional Growth Opportunities:** Staff development opportunities, training, and policy regarding promotions.

_____ **Introduction to Job:** Introduction to the particular job the employee will be doing.

Signed by Employee _____ Date _____

Signed by Person in Charge of Orientations _____

Adapted from Mississippi State Department of Education 1987.

FIGURE 10-1. Employee orientation checklist.

Training

Training is the key to a strong, successful school foodservice program in this country. Training is an ongoing process and should never stop. It is a manager's responsibility to train staff. Some of the advantages of a good training program are

> Reduction in employee turnover
> Lower absenteeism
> Fewer accidents
> Improved job satisfaction, fewer complaints and grievances
> Improved morale
> Lower production costs
> Improved sanitation habits
> Improved utilization of commodities
> Increased productivity

Training should take place when someone is new to a job, when new equipment is purchased, when government regulations or other procedures are changed, and when skills need polishing. Sometimes employees will need to be retrained in order to obtain the standards desired. In addition, some foodservice directors/managers may need training in the areas of cost-effectiveness, quality food production, or compliance with federal regulations. There appears to be a definite need for more training in the accountability requirements under AccuClaim areas. Nutrition education and training monies for these purposes are made available to each state under the Child Nutrition Education Act.

Because learning is so complex, it is important to use many different approaches to teaching. Though a person can listen at 700 words per minute, what is remembered the next day is much less. Just "telling" an employee something is a weak method of teaching. It has been said that—

> 20 percent of what is said to a person generally is remembered.
> 30 percent of what a person sees is likely to be remembered.
> 60 percent of what a person sees and hears will be remembered.
> 80 percent of what a person does will be remembered.

Some basic principles of learning (VanEgmond-Pannell 1987) are as follows:

- The learner must want to learn before learning can take place.
- The learner must be interested in the subject before he or she will learn.
- The learner remembers things taught that he or she can use right away.
- Absorption of information is more effective if it is based on seeing and doing. The learner remembers things which have made a deep impression.
- The learner remembers things best that are pleasant and tries to forget the unpleasant.

"Hands-on" experiences should be provided as much as possible, for maximum retention of learning. On-the-job training can be effective hands-on experience. For a manager to carry out on-the-job training successfully, he or she will need to know how to operate every piece of equipment in the kitchen. If the job of training on the job is delegated, it should be ensured that the person delegated to do the training is using correct methods and knows how to operate the equipment correctly and safely and do the job correctly. When proper methods are not taught, poor working practices become inbred.

PERFORMANCE APPRAISAL

As teacher performance standards and merit pay are developed and become more commonly used in determining increases in pay, performance appraisals for support service employees will become more meaningful. When the yearly raises are not being tied to performance, there may be high labor cost and "low efficiency."

Performance appraisals should be objective, consistent, and fair. They should identify the quantity and quality of work an employee performs and the areas in which improvement or additional training is needed.

Pay for Performance

The trends in the 1990s will be toward wage incentive plans and merit pay programs. Money can be a good motivator when it is a reward for accomplishment. Under a merit pay program, performance is appraised periodically and salary is adjusted to reflect the individual's output or accomplishments. In order for it to work, it is essential to have (1) a written policy, (2) accurate standards and reporting, (3) a bonus worth earning, and (4) incentive earnings or a visible merit bonus (paid by separate check).

Bonus pay for management when they have had a successful year is common in commercial industries. Companies like Hewlett-Packard, General Motors, Ford Motor Company, Aluminum Company of America, and Caterpillar Incorporated have updated their companies' performances with bonus incentive programs. Caterpillar turned their company around in the late 1980s with a pay-for-performance system that included profit-sharing ("Watching the Bottom Line . . ." 1988).

A school foodservice manager's pay raises should be tied to accomplishing goals and running a successful foodservice. Incentives to provide good food and services, develop customer relations, and so on need to be developed. The merit pay program is particularly applicable for managers of individual school foodservices. Gwinnett County, Georgia and Jefferson County, Kentucky have initiated such incentive programs. Aetna Life and Casualty Insurance of Hartford, Connecticut calls its written policy regarding its incentive program "In Business for Yourself." From the management standpoint, it is good for a manager to feel that it is his or her business.

Base pay may remain uniform if the minimum standard is met in a merit pay system. Pay differentials from worker to worker are based on the quality or quantity of work and how each worker performs his or her tasks. There can be levels of performance where there is no reward, and those levels must be surpassed to reach the reward level. Henry Gantt, a pioneer in scientific management, established the Gantt plan, whereby an employee earns an incentive after he or she has exceeded standards by a given amount.

Standards for Evaluating Performance

The supervisor should establish reasonable goals and quotas each year for the foodservice manager, and the manager, in turn, for the staff employees. Should a goal for the manager be to reduce labor costs, then one of the goals for the staff would be to improve efficiency and serve more meals without increasing labor.

There are very few merit and efficiency standards one can use at present in foodservice. The number of meals per labor hour can be used to judge the efficiency of a staff as a whole.

Employee Name	Social Security No.	Cost Center Name	Cost Center No.
Position Title	Employee Status	If Unscheduled Report, check here: ☐	DUE DATE

SEC-TION A	Unsatisfactory	Requires Improvement	Meets Standards	Immediate supervisor must check each category in appropriate column. FACTOR CHECK LIST	SECTION B — Superior performance in any category should be described in detail. Check marks in "Unsatisfactory" or "Requires Improvement" must be supported with documentation.
				1. *Observance of Work Hours:* Dependable and punctual attendance.	
				2. *Productivity/Quality of Work:* Completes an acceptable level of quality work.	
				3. *Job Skill Level:* Demonstrates required skills.	
				4. *Communication Skills:* Communicates well orally and in writing; effectively carries out verbal and written instructions.	
				5. *Working Relationships:* Works with and relates to others effectively.	
				6. *Adaptability/Flexibility:* Accepts change; works effectively under stress; responds to varying needs.	
				7. *Observance of Saftey/Health Standards:* Demonstrates knowledge of district safety/health/sanitary procedures.	ATTACHMENTS ADDED YES ☐ NO ☐

SECTION C

Employee was counseled on noted deficiencies: (Dates) _____ _____ _____

SUMMARY EVALUATION: (Check one)   Unsatisfactory ☐ Requires Improvement ☐ Meets Standards ☐

IF PROBATIONARY: I do not ☐ I do ☐ RECOMMEND PERMANENT STATUS

SECTION D

Goals and Objectives:

Continue to accept new learning experiences when offered. Watch for information on various food related courses offered at local junior colleges and through food service department and City Schools Inservice training classes. These courses help provide a better understanding of our goals and aims within our own food service department.

RATER:		REVIEWER:	
_____	_____	_____	_____
Signature	Date	Signature	Date

My supervisor has discussed this report with me and given me a copy of this evaluation report. I understand my signature does not necessarily indicate agreement.
Comments:

ATTACHMENTS ADDED YES ☐ NO ☐	_____	_____
	Signature	Date

FIGURE 10-2. Example of a performance evaluation report form. (*Source:* San Diego, California City Schools.)

INSTRUCTIONS FOR USE OF THE PERFORMANCE EVALUATION REPORT FORM

The Performance Evaluation Report Form is designed to help those being evaluated to achieve and maintain high levels of work performance and behavior. The form can be used by supervisors as an effective counseling device and as a means for establishing performance goals. Please see the *Performance Evaluation Guide for Classified Employees* for detailed instructions.

General:

1. After marking very lightly with pencil each factor in Section A, the rater shall review the report with her/his principal or department head, if any. Markings and comments shall then be typed or inked in. Either the rater or reviewer (or both) shall then review the rating with the employee in a private interview. All signatures shall be in ink. Changes and corrections shall be initialed by the employee.
2. If space for comments is inadequate, attachments (either typewritten or in ink) may be included, but each must be signed and bear the same date as the Performance Evaluation Report Form.
3. Due dates shall be observed and are particularly important for final probationary reports. Filing dates are flexible; both the first and final reports may be filed at any time between their receipt and the printed due date.
4. All probationers (either new-hire or promotional) shall be evaluated no later than the end of their third full month of probationary service and again after nine full months, but not later than the end of the eleventh full month of such service. Probationers may be separated (or demoted, if permanent in a lesser class) at any time such action is deemed necessary by the principal or department head through use of either a scheduled or unscheduled performance evaluation report.
5. All permanent employees (who have completed at least five months of service in permanent status) shall be evaluated every two years as of the printed due date. Permanent employees may be separated or demoted in the same manner as probationary employees, provided that all pertinent merit system rules and district procedures are observed.
6. Unscheduled reports may be filed at any time to record progress achieved or specific work performance deficiencies.
7. All performance evaluation reports in an employee's personnel department file are subject to review by principals or department heads whenever the employee is certified for transfer or promotion.

Section A: Check ( ) one column for each factor. N/A may be used when a factor is considered "not applicable" to a particular job. Each check mark in Unsatisfactory or Requires Improvement must have a specific explanation in Section B.

Section B: Describe outstanding qualities and superior performance. Give specific reasons for check marks in Unsatisfactory or Requires Improvement columns. Record here any other specific reasons why the employee should not be recommended for permanent status, or—if the employee is already permanent— any specific reasons for required improvement. Attachments, if included, should be indicated in space provided.

Section C: Enter the dates employee was counseled on noted deficiencies. SUMMARY EVALUATION: Check the appropriate box to indicate overall performance here, taking into account all factors and total performance for the full period of service being evaluated.

Unsatisfactory: Performance is clearly inadequate in one or more critical factors as explained or documented in Section B. Employee has demonstrated an inability or unwillingness to improve or to meet standards. Performance is not acceptable for position held. (Note: Such summary evaluation bars the employee from promotional examinations for one year.)

Requires Improvement: Total performance periodically or regularly falls short of normal standards. Specific deficiencies should be noted in Section B. This evaluation indicates the supervisor's belief that the employee can and will make the necessary improvements.

Meets Standards: Indicates consistently competent performance meeting or exceeding standards in all critical factors for the position. Most employees will fall in this category. If margin is narrow and standards are barely met, explain in Section B.

If Probationary: Make a recommendation regarding permanent status.

Section D: Record progress or improvements in performance resulting from employee's efforts to reach previously set goals. Record agreed-upon or prescribed performance goals for the next evaluation period.

Signatures: Both the rater and the employee shall date and sign the report. The employee's signature indicates that the conference has been held and that she/he has had an opportunity to read the report. If she/he refuses to sign for any reason, explain that her/his signature does not necessarily imply or indicate agreement with the report and that space is provided to record any disagreement. Further refusal to sign shall be recorded in the report. Attachments, if included, should be indicated in space provided.

Appeal: Evaluation reports express the judgment and opinions of supervisory authority, and as such, are not subject to appeal under rules of the merit system unless there has been a resultant action taken to suspend, demote, or dismiss a permanent employee.

FIGURE 10-2. *Continued.*

The profit and loss statement can be used to judge a manager's ability to manage finances (if the prices of food offerings are correctly set). Increases in the number served in a prescribed time can be an indication of efficiency. Increased participation can be an indicator of meeting customer needs.

People are motivated by standards that are realistic and will usually meet them or even surpass them if they are the types of employees management wants in permanent positions.

A part of the job of a supervisor and manager is to evaluate employee work performance. School districts usually have their own criteria and standards by which to evaluate employees. The performance appraisal (evaluation) should be tied to the job description. Employees should be made fully aware of the criteria and standards by which they will be evaluated. The formal performance appraisal should be written, and it should include documentation (see Fig. 10-2). The job performance, not personality traits, should be evaluated.

A system of measuring quantity and quality of work and evaluating performance based on standards may take many different forms, but basically it is based on such bench marks as the following (based on Nolan, Young, and DiSylvester 1980).*

150 percent: Super-skilled level
135 percent: Expert pace
120 percent: Incentive pace
100 percent: Fair day's work pace
 85 percent: Acceptable level
 70 percent: Minimum tolerable level
 50 percent: Unacceptable level

Or as follows:

- *Superior performance, exceptional* (150%) = reward and/or promotional opportunity
- *Above average, exceeds requirement or standard* (120-135%) = increment raise
- *Satisfactory, meets all requirements* (85-100%) = cost-of-living raise
- *Below standard, needs improvement* (70%) = maintenance of present pay
- *Unsatisfactory, unable to meet standard* (50%) = removal from position

Importance of Performance Appraisals

The performance appraisal is a motivational tool which can challenge, reward, and provide positive strokes. The appraisal process should help a person determine what to do in order to become a better employee and to grow and be promoted.

The performance appraisal should be tied to pay raises, and raises should not be automatic. In some cases, it is tied to tenure status. The first year may be a probationary period. If it is, a person should receive an informal appraisal at intervals during the first year, so that the employee knows how he or she is doing. The probationary period is the time to terminate a new employee's employment if the employee cannot do the job or is not dependable .

After the first year, a yearly appraisal should be adequate, unless the employee is not performing up to standards. In such a case, less formal evaluations can be made more frequently.

The formal appraisal should be in writing. Once the form has been completed, the evaluator should schedule a private meeting with the employee to discuss the appraisal.

DISCIPLINARY ACTION

Discipline is a necessary part of being a manager. If disciplinary action is not taken for misconduct or when someone fails to do his or her job, management becomes ineffective and is not respected by the other employees. Discipline can be as mild as talking to the employee or as strong as reprimanding and establishing changes that must be made. More stringent discipline includes suspension, demotion, or dismissal.

The following suggestions on reprimand are adapted from Buchanan (1973):

- *Do not ignore.* Impress on each employee the importance of his or her job. Wanting to be liked prevents some managers from functioning at their optimum for the organization.
- *Don't be afraid to praise.* Cash wages are paid by check. Mental wages should be "paid" by expressing appreciation for a job well done.
- *Praise the work*—not the worker. Praise in the presence of others when possible.
- *Be sympathetic in listening* to an employee's grievance. Hear his or her entire story.
- Make sure that *reprimands are always constructive.*
- *Begin all reprimands with a question.*
- *Never criticize intentions*—criticize methods.
- *Reprimand publicly only when absolutely necessary*—when an open violation of an important rule is committed, *for example.*
- *Don't harbor resentment.*
- *Support the school board policy* and the superintendent's rules even if you don't agree with them.
- *Be consistent with your discipline.* Be fair with all employees.
- *Don't be too lenient or too severe.* Seek the middle ground.
- *Don't take yourself too seriously.*

All types of reprimands and discipline should be followed up with a written report. This written report does not have to be any more than a handwritten account of what happened for the files with date and what action was taken. For example, if an employee is continually coming to work late, documentation may be a matter of noting this on the calendar with how many minutes late the person arrives and what (if any) excuse is used. This will be essential when more formal action must be taken.

DRUGS AND ALCOHOL IN THE KITCHEN

Unfortunately, for some foodservice employees a day on the job may be negatively affected by a "snort of coke," or a "break for pot," "shooting up," or a "tug at the bottle." Technical skills and know-how deteriorate when a person is drinking or on drugs. The effects or symptoms the employer may see are poor job performance, high absenteeism, morale problems, irregular behavior, an increased number of accidents and, in some cases, theft. A week's supply of drugs may cost upwards of $250. Theft is common when the habit becomes expensive.

The employee may be drinking and consuming drugs on his or her own time and not on the job with no law broken. However, the effects will be felt on the job. The National Council on Alcoholism reports that workers who abuse alcohol are absent two to four times more frequently than the nonabuser. They also have two to four times more accidents on the job.

Many school districts have employed specialized counselors to deal with problems caused by employees' use of drugs and alcohol. These areas will be an important management concern in the 1990s.

QUALITY CIRCLES

Quality circles are groups of employees (all levels) who work together to identify problems and areas that need improving and who become involved in improvements. These groups may analyze problems and look for solutions in such areas as the following:

- Improving the quality of school foodservice
- Reducing costs
- Providing better customer service and improving relations with customers (both students and adults)
- Improving atmosphere/surroundings in the foodservice facility

The quality circle approach is a form of participatory management that allows employees to be involved in making suggestions and initiating changes.

People will support what they have been involved with and will make things work if they have recommended the change. When an idea comes from the supervisor's office or the manager, however, they may support it but only because they "have to." It is important that employees "buy into" school foodservice. The teamwork approach helps meet social and self-esteem needs of many employees, which are two of the needs identified by Maslow in his "hierarchy of human needs."

Many large companies that use quality circles employ an outside person as the group facilitator (one who keeps the group on track and helps the group determine what the real problems are at the work place). In a school district, the facilitator may be someone from another department. The people who make up the group may be selected by all the employees or they may be the entire staff if the staff is small (no more than six to eight people).

Often quality circles are used when major problems related to morale, the organization, or a kitchen have occurred. The problems may be complex and difficult to identify, or they may be simple.

MOTIVATING EMPLOYEES

Managing human resources means understanding human behavior. Just as people's needs are different, it takes different things to motivate different people; however, most people respond to certain motivational factors. Each employee has basic needs, and each is at some level in terms of need fulfillment. Maslow's theory describes the basic needs and the levels of those needs with physical needs (most basic), safety and security needs, social needs, esteem needs, and self-realization needs (highest level) stacking one on top of the other to form a pyramid-like hierarchy. These basic needs of people can be met in the following ways:

- Work—which meets a basic psychological need by providing job satisfaction and security
- Salary—helps provide for the physical needs; an increase in salary and rewards motivates at a higher level
- Working conditions—a safe environment helps meet the safety needs; an improvement in working conditions may motivate at a higher level
- Social environment—relationships with supervisor and fellow employees will aid in meeting the social needs
- Advancements, achievements, and recognition—help meet the esteem and self-realization needs

Recognition may be as simple as the supervisor's or manager's calling the employees by name, showing interest in them, listening to their ideas, praising them on day-to-day accomplishment, and smiling and being pleasant. Promotions are one form of recognition for good work.

Praise is a powerful tool. It is a form of recognition that is easy to provide, and it should be used often. It is particularly effective when given around peers, relatives, and others. Just about everyone wants to be praised by others—even "proven employees."

What does the employee want from his or her job? According to Hersey and Blanchard (1969), appreciation of work ranks number one with employees. Table 10-2

Table 10-2.   What Employees Want Most from Their Jobs, as Viewed by Supervisors and by Employees Themselves

Items Ranked	Supervisors	Employees
Good wages	1	5
Job security	2	4
Promotion and growth	3	7
Working conditions	4	9
Interesting work	5	6
Personal loyalty of supervisor to employee	6	8
Tactful discipline	7	10
Appreciation of work	8	1
Understanding and help with problems	9	3
Feeling in on things	10	2

Source: Hersey and Blanchard 1969.

shows that supervisors have very different views of what is important to employees than do the employees themselves. This can explain why some supervisors have difficulty motivating employees.

BIBLIOGRAPHY

Altenburg, Randy. 1984. "Fair Play, Just Cause, and Due Process." *School Food Service Journal* 38(1).

Beach, D. S. 1975. *Personnel: The Management of People at Work.* 3d ed. New York: Macmillan Publishing Co.

Biasatti, L. L., and J. E. Martin. 1979. "A Measure of the Quality of Union-Management Relations." *Journal of Applied Psychology* 64: 387-390.

Bittel, L. R. 1974. *What Every Supervisor Should Know.* 3d ed. New York: McGraw-Hill.

Bolton, R., and D. Grover. 1984. *Social Style/Management Style: Developing Productive Work Relationships.* New York: American Management Association.

Boyle, Kathy. 1986. "Scouting." *Restaurant USA* 6(7): 22-24.

Bramson, Robert M. 1986. *Coping with Difficult People.* New York: Simon & Schuster.

Buchanan, R. D. 1973. "Personnel." *School Food Service Journal* 27(7): 43.

Bureau of Labor Statistics. *Occupational Outlook Handbook.* Washington, D.C.: U.S. Government Printing Office.

Department of Health, Education, and Welfare. n.d. *Work in America.* Washington, D.C.: U.S. Government Printing Office.

Deutsch, R. E. 1985. "Tomorrow's Work Force." *The Futurist,* 19(3): 10-11.

Drucker, P. F. 1974. *Management: Tasks, Responsibilities, Practices.* New York: Harper & Row Publishers.

Flippo, E. B. 1976. *Principles of Personnel Management.* 4th ed. New York: McGraw-Hill.

George, C. S. 1985. *Supervision in Action: The Art of Managing Others.* 4th ed. Englewood Cliffs, N.J.: Prentice-Hall.

Griffith, Clyde L., Richard C. Johnson, and Robert Alan Palmer. 1987. *The Legal Problem Solver for Foodservice Operators.* 3d ed. Washington, D.C.: National Restaurant Association.

Hersey, Paul, and Kenneth H. Blanchard. 1969. *Management of Organizational Behavior: Utilizing Human Resources.* Englewood Cliffs, N.J.: Prentice-Hall.

Herzberg, F. 1966. *Work and the Nature of Man.* Cleveland, Ohio: World Book.

Long, Dolores. 1985. "Drugbusters." *Restaurant Business* 84(14): 134ff.

Maslow, A. H. 1954. *Motivation and Personality.* New York: Harper & Row Publishers.

McGregor, D. 1960. *The Human Side of Enterprise.* New York: McGraw-Hill.

McIntosh, Robert W. 1984. *Employee Management Standards.* vol. 4. The L. J. Minor Foodservice Standards Series. New York: Van Nostrand Reinhold.

Minnesota Department of Education. n.d. *Supervisory Management.* St. Paul: Minnesota Department of Education.

Nolan, Robert E., Richard T. Young, and Ben C. DiSylvester. 1980. *Improving Productivity.* New York: AMACOM, American Management Association.

"Pay and Recognition Are Top Work Concerns." 1988. *FoodService Director* 1(11): 4-17.

Peters, Thomas, and R. H. Waterman, Jr. 1982. *In Search of Excellence.* New York: Harper & Row, Publishers.

Plummer, Joseph T. "Changing Values." *The Futurist* 23(1): 8-13.

Richie, J. B., and P. Thompson. 1980. *Organization and People.* St. Paul: West Publishing Co.

Sherer, Gail. 1984. "Good Intentions Are Not Enough!" *School Food Service Journal* 38 (10): 109, 112-13.

Smith, D. R., and L. K. Williamson. 1981. *Interpersonal Communication.* Dubuque, Ia.: William C. Brown Co., Publishers.

Smith, Jason P. 1986. "Bonuses." *Restaurant USA* 6(7): 26-30.

VanEgmond-Pannell, Dorothy, ed. 1987. *Focus: Management Skills for School Foodservice Managers.* Jackson: Mississippi Department of Education.

Vicary, Judith, and Henry Resnik. 1984. *Preventing Drug Abuse in the Workplace.* Rockville, Md.: National Clearinghouse for Drug Abuse Information.

"Watching the Bottom Line Instead of the Clock." 1988. *Business Week,* November 7, 134, 136.

11

Marketing and Promoting School Foodservices

Today's students grew up with thousands of commercials telling them what they ought to eat in order to be big, strong, popular, or "in." Since fast foods are a central part of their lives, to them the perfect lunch may be a Big Mac, fries, and a Coke—not cafeteria sliced turkey and gravy, mashed potatoes, fruit cup, and milk. As a result, many school foodservice managers are beginning to look at the students as "customers" and marketing what they have to sell. If this is not done, a school foodservice can lose out to neighborhood fast food restaurants and convenience stores at lunchtime. The Los Angeles City Unified School District experienced this late in 1988, when only 23 percent of the high school students chose to eat the school lunch, even though 78 percent of them qualified for the free or reduced-price lunch. The same thing happened on many of the military bases in the early 1980s, until foodservice management began treating the troops as customers and "marketed" to them.

MANAGING MARKETING

Marketing is the process of promoting, advertising, merchandising, and selling. It includes defining what the customer wants or needs; providing products or services that meet those wants and needs; informing the customer of the availability of the service or products and the benefits that can be gained by using them; and finally, selling products at prices the customer considers fair. The commercial foodservice industry understands the importance of marketing and spends millions of dollars each year on it. McDonald's spent more than $850 million in 1989 on marketing their products.

Zimmerman (1985) says that school foodservice management should take a few tips from successful commercial foodservice operations. When comparing what successful commercial foodservices had in common, she found the following:

> Products are promoted.
> Popular foods are served.

Food is consistently of good quality.
Atmosphere is pleasant.
Personnel are friendly.
Prices fit students' budgets.
Service is fast.

The image of school foodservice may be negative in a community because of adverse publicity or lack of publicity. Every school foodservice has an image. The image is made up of intangible thoughts and impressions that people hold about it. These are influenced by all the senses, and can be changed. The first thing to determine is what the current image is and what the desired image is.

A dull, institutional-type school foodservice can be turned into a fun place to eat. The image "fun place to eat" can be created by presenting food in a more contemporary way (e.g., fish and chips in a paper cone), by painting the serving line area and dining room area brighter colors, and by having employees smile while serving customers. Adding a "super sack" (not a brown bag lunch) or a "big lunch in a box" in the spring for eating outside is possible. The food can be brought to students in portable serving carts, an option that has been tried successfully by San Diego City Schools.

The National Evaluation of School Nutrition Programs (Wellisch et al. 1983) found that several factors affected the frequency with which individual students participated in the school foodservice program. The factors included the following:

- Price charged students—this was the single most important variable.
- Value parents place on nutrition, and their perception of how nutritious the meals at school were.
- Age of students—older students participated in school lunch programs less frequently than younger students.
- Sex of students—male students participated more frequently than females.
- Urban or city—students from rural areas participated more often than students from urban areas.

Before selecting a marketing approach, foodservice personnel should examine the factors associated with nonparticipation. A study of one major school district's foodservice participation in 1988 showed that

1. There was a lower interest in school lunch at the ninth grade level or at about age 15.
2. Food variety was more of a concern among senior high students.
3. There were substantial differences in food preferences between different ethnic groups.
4. Some ethnic groups of students were more embarrassed by association with free/discounted programs than other ethnic groups.
5. Breaks in the morning reduced the number who ate lunch.

To increase the participation of females or others concerned with losing weight, a salad bar might be opened and promoted with a sign saying "Make it your way" or "You decide how many calories you eat."

To prepare a marketing approach, a school foodservice manager or supervisor also needs to identify the competition. It is usually one or more of the following: fast-food establishments nearby, convenience stores, lunch brought from home, going home for lunch, vending machines (if available), or not eating at all.

The marketing approach should be planned and executed in big chunks or all at one time—not gradually, because the gradual approach does not get attention. Students will not see the marketing approach as anything new. The theme and image to be marketed should be enhanced by the presentation of food, the type of service offered, the appearance of the serving and dining areas, the uniforms the employees wear, and the attitudes the employees display.

Six marketing characteristics are shared by giants in the corporate world that are considered to have the most successful marketing programs, including Mercedes-Benz, Xerox, Federal Express, and Kodak (Lele and Sheth 1987):

1. *They set themselves "impossibly high" standards.*
2. *They are obsessive about knowing, even better than the customers themselves, what the customers want.*
3. *They create and manage customers' expectations.*
4. *They design their products or services to maximize customer satisfaction.*
5. *They put their money where their mouth is.*
6. *They make customer satisfaction everybody's business.*

MANAGING PROMOTIONS

Promotion, or *public relations,* can be described as the "act of promoting goodwill"; it should result in the public's having a positive image of the school foodservice. Dr. R. W. McIntosh, a sales promoter and merchandising authority, says that public relations should be "an attitude of management which places first priority on the public interest when making management decisions."

Promoting goodwill can mean something as simple as giving a straw to a child who brings a drink from home. Though one has to control "freebies," the public relations benefit of giving the straw must be considered by management in making the decision.

Since creating goodwill can be costly, it is usually best to establish clearly what services and products can and cannot be provided by foodservice. For example, if a teacher wants free napkins to serve food cooked in the classroom and the manager says "no," the results may be negative public relations. The manager is not wrong, but if the rule has not been established that napkins must be paid for, the decision may come across negatively. In such a case, it probably would help if prices for the services and supplies are established and teachers informed about them. For good public relations, it is best to announce what can be provided at what price.

Promotions used in the commercial food industry draw on a wide variety of special marketing techniques (Schultz and Robinson 1982), such as special events contests, coupons, and specials (reduced prices, samplings, and bonuses). For example, the Clorox Company, which makes Hidden Valley Salad Dressings, does salad bar promotions to increase its sale of dressing. Their promotions include the popular "rub-off" cards given to each customer who selects the salad lunch. If the rub-off card has a salad under all three dots, the customer receives a free salad lunch; if two, an ice cream. It is fun and creates suspense.

The use of promotions in a foodservice can help keep students interested in eating at the same place each day throughout the school year. The Marriott Corporation Food Services Division calls promotions "monopoly breakers." Looking at the commercial industry can provide ideas for school foodservice promotionals.

A school foodservice promotion might involve a contest to name the dining room and pick a theme for different seasons of the year, the sale of a book of lunch tickets for ten meals at a slight savings, or a coupon for a free ice cream with each book of tickets. It may include capitalizing on holidays and special school events with decorations and menus that create interest, sending home with the student favorite school recipes (adjusted to family size) at Christmas time or during National School Lunch Week, or celebrating birthdays of the month with specially decorated cupcakes. These efforts will usually result in not only higher participation, but also more customer satisfaction.

A promotion can have very positive results. It is an excellent way to encourage students to try something new and buy more than just a lunch (if the customers have the money). As an inducement, the foodservice can, for example, offer a nonfood item such as a customized school cup with the purchase of a milkshake.

Grandparents' day, secretaries' day, and a special Thanksgiving lunch can be very positive community relations activities. The Fairfax County Public School Food Service sponsored a very successful "Pizza Read": Students were rewarded with a "pizza party" if they met the reading requirements for one month. This was an excellent way to encourage students to read more and to relate classroom effort to the school foodservice program.

Promoting good nutrition should be a prime goal of school foodservice. Making information available, such as nutrient analyses of the food served, can be very positive. With the use of the computer, it is possible to provide actual nutrient analyses of the menus served. One of the major commercial management companies, ARA's nutrition promotions involves Nutrisaurus, a registered trademark. It is a grinning, green, dinosaurlike creature with horns, used to extol the virtues of a well-balanced, nutritional lunch ("ARA's Marketing Efforts . . ." 1988).

Some school districts have adopted logos and trademarks that promote good nutrition. Decatur, Georgia, Schools' registered trademark is Smart Bites; Virginia Beach City Schools, Mighty Bite; and Fairfax County, Virginia, Public Schools, Bite Right.

Armistead (1988) identifies four steps in planning a public relations project: (1) research, (2) planning or analysis, (3) communications, and (4) evaluation. Unfortunately, the first two and the fourth steps are frequently omitted in public relations. All four steps are important to planning and managing a successful public relations project.

Some of the characteristics of successful nutrition promotional programs (National Restaurant Association 1986) are the following: (1) The promotions clearly communicate to the customer "how" the items meet their needs; (2) they not only are addressing current nutrition needs but also have the built-in flexibility to adapt to future nutrition concerns; and (3) they are promoted "in house" to the staff (production and service) as well as to the customer. This generates enthusiasm for the program.

MANAGING ADVERTISING AND PUBLICITY

The objectives of advertising and publicity are to create and reinforce an image. Publicity is usually free, while advertising is purchased. Both are techniques used to inform and persuade the public or the customer. Both can be used to call attention to, tell about, or praise someone or something. Just because publicity is free does not guarantee that positive publicity will happen. School foodservice management should be assertive and imaginative in obtaining "free" publicity. This can be done by preparing feature stories and making them available to small newspapers that have lean budgets—they may be used as fillers, but the story is told.

One sure way to obtain positive publicity is through paid advertising. However, paid advertising is rarely used by school foodservices. Why not purchase an ad in the school newspaper? Why not run a 25-cents-off coupon in the school newspaper? The cents-off coupon is one of the most popular and effective sales promotions used in the retail food market (Schultz and Robinson 1982). School districts in the Phoenix area have been able to purchase time on television and radio by forming a corporation through which companies contribute funds for advertising school foodservice in relationship to the products purchased from the companies (Reid 1988).

Advertising of school foodservice activities and offerings usually qualifies for "free time" or "free space." Menus are often published in local newspapers. Even the *Washington Post* carries the local school districts' weekly menus. Surveys have shown that students are one of the prime audiences for early-morning television—just prior to leaving for school. With persuasion, the local television channels may be interested in carrying the menus. Cable television is often looking for fillers.

If book covers are popular, book covers can be printed advertising the school's football schedule as well as foodservice offerings and a la carte prices. These book covers can be given away with a lunch served at the beginning of the school year.

Meeting the Press

Since one cannot expect that all publicity will be positive, it is important to develop a cooperative working relationship with the press. This becomes especially useful in handling any unpleasant situations that may arise. For example, reports of food poisoning or high levels of some undesired nutrient or chemical in school lunches can cause very negative publicity. In the late 1980s, CBS in Washington, D.C., carried a series of feature news items entitled "Flunking School Lunch," which claimed that school lunches were higher in sodium and fat than fast foods. The reporter was good at sensationalizing and turning facts into hot human interest stories during television rating week.

Most reporters will be fair. Honest responses to a reporter are safer in the long run than attempts to cover up an unfavorable situation. In the case of crises, it is usually wise to take the initiative in disseminating information. Facts can stop rumors and gossip and provide reassurance to the public. The best public relations results come from an "act" mode, not a "react" one. The public can usually be won over by frank, candid responses and a sincere concern for the welfare of the customers.

According to National Restaurant Association (1988), every operation, no matter how large or small, should have a written crisis communications policy. Anyone who is to speak to the press on behalf of the foodservices or school district should be a skilled communicator and have the primary objective of getting the right message to the right audience in a believable way. In the case of a food poisoning outbreak thought to be caused by food eaten in a school cafeteria, the goals should include protecting the well-being of the customer, cooperating fully with any investigation, informing the public, and being truthful at all times.

Some tips in working with reporters in a normal situation (Armistead 1988) include these:

- Be honest.
- Do not be afraid to be interviewed.
- Regularly and systematically offer news and feature story ideas to the media.
- Spend as much time as necessary explaining an idea or program so reporters will understand it.
- Keep your head about errors in the resulting story. (Does it really matter?)
- Understand that when you are talking "off the record" this information may be used by the reporter.

MERCHANDISING

Effective merchandising can increase participation in a school foodservice program, and it can particularly increase satisfaction. In narrow terms, merchandising refers to making the customer want to buy a product because of the product itself. In a school foodservice, it involves offering good food that looks attractive at a price the customer considers fair, in a courteous manner, and in a pleasant environment.

One of the greatest downfalls of school foodservice has been lack of merchandising. This may be due to the volume of food being produced, a tight budget, time limits, or just the lack of competition. (Garnishing and presentation of food is discussed in chapter 8.)

COMMUNICATING WITH CUSTOMERS

How can a manager know what the students like or dislike? Certainly, production records help determine preferences. However, there need to be ways the manager can get more definite feedback. Techniques that can be used in getting to know the students' and adults' likes and dislikes include (1) formal questionnaires and surveys, (2) informal interviewing of students, (3) small group discussions, (4) suggestion boxes, and (5) taste parties or sampling.

Small group discussions with students can be very beneficial if suggestions for improvement are obtained along with help in carrying out the changes. Circulating throughout the dining area during lunch time, a manager or designated person can effectively solicit customers' opinions and give them a chance to ask questions in turn. This should be a regular occurrence. Also, employees on the serving line and in the dishroom window can obtain useful feedback and identify happy and unhappy customers. This information should be communicated to management.

Taste parties can be formal or informal, small or large, and can involve students, parents, faculty and/or foodservice supervisors or managers. They provide an excellent means of determining if a new product will be accepted. New recipes can be tested this way. The National Dairy Council has materials and ideas on having taste parties in their kit called "Taste Buddies."

For any taste party or sampling of food on the serving line, some type of form for expressing opinions should be provided. For younger children, a simple graphic form, as shown in Figure 11-1 is appropriate.

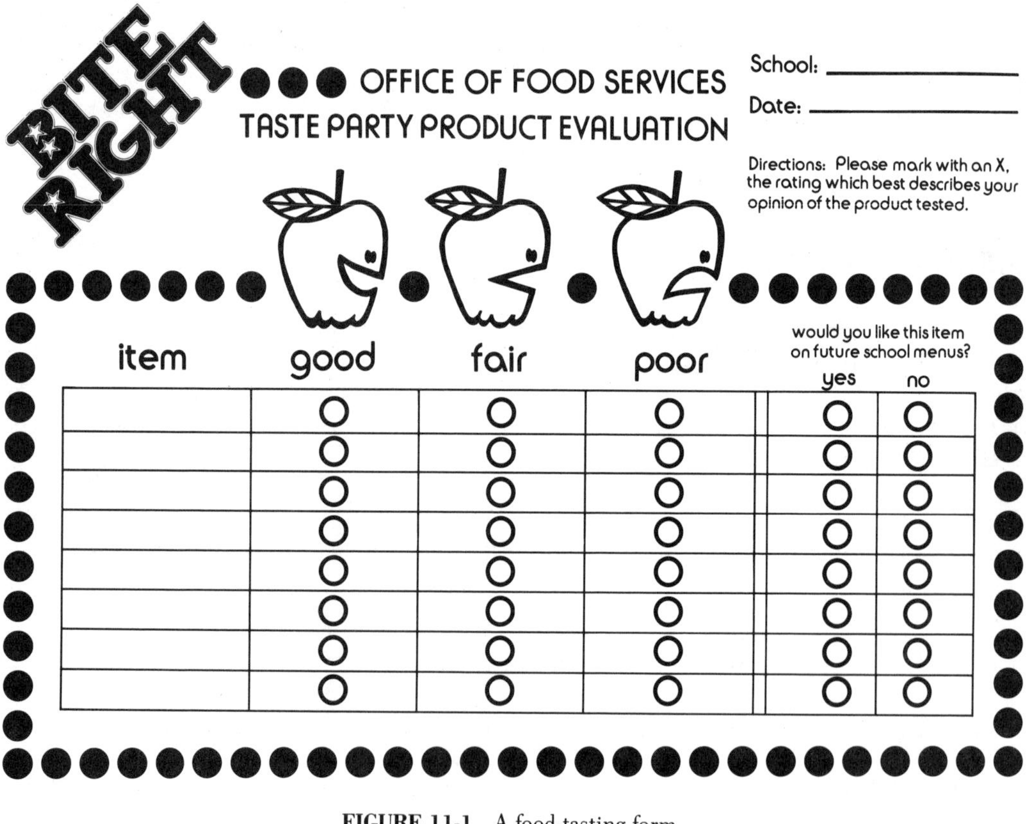
BITE RIGHT

OFFICE OF FOOD SERVICES
TASTE PARTY PRODUCT EVALUATION

School: ____________

Date: ____________

Directions: Please mark with an X, the rating which best describes your opinion of the product tested.

item	good	fair	poor	would you like this item on future school menus? yes	no
	O	O	O	O	O
	O	O	O	O	O
	O	O	O	O	O
	O	O	O	O	O
	O	O	O	O	O
	O	O	O	O	O
	O	O	O	O	O
	O	O	O	O	O

FIGURE 11-1. A food-tasting form.

The Youth Advisory Council (YAC) is an organization made up of students interested in nutrition and school foodservice. It is a national organization sponsored by the American School Food Service Association. The Irving, Texas, Independent School District was one of the first to form such a group; it developed a manual for its Youth Advisory Council. The American School Food Service Association has materials available on how to start a Youth Advisory Council.

Federal regulations require that schools participating in the National School Lunch Program have student and parent involvement. The YACs and other student groups have been excellent ways to involve the students. Since parent involvement has proved difficult to obtain, the U.S. Department of Agriculture has considered dropping this requirement.

SELLING

Selling (like *advertising*) is a new word to some school foodservice managers. Certainly the schools are no place for high-pressure selling, but suggestive selling and using good business sense in displaying food are appropriate in most school foodservices. For example, chocolate chip cookies next to the ice cream cups with the suggestion to make one's own cookie and ice cream sandwich will usually increase the sales of chocolate chip cookies and ice cream cups.

Displaying soft pretzels in a revolving, well-lighted case will increase their sales. Making a la carte food items accessible—easy to reach—will also make a difference in sales. How foods are priced will have an effect on sales. For example, if the price of lunch is $1.35, having a 15-cent item such as a cookie will increase the revenue. (Pricing is discussed in chapter 2.)

To make the foodservice more effective by increasing participation and serving all students in less time, the manager needs to know what the customer wants. Preferences can be determined through surveys, listening, questioning, and staying in touch with the customer. The student needs to know that the foodservice goals are to deliver a top-quality, nutritious lunch at the best price in town. The good price can be proved to the customer with a poster comparing the prices of key items on the menu with prices charged at popular fast food restaurants.

In order to keep the customer's interest and maintain the goals of increasing participation and customer satisfaction, the foodservice should: design products to provide surprises, give more than is expected, put as much of the revenue as possible into the purchase of good-quality food, and train all the employees to be salespersons and to act as if the foodservice is their own business.

Surveys for evaluating the school cafeteria atmosphere and the lunches served are provided in Figures 11-2 and 11-3.

Name: _____ Date: _____

Please place an "X" by your answer or answers.

1. Is the time you spend in line getting your food:
   _____ too long
   _____ okay
   _____ too short

2. How many minutes do you have to eat your meal?
   _____ less than 15 minutes
   _____ 15–30 minutes
   _____ 30–45 minutes
   _____ more than 45 minutes

3. Is the school cafeteria supervised by friendly people?
   _____ yes   _____ no

4. Are the people who serve the food friendly?
   _____ yes   _____ no

5. Do you think the school cafeteria is:
   a. _____ well lit   b. _____ colorful
      _____ okay   _____ okay
      _____ too dark   _____ drab
   c. _____ too quiet   d. _____ messy
      _____ okay   _____ okay
      _____ noisy   _____ clean

6. Would you like to see improvements in the school cafeteria?
   _____ yes   _____ no

7. Would you like to help make improvements in the school cafeteria?
   _____ yes   _____ no

FIGURE 11-2. Sample form for evaluating the school cafeteria atmosphere.

Name: _____ Date: _____

Please place an "X" by your answer or answers.

1. How often do you eat the school lunch?
   _____ never
   _____ sometimes
   _____ always

2. If never, why?
   _____ food does not taste good
   _____ food does not look good
   _____ too expensive
   _____ don't like menu choices
   _____ my friends don't eat there
   _____ don't like cafeteria
   _____ lines too long
   _____ too expensive
   _____ I have no choice

3. If always, why?
   _____ food tastes good
   _____ food looks good
   _____ inexpensive
   _____ like menu choices
   _____ have no choice.
   _____ my friends eat there

4. What do you prefer for lunch?
   _____ hot dinner-type lunch
   _____ soup and sandwiches
   _____ fast-food type lunch
   _____ box or bag lunch
   _____ salad bar
   _____ yogurt
   _____ snack items
   _____ other

5. List five of your favorite foods that are served for school lunch.

   _____   _____

   _____   _____

6. List five foods that you would like to see served for school lunch.

   _____   _____

   _____   _____

   _____

FIGURE 11-3. Sample form for evaluating school lunches.

BIBLIOGRAPHY

"ARA's Marketing Efforts Help Keep Clients Satisfied." 1988. *School Business Affairs* 54 (8): 51.

Armistead, Lew. 1988. "A Practical and Positive Approach to Public Relations." *School Business Affairs* 52(12): 15-19.

Barker, I. M. 1982. *The Psychology of Human Food Selection.* New York: Van Nostrand Reinhold.

Feltenstein, T. 1983. *Restaurant Profits through Advertising and Promotion.* Boston: The CBI Publishing Co.

Irving Independent School District. 1979. *Youth Advisory Council Resource Manual.* Irving, Tex.: Irving Independent School District.

Lele, Milind M., and Jagdish N. Sheth. 1987. *The Customer Is Key: Gaining an Unbeatable Advantage Through Customer Satisfaction.* New York: John Wiley & Sons.

McNeal, James U. 1987. *Children As Consumers: Insights and Implications.* Lexington, Mass.: Lexington Books, D. C. Heath and Company.

National Restaurant Association. 1986. *A Nutrition Guide for the Restauranteur.* Washington, D.C.: National Restaurant Association.

———. 1988. *The Foodservice Operator's Crisis Management Manual.* Washington, D.C.: National Restaurant Association.

Rednak, Jon. 1987. "Building High Participation in School Food Service." *School Business Affairs* 52(11): 22-27.

Reid, Joyce E. 1988. "School Lunch in Crisis: An Arizona District Takes an Innovative Approach." *School Business Affairs* 54(11): 32-33.

Reid, Robert D. 1983. *Foodservice and Restaurant Marketing.* Boston, Mass.: CBI Publishing Co.

Schultz, Don E., and William A. Robinson. 1982. *Sales Promotion Management.* Chicago: Crain Books.

Watkins, Edward. 1988. "Teaching the School Foodservice Market to Merchandise." *The Foodservice Distributor* (May): 80-82.

Wellisch, Jean, et. al. 1983. *The National Evaluation of School Nutrition Programs: Final Report.* vols. 1 and 2. Santa Monica, Calif.: System Development Corporation.

Zimmerman, Kathy. 1985. "Changing with the Times." *School Food Service Journal* 39(6): 28.

12

Reducing Cost and Increasing Efficiency

FINANCIAL CRISES

Some school districts have already experienced financial trouble. For many, the 1990s will be the first time their foodservices will have a difficult time breaking even. These financial problems develop mainly because the increase in revenue (price charged students and federal reimbursement) has not kept pace with the increase in expenditures. Labor costs will be a major factor in the financial picture in the 1990s.

Foodservice employees often receive the same raises and fringe benefits as employees in other school district departments. The average labor hour with fringe benefits may be costing in excess of $15. The other departments are probably being funded by tax monies and do not have to be as concerned with productivity and costs. Unfortunately, those departments are not the competitors that school foodservice management has to deal with. The competitors, who are the fast food restaurants, the management companies, and the foodservice industry generally, are often paying much less per labor hour than a school district-managed foodservice. The fast food industry is built around turnover and has little to offer for longevity, whereas many school districts' pay scales have seven- to ten-step raises, based on years of service (and often not on performance).

Fringe benefits, especially health insurance, have undergone steep increases in the last 5 years. In some cases the fringe benefits exceed 30 percent of the pay an employee receives. During the 1970s fringe benefits were provided for foodservice employees, with little thought given to costs in 10 to 15 years. The 15-minute break in addition to the lunch break for part-time employees provides an example of the cost of fringe benefits. Although not required by federal law, the 15n-minute break may be a part of the union contract agreement for all employees including part-time employees. If a kitchen has four employees and the average labor hour with fringe benefits is costing $12.50, a 15-minute break would cost $2,312.50 a school year or $12.50 per day.

Food costs have increased as USDA-donated foods have added processing and delivery fees and the supply of bonus commodities has decreased (as "bonus" donated commodities are becoming nonexistent). Weather conditions and the mergers of food companies also influence food costs. For example, as a result of the drought in 1988, the price of some vegetables increased as much as 50 percent in 1989.

The cost of producing and serving a lunch varies across the nation, as do the prices charged students for lunch. In many cases not all costs are being identified, and the subsidy by the school district is a considerable amount. An example of the average cost of producing and serving a lunch in Florida (1987) was $1.40, not including commodity value (see the following breakdown, which is from the Florida Annual Report of School Nutrition Programs 1987).

Salaries	$ .5118
Benefits	.1684
Purchased services	.0482
Supplies	.0538
Purchased food	.5060*
Other materials/supplies	.0106
Other expenses	.0348
Total direct costs	$1.3337
Indirect costs	.0699
Total costs	$1.4036

New York state (1987) estimates the average cost of serving a lunch at $1.72; Fairfax County, Virginia Public Services (1988) estimates the average cost at $1.63. At the same time that school foodservices are needing some financial relief, school district general budgets are also under pressure. As a result, foodservice programs are being charged for services they have never had to pay for in the past. More and more school districts are charging the foodservice program for utilities, for example.

When revenue does not cover the cost, the first impulse is to increase the price charged. This is certainly one way, but the customers and community may resist. School boards are telling foodservice directors to reduce costs.

Although some school districts are turning to management companies to resolve their financial problems, the financial problem often can be resolved by the school foodservice director/supervisor with the support of the administration. If the school district decides to take on the challenge of solving a financial problem, it will usually mean a combination of raising prices and reducing costs. (Pricing is discussed in chapter 2.)

One of the main qualifications for a director or supervisor in the 1990s will be a good financial management background. It will be necessary for management to "control cost," which means direct, regulate, and restrain actions to achieve a financial goal.

Since labor and food costs consume usually 90 percent or more of the foodservice budget, this section will concentrate on reducing the costs in these two areas.

REDUCING LABOR COSTS

During the 1960s, labor costs consumed between 28 and 32 percent of the school foodservice revenue. During the 1970s, with the addition of fringe benefits and a popular

---

*The value of commodity food was not considered, which would add approximately 20¢.

annual cost-of-living raise and step raise, the percentage inched up. Studies on equal pay for equal work in the 1980s resulted in foodservice employees in some school districts receiving large raises. All the school districts in Minnesota are required to adjust their pay.

Even though a school district's starting pay for foodservice workers may be only $6.34 ($8.37 per hour with fringe benefits), the average cost per labor hour may be as high as $14.00. This is due to employee longevity, different position guidelines, and managers' salaries.

Today the labor costs in many school districts exceed 60 percent of the revenue. It may be because (1) revenues are not high enough, (2) pay scales are out of line with the industry, (3) productivity is low and schools are overstaffed, or (4) there is no control on use of overtime and substitutes. High labor costs may be a combination of these factors.

Some school districts need to do a thorough salary study, reclassify employees, and establish new pay scales that more closely resemble the competitor's pay scale. The step raises need to be tied to performance. Restrictions may need to be placed on fringe benefits—that is, either staff employees are eligible for the retirement program *after one year of employment*, or only managers are eligible for this program—and the employer should be paying less of the cost of health insurance for part-time than for full-time employees.

There are some trade-offs to be considered. When a school district begins reducing wages and fringe benefits for foodservice employees, the results are often higher turnover, low morale, and employees who are less dedicated, motivated, and qualified. This usually means negative changes in the quality of the school foodservices. However, many of the fast food restaurants function successfully with high turnover and employees with no previous foodservice experience. Their secrets are a very limited menu, standardized recipes and procedures, and a good training program.

Increasing Efficiency

One of the main reasons for high labor costs may be low productivity. To determine why labor costs are so high, the productivity rate needs to be evaluated. It is usually based on meals per labor hour (see the guidelines discussed in chapter 5).

Increasing productivity means increasing speed or efficiency. It means producing more with the present number of labor hours or producing the same with fewer labor hours. Preparing work schedules is essential to an efficient operation (see chapter 5).

The most important ways of bringing about an increase in productivity in a kitchen are the following.

Training to improve job efficiency
Applying work simplification methods
Arranging the kitchen for an efficient flow of work
Scheduling work effectively
Establishing time standards
Utilizing automation
Utilizing processed foods and disposable supplies
Changing the foodservice system
Motivating employees to improve productivity (see discussion in Chapter 10)
Paying for performance (see discussion in Chapter 10)
Using volunteers or other labor

Management costs can be reduced by increasing the span of control, for example, by giving one manager responsibility for two nearby schools.

Training to Improve Job Efficiency

The manager should be trained in the basic principles of motion economy, the steps to improving productivity, using the principles of motion economy, and motivating employees to increase productivity. If the manager knows these steps and principles, he or she can use them in on-the-job training as well as in the kitchen to improve jobs.

The principles of motion economy described by Barnes (1968) and Kazarian (1979) can be used in school foodservices to increase productivity. Motion economy can be divided into three principal segments: (1) hand and body motions, (2) work process or sequence, and (3) design of tools, equipment, and the workplace.

Observation is one of the main ways of determining if a job can be improved. The six steps toward improving productivity are as follows:

1. Select the job to be improved and define the situation (problem).
2. Break down the job into parts by flow charting.
3. Question each step and each process to determine: Is there a better way? Can steps be eliminated? Can steps be simplified?
4. Arrive at a new method.
5. Put the new method into action.
6. Follow up and evaluate.

Applying Work Simplification Methods

Motion economy principles can be applied to school foodservices in the form of work simplification methods. Examples are provided below.

- Use both hands at the same time to do useful work whenever possible. Examples:
    —Panning rolls: pick up a roll in each hand and put onto the pan.
    —Racking dishes: pick up a plate in each hand to put into the dishwashing racks. Use both hands to take dishes out of the racks and stack.
    —Serving food: pick a plate up with one hand and bring midway to meet the food that has been dipped or picked up by the other hand.
- Perform work in a rhythmic way. Examples:
    —Using a French knife: place the knife point on the cutting board and with other hand move the food under the knife; rock the knife up and down, cutting the food and developing a rhythm.
    —Developing a natural rhythm: practice with motions such as stirring, racking dishes, rolling, or cutting rolls and biscuits.
- Use smooth, continuous, curved motions when possible rather than straight-line motions with sharp changes in direction. This could increase productivity by 25 percent. Examples:
    —Wiping tables: use a wide arch-like motion rather than a straight-line one.
    —Spreading sandwich fillings on bread: spread with circular motion without lifting the tool.

- Use the fewest, shortest, and simplest motions. Examples:
  —Brushing and spreading: use a 2-, 3-, or 4-inch pastry brush instead of the hand or a 1-inch brush for greasing pans, or the spatula for spreading mayonnaise and butter on bread; reduce strokes by using the largest brush feasible.
  —Measuring: use the largest measure practical, not multiples of a smaller one (e.g., a 1-cup measure instead of 16 tablespoons, and a 2-ounce ladle for a 2-ounce quantity).

- Combine operations and eliminate all unnecessary parts of the job. Examples:
  —Cooking in serving pans.
  —Adding dry milk to dry ingredients, then adding water, eliminating reconstitution of milk.
  —Hardening gelatin in the portion cup or dish in which it is to be served.
  —Combining peanut butter and jelly before spreading on bread for sandwiches.

- Eliminate unnecessary walking, reaching, stretching, and bending. Examples:
  —Using a cart to carry supplies needed from the storeroom to the work center.
  —Using foot pedal controls and knee levers when possible.
  —Arranging work where reaching or stretching will be kept to a minimum. The normal reach of most people is 12 to 14 inches, and the maximum reach without stretching is 22 to 24 inches.

- Develop standardized procedures.
  —Eliminating "to taste" directions in recipes by determining how much salt, sugar, or other flavoring is needed and adding the information to the recipe.
  —Putting the same number of items (hamburger patties, cookies, and so on) on a pan each time.

Several of the above principles of motion economy are illustrated in Figure 12-1, "Assembling Sandwiches."

Arranging the Kitchen for an Efficient Flow of Work

The kitchen should be divided into work centers—separate areas as baking, preparing salads and fresh produce, and cooking. The equipment should be arranged within each center according to the sequence of its use, to avoid crisscrossing and unnecessary walking and reaching. Food and supplies should flow from receiving through the kitchen to service. Foods such as French fries, which are batch-cooked and served hot, should be prepared as close as possible to the serving line. Equipment that needs to be used by more than one work center should be put on wheels if possible. Otherwise, it should be located in the center that uses the equipment most, or a duplicate piece of equipment should be purchased, if feasible. Tools, as well as materials and supplies, should be located close to the point of use and in a definite place.

If work centers are color coded, the coding can be used on the equipment and tools so that they are returned to the center. Refrigerator doors that contain each center's supplies should be color coded to reduce time spent locating ingredients.

COLD SANDWICHES

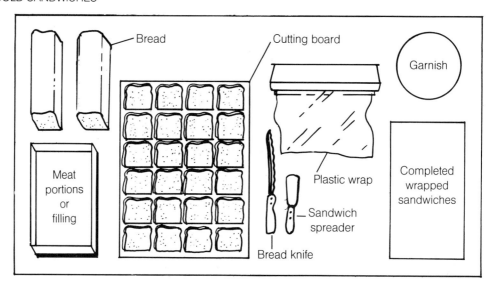

Step f:

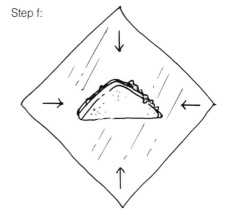

Steps to making cold sandwiches:
1. Pull recipe and read thoroughly.
2. Prepare ingredients and garnishes.
3. Set up work station. Make sure all ingredients, utensils, and pans are within easy reach.
4. For egg salad or tuna salad sandwiches:
   a. Place sliced wheat bread on cutting board to cover board or for number of sandwiches needed.
   b. Portion filling with proper scoop on all slices of bread. Spread filling evenly to edges using a sandwich spreader.
   c. Top with sliced white bread.
   d. Slice diagonally with bread knife.
   e. Garnish with pickle chip.
   f. Wrap with plastic wrap cut-side down.

FIGURE 12-1. Assembling sandwiches. (*Source:* Lina 1988.)

The arrangement of the storeroom should be planned carefully. The inventory form should be set up in the same order as the physical facility.

Establishing Time Standards

Since there are so many variables in accomplishing a job, each individual district (or region or state) needs to determine what is a reasonable amount of time for doing each job. For example, how long should it take an employee to portion 250 portions of fruit cups and tossed salads or make 50 chef salads? (Figure 8-2 illustrates a form for establishing time standards.)

Knowing how long a job should take (1) acts as a motivator to the employee, (2) provides a goal, (3) provides a standard for evaluating the productivity of an individual, and (4) is information needed for work scheduling.

Utilizing Automation

Computerization and automation have been slow to take hold in the foodservice industry. However, the next ten years will see unbelievable progress in this area. When it becomes necessary to purchase a new piece of equipment, an automated version should be considered. Among the automated types of equipment presently available are deep fat fryers with automated baskets that will remove the product from the fat when it is done, and with an automated filtering system. These features save time and make a process almost foolproof.

It may not be practical for each individual kitchen to have automated portioning machines and similar equipment. However, in a central kitchen, computerized automation can be better utilized and reduce labor costs substantially. (See chapters 13 and 14 for discussions of other automated equipment and the use of robotics and computers in school foodservice.)

Utilizing Processed Foods and Disposable Supplies

The use of convenience foods and disposable supplies instead of cooking from raw ingredients and washing dishes will reduce the number of employees and labor hours needed. The cost of food, however, will increase. Will the labor cost be lowered more than the cost of the food will increase? Will the finished products be the foods the majority of customers prefer? Will the nutritional value be comparable or improved?

Using more processed (convenience) foods and utilizing disposable supplies are rather major steps and should be carefully weighed to determine the real cost per meal as compared to making the items from raw ingredients.

It is important that the addition of convenience foods and disposable dishes be matched by a cutback in staff or hours. Otherwise (according to Parkinson's Law—"Work expands to fill the time available") the staff will gradually slow down and adjust to the workload.

Using disposable supplies is not always cost-effective. (See table 5-4 for a comparison of the costs of washing dishes with the costs of using disposable supplies.) In a small rural school district, where labor costs are low and paper supplies are high, washing dishes may cost less than using disposables.

Changing the Foodservice System

The highest productivity can be obtained with preplated meals prepared in a central kitchen that serves 20,000 or more. Bulk satellite food for portioning on location can obtain higher productivity than on-site production in most situations. The larger the central kitchen and the more automated it is, the higher the productivity will be.

The Corpus Christi, Texas, Independent School District has been able to maintain one of the lowest labor costs (28 percent including fringe benefits) in the industry. With a central kitchen preparing 20,000 meals for bulk transporting to satellite schools, this foodservice has been able to maintain very high productivity. The central kitchen has been studied by Japanese school foodservice administrators to learn how to obtain similar results. Staffed with 16 employees producing 128 hours, the central kitchen produces at the rate of 156 meals per labor hour. At the satellite schools, the employees heat, portion, and serve. These schools are staffed on the average at 37 meals per labor hour.

Other examples of high productivity are in the automated, high-volume central kitchens of the Dayton, Ohio, Public Schools and the Los Angeles Unified Public Schools.

Reducing the need for employees is one of the solutions to high labor costs. Having on-site production kitchens in every school, for example, requires more employees than when food is prepared at a central kitchen and delivered to finishing kitchens. By making all but one kitchen a "finishing kitchen," labor hours can be reduced substantially. With the finishing kitchen concept, food is prepared for finishing on-site (heating or maintaining at cold temperature, portioning, and serving).

Preplated meals prepared by a central kitchen in an automated assembly line approach require the least number of employees and labor hours and the least amount of training for employees.

The costs of processed foods have not become competitive enough yet with either of these systems for a volume of over 20,000. If the capital for building and equipping a central kitchen is an issue, processed foods are an alternative. Large school districts such as St. Louis, Fairfax County, and Detroit use many processed foods.

Henry Ford II is given credit for saying, "Productivity is a measure not of how hard we work but of how well we use our intelligence, our imagination, and capital." Foodservice directors/supervisors need to use their intelligence and imagination to provide school breakfasts and lunches at the lowest prices possible.

According to the South Carolina Office of School Food Service's Training Manual, the objectives of increasing productivity and work simplification are to (1) reduce the cost of the operation, (2) eliminate all unnecessary or nonessential activities, (3) increase the effectiveness of each necessary activity, (4) eliminate duplication of activities, (5) make work safer and less fatiguing, (6) eliminate waste of time, energy, and material, (7) improve customer relations, and (8) develop an attitude of receptiveness to change.

Using Volunteers or Other Labor

Another way to reduce labor costs is to use volunteer labor. Many school districts use parent volunteers. However, working in the kitchen may not be the most popular job among volunteers unless there are incentives. Another source of labor is high school students, paid as substitutes, or a club and class in the high school that can be paid for providing students to run a snack bar. Clubs and classes are always looking for ways to raise money. A volunteer or group of students can provide needed "hands" at the peak hours, especially lunch periods, if the motivation is provided. An hourly rate, percentage of profits, or a flat sum that is much lower than an employee labor hour cost is paid to the club, class, parent-teacher association, or school.

The Fairfax County Public Schools Foodservice have a program called "Volunteers for Computers," with funds going toward the purchase of a computer for the particular school. In the case of a club or class operating a snack bar, a contract is drawn up between the club and the foodservice. Tight inventory controls have to be in place and definite procedures followed. The arrangement can work to the advantage of both the club and foodservice.

REDUCING FOOD COSTS

Food costs can be reduced in a number of ways, including the following:

- Reducing waste
- Utilizing leftovers
- Using less expensive products
- Changing menus and other food offerings
- Reducing portion sizes
- Extending "offer versus serve" in elementary and intermediate schools
- Utilizing USDA-donated commodities more economically
- Ordering only what is needed
- Checking in orders and storing properly
- Eliminating theft

Also to be considered: Will employees' lunches be a fringe benefit, or will employees be charged for their lunches? If the meal is costing $2 to prepare and serve, it would cost approximately $364 per year to feed each employee.

Reducing Waste

Controlling waste is always desirable, because waste is an unnecessary cost. The following should be considered in controlling production (Miller 1987):

Produce to a forecasted number.
Plan use of leftovers and by-products.
Reduce holding time to improve quality and reduce loss.
Practice portion control.
Preportion when possible.
Have close supervision during preparation and service.

Miller further recommends auditing waste. First, returning plates should be watched for plate waste and then kitchen waste (checking garbage cans). There are two concerns:

(1) waste in preparation and (2) the food students are throwing away. Waste in preparation usually results from

- Burning or overcooking a product and having to throw the product away
- Failure to obtain all the product with the use of a spatula from the can or bowl
- Throwing away less than perfect products, such as broken cookies and ends of breads which could be utilized
- Excessive paring when cleaning vegetables and fruits
- Improperly storing items not used
- Failing to utilize products before they spoil

If the plate waste is heavy, why? Is it because the students do not like the food? Is it because the portion is too large? It may be a combination of these. "Offer versus serve" and offering choices (discussed below) are recommended ways of reducing plate waste.

Utilizing Leftovers

Overproduction is common, particularly in schools which offer choices and take no lunch counts. Leftovers can be a food waste, a choice the next day, or part of another dish. Working leftovers into already planned menus is an art; the returns are lower food cost.

No food (either leftovers or their own portion) should go home with employees. Allowing leftovers to be taken home can encourage employees to cook more than is needed.

Purchasing a Different Product

Using Grade A fruits and vegetables may not be necessary. For example, Grade A sliced peaches are not needed for fruit cobbler. But you should use seasonal foods in season and plan menus accordingly. Purchasing beef products that contain soybean product will reduce the cost per pound. In some cases, the product will be improved in flavor, moisture content, and nutritional value. Using a different piece of chicken or cut of meat may reduce costs.

Salad dressing, for example, may be a satisfactory substitute for mayonnaise and cost less. Other imitations or substitutes should be considered: for example, imitation cheese, whipping cream, and sour cream.

Changing Menus and Other Food Offerings

The menus should be planned to meet basic requirements. Any additional foods may consist of the condiments needed with the foods. However, extras may be limited *or* eliminated from the menu in order to reduce waste and costs. Examples of extras are potato chips and desserts, which, in any case, may be sold a la carte for those who need or want the additional calories. Still, providing more items on the menu than are needed is nice, if one can afford the extra cost.

There may be some menu items that can no longer be afforded, or must to be sold a la carte or as part of a higher lunch price. If 80 percent or more of the students pay for their lunches (20 percent or less free and reduced-price), two different price lunches may be a solution. This approach works particularly well in high schools, where the needs of students with widely different appetites—from athletes to weight-conscious girls—must be met. On the higher-priced lunch menu can be the quarter pounder, 8-inch French bread pizza, chicken breast, and so on. Note that the students eligible for free and reduced-price lunches must have the option of the higher-priced lunch if the lunch is to be claimed for reimbursement.

Reducing Portion Sizes

The school lunch pattern has three different portion sizes that can be used in the public schools. Varying the meal pattern provides a built-in flexibility that reduces waste.

Portion control is often a problem, and a manager should always be aware that this needs supervision. Preportioning can help ensure that a standard portion is being given.

Extending "Offer versus Serve"

Though "offer versus serve" is required by regulation at the high school level, the local school district can decide whether it will be carried out at other levels. It can reduce plate waste by 10 to 20 percent, particularly in elementary school.

Better Utilization of USDA-Donated Commodities

Considering commodities at their purchased value rather than as a "freebie" is important to the attitude toward and the use of donated foods. The fact that it is donated does not justify giving very large portions or serving the food simply to "use it up." This is a philosophy that was taught in the early days of commodities. Then the commodity became an "entitlement" and a specific dollar amount had to be provided each year.

If the commodity can be used to take the place of having to purchase an item, it then adds *real value* to the program. Some commodities are not easy to use, and some should be refused. Refusing a commodity that requires preparation of a product that has poor acceptance will save money in the long run, since it may save time and the cost of other ingredients needed to use the commodity, as well as avoiding lowered participation.

Order Only What Is Needed

Ordering (discussed in detail in chapter 7) should be done by menu based on what is in inventory. Overordering may result in waste, particularly with produce. It takes careful planning to order just enough for delivery at the right time. Inventory should be kept low.

Checking Orders In and Storing Properly

When a manager does not carefully check in orders, the foodservice may be short-changed, given an inferior product, or not receive what was ordered.

As soon as possible after delivery, foods and supplies should be stored at the proper temperature, with good air circulation. Improper storage can result in food waste.

Eliminating Theft

High food costs may be caused by theft—either of food or revenue (either will cause food cost percentages to increase). The most important safeguard against theft is a good system of accountability. Such a system accounts for every item received and used, and will bring shortages or losses to the attention of the manager. Perpetual inventory is an excellent accountability tool, particularly when computerized and tied to the food rung up on the cash registers.

Legally Bypassing Federal Regulations

Some school districts take rather drastic measures to resolve financial problems. For example, Pulaski County Special School District in Little Rock, Arkansas, pulled their junior and senior high schools out of the National School Lunch Program in 1984. The Glendale, Arizona, Union High School District also pulled out of the National School Lunch Program when faced with a financial crunch in the early 1980s. Their school foodservice was operating at a yearly loss of over $186,000. Management decided against using a Band-Aid approach: simply raising prices charged students. They narrowed down their menu offerings, served the more popular items, and overhauled their staffing and employee benefits program.

In the Glendale, Arizona, Union High School District only 3 percent of the student population received a free or reduced-price meal. The district could afford to provide meals for those students. The percentage of students qualifying for free and reduced-price meals would have to be considered seriously in a decision to go off the National School Lunch program. If only the federal funding for the paying child's meal were eliminated, withdrawing from the National School Lunch program would be considered by several thousand schools. The National School Lunch program requires that the paying students as well as those who qualify for free and reduced-price meals be served in order to qualify for any federal funding. Funding for free and reduced-price meals is also a considerable help to a budget, and giving it up may not be a feasible alternative. Also, some state regulations may require schools to provide meals free and at reduced prices to the needy. Volume of meals served is also a factor—the paying student and free and reduced-price students all contribute to the larger volume.

BIBLIOGRAPHY

Barnes, R. M. 1968. *Motion and Time Study: Design and Measurement of Work.* 6th ed. New York: John Wiley & Sons.

Bureau of Business Practice. 1986. *Quick-Action Productivity Ideas for the Supervisor.* Waterford, Conn.: Bureau of Business Practice.

Dittmer, Paul R., and Gerald G. Griffin. 1984. *Principles of Food, Beverage, and Labor Cost Controls for Hotels and Restaurants.* New York: Van Nostrand Reinhold.

Florida Department of Education. 1987. *Annual Report of School Nutrition Programs.* Tallahassee: Department of Education, Food and Nutrition Management.

Food Research and Action Center. 1983. *Doing More With Less.* Washington, D.C.: Food Research and Action Center.

Kazarian, E. A. 1979. *Work Analysis & Design for Hotels, Restaurants & Institutions.* 2d ed. New York: Van Nostrand Reinhold.

Lina, Cathy C. 1988. *Food Services Basic Skills Training Manual.* Fairfax, Va.: Fairfax County Public Schools.

McIntosh, Robert W. 1984. *Employee Management Standards.* The L. J. Minor Foodservice Standards Series, vol. 4. New York: Van Nostrand Reinhold.

Miller, Stephen G. 1987. "Improving Production Standards—Reducing Waste." Presentation at National Restaurant Association Convention in Chicago.

Minor, Lewis J., and Ronald F. Cichy. 1984. *Foodservice Systems Management.* New York: Van Nostrand Reinhold.

Rinke, Wolf J. 1989. *The Winning Foodservice Manager: Strategies for Doing More with Less.* Rockville, Md.: Aspen Publishers.

State of New York Department of Education. 1987. *Financial Management: Training for School Food Service Personnel.* Albany, N.Y.: The University of the State of New York and the State Department of Education.

Tolve, Arthur P. *Standardizing Foodservice for Quality and Efficiency.* New York: Van Nostrand Reinhold.

U.S. Department of Agriculture. 1983. *Using Vegetable Protein.* FNS Notice 219. Washington, D.C.: Food and Nutrition Services, U.S. Department of Agriculture.

VanEgmond-Pannell, Dorothy. 1983. "Strategies for the '80s." *American School and University* 56(12): 32-38.

———. 1986. "Labor Costs Are Overcoming Food Costs." *School Business Affairs* 52(2): 38-39.

———. 1987. *Management Skills for School Foodservice Managers.* Jackson, Miss.: State Department of Education, Child Nutrition Division.

13

Planning Facilities and Large Equipment

TRENDS IN FOODSERVICE FACILITIES

In urban areas, there is a steady trend toward central kitchens, commissaries, and satellite foodservice, which means a considerable savings when building additional schools. Even rural schools' kitchens are being built to provide food for other schools in the district. If the distances between schools is reasonable, the central production of food means a reduction in the cost of producing and serving a lunch and equipping a kitchen.

Some schools, however, are still being built with self-contained kitchens. The challenge is to plan flexible foodservice facilities that can be adapted to the needs of the future, which may include more summer meal programs, serving the elderly, and other special programs.

FACILITY PLANNING

Good planning is necessary for high productivity and the greatest efficiency. When working in an old building with construction faults and a poor layout, the waste of time and motion is costly but often unavoidable. However, when a new facility is being planned and constructed, it would be expected that these faults could be avoided. Frequently, however, the same mistakes are made.

Foodservice management must insist on being a part of the planning team for a new school. The local and state health departments should also be consulted during the planning stages. The factors to be considered in planning include (1) the capacity of the school and its potential for future expansion, (2) the number of meals to be served, (3) the age of the children, (4) the type of foodservice system to be used, (5) menu and food offerings to be provided, (6) the type of equipment needed, and (7) the utilities to be used. See Table 13-1 for a guide to space planning.

"Bigger is not necessarily better" when planning the kitchen space. Enough space, but not too much, is the first requirement for an efficient kitchen; the second essential element is good layout.

Table 13-1.   Guide to Space (in sq ft) for School Foodservice On-Site Preparation

	Meals			
Area	Up to 350	351-500	501-700	701-1000
Receiving area				
Loading platform	60	80	100	100
Receiving area inside building	48	48	60	80
Storage				
Dry storage (⅓-½ sq ft per meal)	175	250	325	450
Nonfood storage	30	50	70	90
Office space	40-48	48	60	80
Lockers and toilet for employees	45	60	75	85
Kitchen and serving preparation including refrigeration (1.1-1.5 sq ft per meal)	500	650	800	980
Serving	200	300	400	600
Dishwashing	150	150	180	210
Maintenance area				
Mop area	25	25	30	30
Garbage area	30	48	60	75
Total kitchen and serving area	1303	1709	2135	2780
Dining area (based on two seatings)				
Elementary (10 sq ft/meal)	1750	1750-2500	2500-3500	3500-5000
Secondary (12 sq ft/meal)	2100	2100-3000	3000-4200	4200-6000
Total dining, kitchen, and serving area				
Elementary	3053	3459-4209	4635-5635	6280-7780
Secondary	4303	3809-4709	5135-6335	6980-8780

General requirements and considerations that should be provided to the architect for the foodservice area are the following:

Kitchen location
  Near a back loading dock
  On the first floor or ground floor
  Adjoining the dining room
  In the center of the classroom area
Dining seating capacity
  Ability to seat a third to a half of the student body at one time
  A combination of round and rectangular tables
Physical conditions
  Adequate lighting
  Bright-colored accents included in the decor
  Good air circulation
  Air conditioning (kitchen included)

Adequate hot water supply (140°F all year round, with booster heaters to raise the temperature to 180°F)

Electrical outlets to be noted on plan

Kitchen layout

Planned around work centers

Manager's office to be enclosed in glass panels 3 to 4 feet above floor level

Rest room with employees' lockers off kitchen

The work centers of a kitchen should be planned so that the flow of work is natural, logical, and follows the sequence of food processing (Fig. 13-1). Normally, the flow

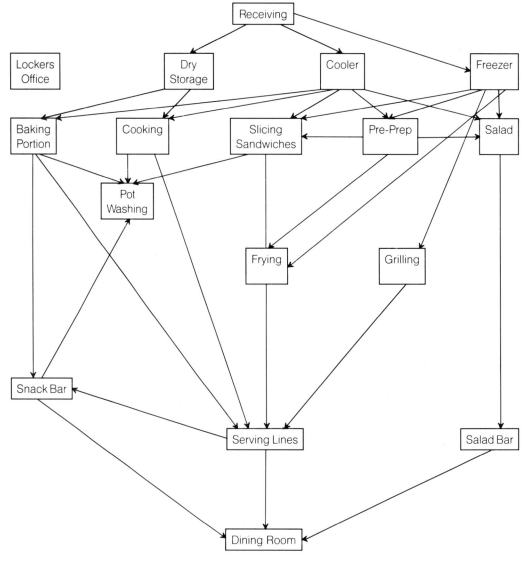

FIGURE 13-1. Layout based on flow of food in the kitchen.

of foods is from receiving to storage, to prepreparation, to preparation, to service, and to cleanup.

Basic Physical Considerations

The following physical conditions are most conducive to work:

> *Light:* 35 footcandles on equipment; 35-50 footcandles on work surfaces; 50 at the cashier's stand; 75-100 in the serving area; warm white fluorescent lights in the serving areas
> *Temperature:* 68° to 78°F
> *Relative humidity:* 40 to 45 percent
> *Ventilation:* change of air every 5 minutes
> *Height of work surfaces:* 35-37 inches
> *Wall and ceiling color:* light without producing glare

When selecting wall colors, an institutional look should be avoided. Among the physical features and conditions that affect customers' perceptions and well-being are the choice of colors; illumination; noise levels; temperature and relative humidity; odors; the type of seating; furnishings, including floor and wall coverings and drapes; the shapes and sizes of rooms; the layout of tables; the appearance and dress of employees; and sanitation (Kazarian 1983b).

The choice of colors can have a significant impact on foodservice customers. Different colors promote different feelings, moods, and mental associations:

> *Yellow:* sunny, warm, cheerful, inspiring, high spirited; boosts morale and enhances food
> *Orange:* bright, warm, jovial, lively, forceful, energetic; enhances food
> *Green:* clear, cool, quieting, refreshing, low spirited; sells more salads
> *Blue:* transparent, cold, subduing, melancholy
> *Purple:* deep, cool, dignified, mournful
> *Red:* brilliant, hot, exciting, active, intense

Bright accent colors should be used to enliven the decor.

Dining Room Atmosphere

Few of the older school dining rooms show any indication that the person drawing the plan considered atmosphere. Atmosphere is identified as one of the prime inducements for people to want to dine out, as can be seen from the importance fast food restaurants place on decor. Though students may not be "dining out," the school dining room will be the scene for many a meal. It should be pleasant, attractive to the age group it serves, and a fun place to eat. That type of atmosphere does not have to add much cost to the building.

The atmosphere will have an effect—negative or positive—on the students' behavior in the dining room, as well as on the degree of participation. The atmosphere can create a fun place to be or an unpleasant place to be.

LARGE EQUIPMENT

Much of the equipment in schools today was purchased during the 1960s, when the number of schools being built was at a peak and when federal monies were available for equipment. Much of the equipment bought in the 1950s and 1960s had a "life" of 25 to 30 years, is wearing out today, and needs to be replaced.

According to Minor and Cichy (1984), equipment standards and specifications must be based on certain fundamental parameters, including the following: (1) the menu and number of meals served, (2) personnel, (3) location, (4) safety, health, and sanitary standards, (5) equipment and installation costs, (6) available space, and (7) efficiency standards for equipment.

When determining equipment capacity requirements, the menu items and quantities to be processed should be considered. For example, what is the maximum number of pans that can be put in the ovens at one time? What quantity of French fries will be needed over a lunch period? What size and how many fryers will be needed?

Equipment is generally purchased for one or more of the following reasons: (1) to improve sanitation, (2) to reduce labor costs, (3) to maintain the nutritional value of foods, (4) to lower food costs, (5) to add appeal and variety to the menu, or (6) to increase productivity and make the work easier.

Table 13-2 may be of some help in determining equipment needs; however, equipment should not be chosen on the basis of a chart in a book, but determined by the operation's needs. A variety of questions need to be considered. How often will each piece of equipment be used—daily, weekly, or monthly? How many work tables will be needed? Will the foodservice need more work tables than workers? Does the equipment allow for changes or expansion of services? When determining quantities and items of equipment needed for a new school, one should anticipate needs a reasonable period into the future. It is unwise, however, to buy oversized equipment in anticipation of future growth many years away. Overequipping and overdesigning a kitchen wastes funds and will hamper efficiency.

Writing Specifications

Written specifications for equipment should describe to the potential bidder or company filling the order exactly what is wanted. See Figure 13-2 for sample specifications. There are a number of guidelines that can be used when writing equipment specifications. Besides experience with the particular type of equipment, the best aids are printed literature from equipment manufacturers' representatives or salespeople, the U.S. government bid specifications, and the National Sanitation Foundation standards. Specifications can be broad or detailed; they may specify manufacturers and models as standards. Usually when brands and models are specified, the specification will include the phrase "or the equivalent" to allow for a range of similar brands qualifying.

Specifications should include special features that are not standard for a particular piece of equipment, such as additional attachments for a mixer. A mandatory demonstration of the equipment and the calibration of ovens following installation should be specified. At least two operating manuals should be obtained—one for the foodservice and one for maintenance. In the specification it should be indicated whether the equipment is

tigma of poverty in breakfast program

ng to state officials.

ast October, the Bridgewater
nts sent a questionnaire to 200
: schools in Massachusetts, ask-
nose that offer the program to
ate problems they have imple-
ing it.

ow student participation, sched-
problems and lack of personnel

term."

The researchers learned of students who do not bring home the eligibility forms because they are
afraid of being teased by other children for eating a subsidized breakfast. Parents, too, sometimes do not
send back the application for fear of
exposing their poverty.

> 'This issue of stigmatization and pride is
> important, and in America, being poor
> means not being able to afford your
> pride.'
>
> DONALD RAPP
> *Bridgewater State College professor*

---

mplement the program were
ng the impediments cited. Some
ol officials also said they were
eing reimbursed for the entire
of the program.

ew school officials indicated
stigmatization was an issue.
ever, according to their report,
ter interviews, Rapp and his stu-
s heard "countless stories" of
ents and parents embarrassed
ke part in a program "that has
 cast ... as a 'welfare' program,
e most negative sense of that

"I can't have everybody in town
know that I can't even provide
breakfast for my children," one parent was reported to have told a
school counselor.

"This issue of stigmatization and
pride is important," said Rapp, "and
in America, being poor means not
being able to afford your pride."

Adding to the program's stigma,
the researchers said, are procedures
that distinguish children receiving a
subsidized breakfast from those paying full price, procedures that clearly

violate federal antidiscrimination
regulations.

Some schools, for example, gave
students getting the subsidized
breakfasts different colored tickets
from those paying for their meal;
others punched holes in the tickets
of those getting the free breakfast.

At one school, students receiving
the free breakfast had to yell
"Free!" at the cash register, while
other schools used separate en-
trances, lines or dining areas for
children eating the subsidized meal.

"You just don't go in that breakfast line, I don't care what color ticket you have," a 1990 high-school
graduate was reported by the study
as saying. "You eat that and it means
your momma's on welfare!"

A counselor at one school told the
researchers of a third-grade girl who
was caught stealing breakfast tickets
from other children. The counselor
said the girl told her "that she wanted a ticket that didn't have holes
punched in it so 'the kids won't say
I'm poor.'"

Mary Jo Cutler, acting director
of nutrition for the state Department
of Education's Bureau of School Nutrition Services, said she was sur-
prised at the schools' noncompliance
with the antidiscrimination regulations, because "numerous education
programs" are offered to food service administrators several times a
year around the state.

More critical than such procedur-

al problems, however, Rapp and
Cutler contend, is the inescapable
stigma associated with any social-
welfare program. The solution, they
say, is to make the breakfast
program more attractive.

The report mentions one principal in a low-income neighborhood,
for example, who went out to the
playground and surrounding streets
to call children in to breakfast. Also
mentioned were teachers who ate
breakfast with students in the cafeteria to help lift the stigma.

"It's marketing," said Cutler.
"You don't start with the ticket. You
want to entice everyone into the
cafeteria. ... There are children
across economic groups that could
benefit from breakfast."

One of the recommendations in
the report is for the Department of
Education to study the comparative
cost of a universal free breakfast, offered to all public school children,
with that of the current program.
While Cutler agreed that a universal
free breakfast would be a good idea,
she wondered whether state officials
would find the cost prohibitive.

The report also urged the state
to communicate to local schools the
importance of the breakfast program
as a fundamental way to fight hunger. Otherwise, it will remain a
program "without a political con-
stituency," said Rapp. And "because
it's a poor person's program, you
don't get quality."

Poverty stigma cited in underuse of free breakfasts

By Laura Batten
CONTRIBUTING REPORTER

Social-work professor Donald Rapp and his student research team call it the "dirty little secret."

Many low-income children are not benefiting from the state's subsidized school-breakfast program, the students found in their survey of 159 public schools last fall, for a reason they say has been overlooked by hunger advocates and state officials:

"Kids are embarrassed, parents are embarrassed," Rapp said. They "just don't want to be associated with 'a program for poor kids.'"

When the 26 juniors and seniors in Rapp's research methods class at Bridgewater State College set out to identify barriers to participation in the breakfast program, they expected to find late buses, staffing shortages or children missing out because they went to schools where the program was not offered.

While those problems do exist, interviews with

BREAKFAST, Page B8

Students' report cites

BREAKFAST
Continued from Page B1

parents, school administrators and students revealed that students and their parents are dissuaded from participating mostly by school procedures that clearly identify the children who receive free or reduced price meals and label them as "poor."

The study, dubbed "We Are Your Neighbors' Children," culminated this spring with a 33-page report written by four of Rapp's students. The project grew out of a suggestion by Project Bread, a Massachusetts antihunger organization, to examine shortcomings in the federally funded breakfast program.

Rapp, a longtime social worker before going to Bridgewater two years ago, said he wants to turn out "social advocates," not "private scholars." He said he regularly engages his students in "advocacy research," which, in this case, "became something of a cause" for them.

Michelle Mitchell, one of the four research assistants who wrote the study, graduated last spring with a degree in social work.

The breakfast program, she lamented, "isn't a big issue to a lot of people. ... Before, it might have been a bigger thing, but with everything being cut and slashed," it is not a priority.

Studies linking a nutritional breakfast and increased school performance are documented in the report, including a 1987 study of 1,000 third- to sixth-grade children in Lawrence. Improvement in achievement-test scores and a decrease in tardiness and absenteeism were evident after the breakfast program was implemented.

Annette Rubin Casas, director of Advocacy and Programs at Project Bread, said the students' report "was valuable to us" and "supports our recommendations about the school breakfast program" made to the state Department of Education, which administers the breakfast program in Massachusetts. Last year, the US Department of Agriculture reimbursed the state $9.6 million for the program.

Those recommendations include expanding the program, both by getting more schools to provide breakfast and increasing participation in schools that already do.

Under state law, schools in which 40 percent of students qualify for free or reduced-price meals under the school lunch program must offer breakfast as well. Eligibility is based on an application that reports total income and whether the family receives food stamps or Aid to Families with Dependent Children.

Currently, 45 percent of the state's public schools offer the subsidized breakfasts, and 17 percent of the students statewide receive it, ac-

Table 13-2. Sample List of Large Equipment Needed

Item	Finishing Kitchen Elementary[a] (quantity)	Finishing Kitchen Intermediate[b] (quantity)	Production Kitchen High School[c] (quantity)
Service			
Milk cooler, drop front	2	3	6
Serving line:			
Hot table	2	2	4
Cold/display table	2	2	4
Cashier stand	2	2	4
Cash register	2	3	6
Solid top portion	4	4	8
Ice cream cabinet	2	3	6
Ice machine, large	—	1	1
Ice machine, small	1	—	—
Refrigerator, pass-through two-door	—	1	2
Heated cabinet pass-through two-door	—	1	2
Salad bar w/table and cashier stand	1	1	1
Soup pot	1	1	1-2
Vending machine	—	1	2
Milkshake machine	—	—	2
Precision Cabinet	2	1	2
Preparation			
Oven, convection, double	2	3	4
Oven, microwave	1	1	1
French fryer, double	—	1	—
French fryer, triple	—	—	1
Slicer, automatic w/table	—	—	1
Steamer-jet trunion combo	1	1	1
Braiser	—	—	1
Trunion kettle, sized per unit	—	—	1
Mixer and parts			
30 quart	—	—	1
60 quart	—	—	—
VCM	—	—	—
Qualheim	—	—	1
Table, work, ss w/wheels	2	4	6
Table, work, ss, enclosed shelf and wheels	—	—	2
Sink, 3-compartment w/booster heater	1	1	1
Sink, food prep w/disposal	—	1	1

(continued)

Table 13-2.   Sample List of Large Equipment Needed *(continued)*

Item	Finishing Kitchen Elementary[a] (quantity)	Finishing Kitchen Intermediate[b] (quantity)	Production Kitchen High School[c] (quantity)
Service container			
Hand Sink	1	2	2
Storage			
Cart, Colson	2	3	5
Cart, Rubbermaid	2	3	4
Pan rack w/o doors	2	4	6
Receiving scale w/stand	—	—	1
Mobile wire shelf			
4 ft	6	10	15
Utility carrier truck	1	2	3
Dunnage rack	2	3	4
Fans	1	2	4
Freezer, reach-in			
Single	—	1	—
Two-door	—	—	—
Three-door	1	1	1
Refrigerator, reach-in			
Two-door	—	—	—
Three-door	1	1	1
Freezer, walk-in	—	—	1
Refrigerator, walk-in	—	—	1

[a]Student enrollment of 990 and on all disposables
[b]Student enrollment of 1440 and on all disposables
[c]Student enrollment of 2200 and on all disposables

to be installed by the company, the method of delivery, the type of warranty or guarantee expected, and when delivery is expected or required.

The following questions should also be considered when writing a specification:

- Is there a service representative within 50 to 70 miles?
- Is a demonstration on site needed?
- Are the certification requirements met?
     Underwriters' Laboratories (UL), for electrical;
     American Gas Association (AGA), for gas;
     National Sanitation Foundation (NSF), for sanitary design requirements
- Is there a minimum of a one-year warranty for parts and labor?
- Is delivery to be within the building or on the dock?
- Should installation be included in the price?

Federal regulations do not require public bidding for purchases of $10,000 or less unless required by state or local governments. Competitive bidding will usually result

ITEMS WILL BE AWARDED AS AN AGGREGATE

QUANTITY:20

9. 3587009011—Refrigerator

STANDARD: Beverage-Air Model ER-48, Hobart Model QV-2 or equal.

DESCRIPTION: Self-contained, two full doors, front opening unit. Automatic defrosting and evaporation system. Refrigeration system located on top of cabinet.

MATERIAL: Exterior—all carbon steel with front, doors, and sides faced with scratch-resistant vinyl or acrylic enamel.

Interior—Scratch-resistant interior with ⅜" radius bends. Automatic interior lighting.

Legs—6-inch stainless steel, adjustable.

Insulation—minimum of 2-inch polyurethane foam insulation, poured into place, bonded to shell and liner.

Shelves—to be adjustable at one-inch intervals.

CAPACITY/SIZE: 46–50 cubic feet of storage space. 52"–55" wide; 32"–34" deep; and 82"–84½" high (including legs).

COLOR: Exterior to be bright yellow or lemon yellow (gold or avocado not acceptable).

ELECTRICAL: 115 volts; 60 cycles; 7–11 amps; single phase; ⅓ HP; 90° Ambient Temperature; 20°F Evaporated Temperature.

PLUMBING: none

APPROVAL AND LABELS REQUIRED: NSF and UL

ACCESSORIES:
1. Dial thermometer on exterior of unit, very visible. Calibrated adjustment. Power "on" indicator.
2. Heavy-duty wire shelves that are rust resistant and will withstand heavy use. QUANTITY: 12 shelves.
3. Heavy-duty, chromium-plated handles, with positive action hinge mechanism, magnetic gaskets, and cylinder locks on all doors.

WARRANTY: One-year, including labor and parts.

SERVICE: Must be service representative in metropolitan Washington area.

DELIVERY: See special provision 11.

FIGURE 13-2. Sample equipment specifications.

in considerable cost savings, particularly if more than one brand is acceptable. When bidding equipment, requesting price for award of bid by line item or group of similar products (two different sizes of refrigerators, for example) will probably yield the best prices.

Equipment Design

The trend in design of equipment is toward modular and movable, which provides flexibility. Modules allow for changing the facility design according to changing conditions. For example, when serving lines are purchased by sections and on wheels, it is easy to change the location or length of the line.

A nice change is the trend toward bright colors, versus only black, white, and shiny stainless steel. A kitchen can be brightened up with the addition of a colorful piece of equipment.

The materials used in kitchen equipment now allow not only the free use of color but also reduced costs and increased durability in some cases. As a matter of fact, the plastics being used are often more durable, more lasting, more attractive, and easier to keep clean than more conventional materials.

Other questions to be considered when planning a purchase of equipment are how efficient the equipment itself is and whether it will help employees work efficiently. One of the first features to consider is the height of work surfaces. Stress may be caused by surfaces that are either too high or too low. A person is most productive when the trunk of the body is vertical, the lower arms are at a right angle to the upper arms, and the work surface is 1 to 3 inches below elbow height. The following heights may be needed: 33-36 inches for women and 36-38 inches for men. Adjustable feet are recommended as a way to provide for differences in height needs.

An important need of school foodservices is good food-holding equipment. The manufacturing industry needs to pay more attention to temperature control in food-holding cabinets, and the effects of holding temperature on food quality. One of the main complaints of students about school food is that it is often cold by the time it is served.

Although technology and automation have been slow to come to the foodservice industry, labor costs will provide the needed impetus in the 1990s. Labor-saving equipment and robots of all types will hit the market, and computerization will be a standard feature of the new equipment.

BIBLIOGRAPHY

Avery, Arthur C. 1980. *A Modern Guide to Foodservice Equipment*. Boston: CBI Publishing Company.

Birchfield, John C. 1988. *Design & Layout of Foodservice Facilities*. New York: Van Nostrand Reinhold.

Kazarian, Edward A. 1983a. *Foodservice Facilities Planning*. 2d ed. New York: Van Nostrand Reinhold.

———. 1983b. *Work Analysis and Design for Hotels, Restaurants and Institutions*. 2d ed. New York: Van Nostrand Reinhold.

Kotschevar, Lendal H., and Margaret E. Terrell. 1985. *Foodservice Planning: Layout and Equipment.* 3d ed. New York: Macmillan Publishing Company.

Milton, A., and D. Kirk. 1980. *Principles of Design and Operation of Catering Equipment.* West Sussex, England: Market Cross House.

Minor, Lewis J., and Ronald F. Cichy. 1984. *Foodservice Systems Management.* New York: Van Nostrand Reinhold.

Scriven, Carl, and James Stevens. 1989. *Food Equipment Facts: A Handbook for the Foodservice Industry.* New York: Van Nostrand Reinhold.

Unklesbay, Nan, and Kenneth Unklesbay. 1982. *Energy Management in Foodservice.* New York: Van Nostrand Reinhold.

Wilkinson, Jule. 1981. *The Complete Book of Cooking Equipment.* 2d ed. Boston: CBI Publishing Company.

14

Computerization and Automation

PROGRESS IN THE 1980s

In the early 1980s, computer mania was seen in all industries, including school foodservice. Many directors/supervisors became computer literate, and some became slaves to the computer as they spent long hours feeding data into their microcomputers. The prices of microcomputers were affordable and could be covered by most school foodservice budgets. For some, the computer became a status symbol, and then came the slow-down in computer interest, which was rather dramatic in late 1980s.

Some of the most successful users of the computer are not the large school districts, but the small to middle-size districts. Over 72 percent of all school districts are now using computers in foodservice. Software systems designed strictly for the school foodservice market and those that have been altered to include this market have begun to mushroom. A directory of school foodservice software dealers is included at the end of this chapter.

There has been a hesitancy among some school foodservice districts to commit the time and money needed to computerize their districts completely. Regrettably, computerization is for the most part done piecemeal, with numerous small programs that do not interface with one another. It is not uncommon for a school district to enter the same data into more than one data base to provide for the foodservice manager's needs for precosting and nutrient analysis, inventory control, production records, and detailed profit and loss analysis. As a result, the controls, the management information, and time savings that are possible to obtain are not realized.

The importance of computerization has been realized by large foodservice management companies, such as Marriott/Saga and ARA. They have made considerable progress with computerization, as have the giants in the fast food industry. McDonald's has put millions into the development of an integrated services digital network that is the ultimate in computerization.

ADVANTAGES OF COMPUTERIZATION

There is probably no department in a school district with as much need for computerization as the foodservice department, which must meet strict standards of accountability and requires various types of reports and detailed technical analysis for efficient management. The information needed to run a successful school foodservice program is extensive and varied.

AccuClaim, the federal meal accountability audit that was started in 1988 as a result of federal legislation, is reason enough for any school district to computerize foodservices. However, computerization is no guarantee of correct reports. Self-audits should be built in, so that large data entry errors will be caught in "exception reports." Computerized programs must have correct data entered and must be updated; otherwise meal claim reports will be incorrect. Here are some of the problems identified by federal auditors in test audits done in 1987 (*Foodservice Director* 1988):

- *There were deficiencies in point-of-service meal counts.* Cashiers did not identify the eligibility status of children passing through the serving line. Cash registers were not used to make point-of-service entries for each transaction. Manual records either did not support cash register totals or were not maintained at all.
- *Incorrect data were transmitted over the computer terminal* from the schools to the central office.
- *The automated data on student eligibility category were inaccurate* because schools did not keep the system updated. (For example, students were listed as eligible for free or reduced-price meals though their parents had not applied for benefits.)
- *School districts did not reconcile meal claims* against either the number of eligible children or the number of children in attendance—or, on the other hand, school districts replaced school counts with the maximum number eligible.

Some of the benefits of a well-thought-out computerized system with "checks and balances" and accurate data entry are (1) increased efficiency and speed of data handling, (2) more reliable information, (3) more timely report processing, (4) improved inventory control, (5) comprehensive management reports and analysis, (6) nutrient analysis of meals served, and (7) reduced food and labor costs.

Competing with the fast food industry and management companies in the 1990s will be nearly impossible for any foodservice without both the savings and improved information provided through computerization. The advantage will go to the "knows" rather than the "know-nots" or guessers. Savings will vary depending on the type of school operation and the scope of computer use. Some of the potential savings as a result of computers include

- Reduced inventory because of better projections and more accurate ordering
- Error-free recipe calculations when altering the batch size, which helps prevent overproduction
- More rapid payment of bills and processing of federal and state monthly claims for reimbursement
- Fewer overclaims found during the state and federal audits (AccuClaim)
- Precosting and postcosting of foods on a timely basis, providing management with the information to make better decisions
- Reduction of time spent preparing reports manually
- Faster service (for example, reduced time between ordering and the delivery of goods)

WHAT CAN BE COMPUTERIZED

The list of activities that can be computerized is almost endless. In general, the activities that are best suited for computerization include the following:

> Payroll, accounts payable, and accounts receivable
> Free and reduced-price meal application processing (Table 14-1 is an example of a free and reduced-price list of students.)
> Inventory
> Procurement, including bid evaluation
> Recipe calculations and production planning
> Participation and revenue reporting
> Pre- and postcosting of meals
> Forecasting, ordering, and work scheduling
> Nutritional evaluation of menus (analysis)
> Menu planning
> Meal tickets and rosters

The parts of the accounting process that can be easily computerized are shown in Figure 14-1. Some of these activities are discussed below.

With computerization, the reams of paper can mount and still not provide the information a manager/supervisor needs to manage. The information may be in an unusable form or too massive. The manager/supervisor may need the information analyzed and interpreted. Groups of figures may need to be compared with prior years, prior months, or other schools to become meaningful. Percentages are usually more meaningful than lists of dollar amounts. Finally, the real success of computerization may be determined by how useful the reports generated are to management.

Procurement

In many school districts automation in foodservice is coming through the back door. Distributors are computerizing their operations and are using the computer for "scientific buying." More and more foodservice companies and manufacturers are utilizing the Uniform Communications Standard (**UCS**) (see below) and telecommunications. This enables buyers and sellers of products to communicate through computer links with the school district or individual school foodservice manager. With an order entry system, which is designed to provide on-line communications between foodservice managers and their vendors, managers transmit their orders to the central or host computer at the food vendor's office. Current prices can be downstreamed, or sent from the host to the manager.

The grocery industry was the first in the food industry to utilize this system successfully. UCS was developed by the Uniform Code Council in Dayton, Ohio. It allows a school foodservice manager/supervisor with a computer and a modem to talk to a distributor for ordering and billing purposes. It eliminates a great deal of paperwork and manager/clerical bookkeeping time. Orders can be processed more quickly.

Table 14-1. Sample School List Coded With Students Approved for Free and Reduced-Price Meals

| Location: 1120 Brown High School | | | | | | | Run Date: 01-06-89 | |
Student	Gr	Homeroom	Teacher	Student #	Status	Comments	Notified	Family #
ABAB, JOHN	12				Reduced		10-21-88	4822
ABAD, MARY	9				Free		10-07-88	2145
AKARI, GEORGE	11				Free		11-23-88	6987
AKARI, SUSAN	10				Free		10-05-88	782
ALLAN, JOSEPH	9				Free		11-23-88	2301
ALLEN, SUSAN	9				Free		10-05-88	303
AMAN, ROBERT	11				Free		10-05-88	1773
AMEN, CALEB	10				Free		12-07-88	7004
BAMBI, JOSEPHINE	11				Free		10-21-88	5323
BEAN, STEVEN	10				Free		10-05-88	546
BI-BABY, JANE	11				Free		10-05-88	546
BLARNEY, WILLIAM	12				Reduced		10-07-88	2152
CARNEGIE, WILLIS	9				Free		11-18-88	6802
DANIELS, VIOLET	11				Free		10-07-88	3321
DANIELS, ZEMINA	12				Reduced		11-23-88	6914
DEAN, JOHN	9				Reduced		10-20-88	4673
DEAN, ROBERT J.	11				Free		10-05-88	807
DE, NAM	9				Free		10-07-88	3308
DUM, XUAN THU	11				Free		10-07-88	3308
EL-MEMAWAWY, RUS	10				Free		10-05-88	1152
ESCOBAR, RUDOLPHO	?				Free		11-23-88	6933
FARHARI, THOMAS	10				Withdrawn on 09-06-88	OUT OF STATE		1152
FEAGAN, RONNALD	10				Denied $$$		10-20-88	4587
FREEMAN, FAITH	9				Free		11-23-88	771
HSING, HUI HSI T.	12				Free		10-20-88	4626
HYUNH, THI THU	12				Free		12-13-88	3670
JACOBS, JOHN	11				Free		10-05-88	1118
JACOBS, MEGAN	9				Free		11-17-88	6494
JACOBS, SUSAN	11				Free		11-17-88	6418
JOHNSON, CAREY	11				Reduced		11-23-88	6942

continued

195

Table 14-1. Sample School List Coded With Students Approved for Free and Reduced-Price Meals (*continued*)

Location: 1120 Brown High School   Run Date: 01-06-89

Student	Gr	Homeroom Teacher	Student #	Status	Comments	Notified	Family #
JOHNSON, GEORGE	9			Free		10-05-88	800
JOHNSON, KAREN	9			Reduced		12-13-88	3663
KE, KIM	9			Reduced		10-07-88	2162
LAMAS, LLAMA	11			Free		10-05-88	803
LEMUS, JANET	9			Free		10-05-88	676
MORTON, JOHN	9			Free		10-07-88	2042
MORTON, SEE	9			Free		10-07-88	1942
NGUYEN, THAO	11			Free		10-07-88	2302
NGUYEN, THAO THI	?			Free		12-29-88	7192
NGUYEN, THAO THU	VO2090 HOME BASE			Free		10-05-88	126
NORTON, ART C.	9			Free		12-29-88	7192
POWELL, JANE	11			Free		10-24-88	5995
POWELL, JOHN	9			Free		10-05-88	878
RESPASSE, MIMI	11			Reduced		10-07-88	2655
RHOSHOVSKY, JON	10			Reduced		11-23-88	5624
SEROUPHANIVAXY, TIM	11			Free		10-21-88	5320
SHAKER, JOHN	12			Denied $$$		12-13-88	3695
SHEETS, FLORIS	9			Free		10-24-88	5645
ZEBRA, STEPHEN	10			Free		10-24-88	5645

Source: MAPS Software, Inc., Columbus, MS.

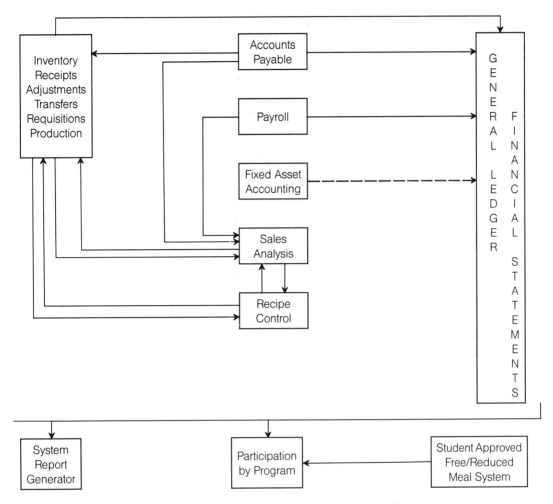

FIGURE 14-1. Sample foodservice information system configuration.

With the Universal Product Code (**UPC**) and a bar code reader, the customer's perpetual inventory can be updated while checking in the order. At the same time, products that do not meet specifications will show up with a "buzz." The UPC is a national system of product identification consisting of small blocks of parallel lines and numbers unique to each product. The UPC symbol is printed or applied on many food packages. These symbols can be read by moving a bar code scanner over the code. With a laser beam device the code can be read at a greater distance. The use of a scanning device and portable handheld computer can reduce the taking of inventory to a few minutes.

Free and Reduced-Price Meals

With a computer program, free and reduced-price meal applications can be acted upon, parents and schools notified, and meal tickets or rosters generated. If the action taken becomes a part of the student roster, it moves with the student when he or she transfers from one school to another in the same school district. Preprinted applications containing student names, grades, schools, and social security numbers of family members in five different languages (or more) can be provided for parents to update yearly.

Computer programs, like **SNAP,*** that contain the names of those qualifying for free and reduced-price meals in the system can interface with the cash register. Then, when a student who does not qualify is served, the system will tell the cashier. Charging and drawdowns can also be handled with systems like this. These systems can prevent a number of irregularities, including overclaiming, from occurring.

Interfacing Cash Registers

An automated or electronic cash register (ECR) works at high speeds to store data and information. It generates information by doing computations with input data and then printing out the results. ECRs can communicate with microcomputers, making it possible for a manager to have a reading of all ECRs without leaving the office.

The "master-slave" network (Fig. 14-2) is frequently used where more than two cash registers are providing information that must be consolidated. The master unit may be

---

*SNAP (School Nutrition Accountability Program) is a computer software program sold by SNAP Systems, Inc., Santa Monica, California.

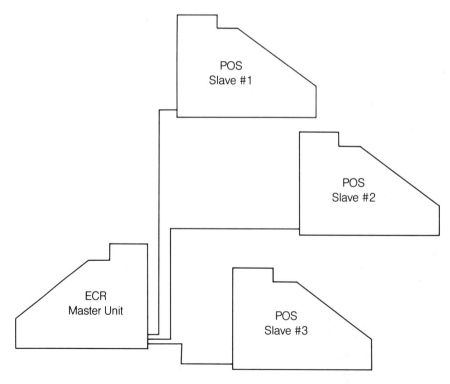

FIGURE 14-2. Master-slave network. (*Source:* Kasavana 1984.)

relatively high priced; however, a number of slave terminals can be connected to the master and depend on it for processing needs. ECRs and a point-of-sale (POS) system have become common in the commercial restaurant industry. As previously explained, inventory and reordering can be controlled on the serving line.

COMPUTER SYSTEM

Determining the best type of computer system for a school foodservice is made more difficult by rapid changes in the electronics industry. The decision requires technical knowledge in both the computer field and school foodservice. One of the recommended ways to start is to conduct a feasibility study. According to Pugh (1989) a feasibility study should define "the specific needs [and] requirements that the computer software must satisfy." It starts with determining the answers to a number of questions. What is the computer system going to do? At what level will computerization begin? What are the purposes? Once questions like these are answered, a list of what is to be computerized initially or later on should be drawn up. The list can then be turned into a flow chart such as that shown in Figure 14-3.

The first decision to consider is how data will be entered and at what level. There are three basic methods:

- *Batch:* information is collected and sent by courier or taken to a central location for data entry.
- *On line:* data are entered into a terminal at the school and warehouse level.
- *Networking:* microcomputers with memory are located at each of the schools (in the manager's office) and used to transmit data electronically to a central location. The communication can be in all directions.

Networking is the most progressive approach and will be commonly used in the 1990s. Telecommunications have added an entire dimension to the ECR industry. With a network, schools in a centralized system can be polled at a specific time for daily participation and revenue data. It is possible to have the automated cash register programmed so that when one hamburger is sold the perpetual inventory shows one less hamburger bun, one less hamburger patty, and one less portion of ketchup; and this daily information triggers the placement of orders for these items.

PREPARING FOR COMPUTERIZATION

Computerization will not transform a poorly organized foodservice with high costs into a well-organized, profitable operation. Management is still responsible for good organization and decision making. As a matter of fact, the foodservice has to become well-organized and standardized to computerize the entire operation successfully.

When preparing for computerization, the following suggestions may be useful:

- Prepare the staff by making them computer literate.
- Begin standardizing recipes. Inaccurate, ballpark figures on yield and ingredients will not work.

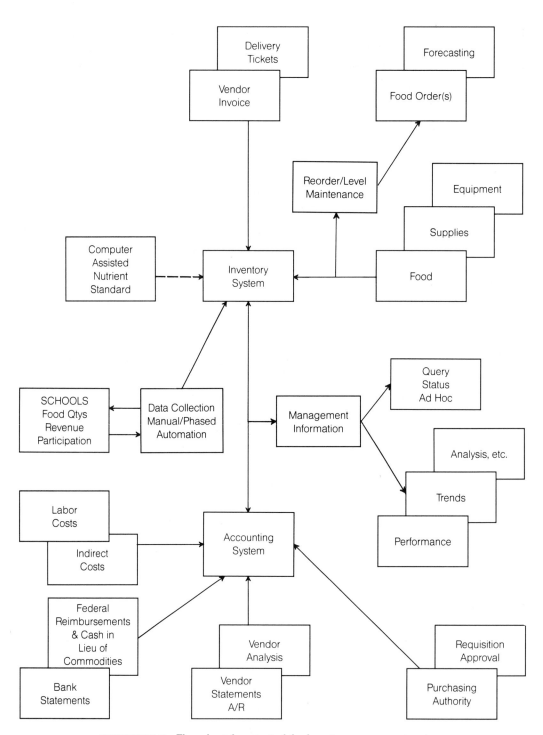

FIGURE 14-3. Flow chart for a typical foodservice management system.

- Design forms for collecting data to fit the computer programs. Highlighting or shading blocks with data that are used frequently will help.
- Plan to run dual systems (manual and computerized) for two to three months until any problems ("bugs") have been worked out.
- Consider the consequences if the computer system is down for a day or more. Be sure the foodservice maintains a backup so that it can continue to operate.
- Have someone who is familiar with recipes and foods input or proof the data when setting up files in these areas.

SOFTWARE

Many school districts have chosen to write their own programs. In order to do this, or to determine if a commercial package will meet the facility's needs, the list of what is to be computerized should be determined. One entire aspect unique to school foodservice is the free and reduced-price meals accountability requirement.

Software needs to be considered before selecting the computer hardware. Software can be more of a limiting factor and more costly than the hardware. Some of the popular software programs generally used are Lotus 1-2-3 and Multiplan for spreadsheet, Wordperfect and Writing Assistant for word processing, and a variety of graphics programs.

Although commercial software companies were slow to enter the school foodservice market, a number of software packages have been designed for school foodservice, or altered to fit the industry. The following are some sources of information on special application software:

1. *Annual Journal of Dietetic Software*, 1988, P.O. Box 2565, Norman, OK 73070.
2. *Directory of Computer Hardware and Software for the Foodservice Industry*, 1987, published by the National Restaurant Association, 1200 Seventh Street, N.W., Washington, D.C. 20036.
3. *Nutrient Data Bank Directory*, 5th edition, 1986, College of Home Economics, 217 Gwynn Hall, University of Missouri at Columbia, Columbia, MO 65211.
4. *Food and Nutrition Information Center: Microcomputer Software Collection*, 1988, published by The Food and Nutrition Information Center, National Agricultural Library, USDA, Beltsville, MD 20705. On-site software demonstrations are provided; the library has nearly 150 programs in food-related fields.

Among the best-known school foodservice programs are (1) School Nutrition Accountability Program (**SNAP**), (2) **MAPS** (Table 14-1 is an example of a free and reduced-price list by school), (3) **Bon Appetit,** marketed by IBM, (4) **CBORD Menu Management,** which is best known in college foodservice, and (5) **COMPUTRITION.**

TECHNOLOGICAL CHANGE IN SCHOOL FOODSERVICES

Telecommunication, the fastest-growing area in school foodservices, will affect all aspects of the industry in the 1990s. With a communication program and modem in place, the central computer in the foodservice manager's office will talk to computers at the state department of education and in purveyors' offices.

By the mid-1990s, student electronic ID cards will be used to activate electronic fund transfers, switching funds to cover purchases from the customer's (or parent's) bank account to the foodservice account. Wendy's International and Roy Rogers Restaurants are among the foodservices testing electronic banking cards.

Students in Salt Lake City Public Schools (Luckman and Adamson 1988) are already using a credit card to pay for their meals. Parents send the school monthly or yearly payments, which are credited to the children's accounts. The cash register is programmed with this data and with free and reduced-price meal information. Laurens County, South Carolina, Public Schools has increased line speed with a computerized credit system it has initiated.

Many other aspects of school foodservice will be affected by the new technology. Menu engineering, the planning of menus by computers, may be a common procedure in the future. The advantage is that costs, student preferences, and nutritional balance can all be determined in minutes. Nutritional analysis can be provided at the same time menus are planned. Customers will have the option in the near future of receiving nutritional analyses on the foods ordered.

Computerization could revolutionize the bid process in very large school districts, making it more like transactions on the New York Stock Exchange. Other changes could affect human resources management. It would be possible to track an employee's productivity. An electronic job bank connected to local employment offices and social service organizations could identify all the available applicants for a job.

Computer-programmed robots can automate repetitive, mundane, or dangerous tasks, alleviating labor shortages and freeing staff for decision-making jobs (Phillips 1987). Several jobs in the foodservice industry can be done by robots, including dishwashing, food preparation, and portioning activities, particularly for preplated meals.

Technology will have a considerable impact on school foodservice in the next 10 years. Although computers are unlikely to make paper obsolete or to hand over the industry to robots, electronic data storage and automation will offer management many opportunities to improve the efficiency and productivity of foodservice operations.

DIRECTORY OF SCHOOL FOODSERVICE SOFTWARE VENDORS*

Accu-Tab Systems, Inc.
P.O. Box 953
Parsons, KS 67357
(316) 421-3190

Bon Appetit
9205 Youree Drive
Shreveport, LA 71115
(318) 797-2361

CAFS (Computer Assisted
  Food Service)
1301 West Garden
Pensacola, FL 32501
(214) 343-8915

The CBORD Group, Inc.
202 E. State, #300
Ithaca, NY 14850
(607) 272-2410

CENTEC
Box 54366
Jackson, MS 39208
(601) 932-1901

Commercial Data Systems
P.O. Box 2126
Tupelo, MS 38803
(601) 842-3282

*From the *School Food Service Journal* 1989.

COMPEL, Inc.
5113 27th Ave.
Rockford, IL 61109
(815) 229-6800

Computrition, Inc.
21049 Devonshire St.
Chatsworth, CA 91311
(818) 341-9739 or
    (800) 222-4488

Diversified Data Systems,
    Inc.
2601 N. Fairview Ave.
Tucson, AZ 85705
(602) 792-3250

Gulf South Analytical
    Service
60 Freehill Court
Brandon, MS 39042
(601) 374-7544

J & K Computer Systems,
    Inc.
1201 S. Alma School
Mesa, AZ 85210
(602) 464-0023

MAPS Software, Inc.
P.O. Box 821
Columbus, MS 39703
(601) 328-6110 or
    (800) 992-6277

Menu Planner
    Management Software
3830 Stone Way North
Seattle, WA 98103
(206) 632-9335

Microcheck Systems, Inc.
11320 S. Post Oak, #201
Houston, TX 77053
(713) 341-7771 or
    (800) 721-0080

Practorcare, Inc.
10951 Sorrento Valley
    Road
San Diego, CA 92121
(619) 450-0553 or
    (800) 421-9073

Precision Computer
    Systems
575 W. Riordan Road
Flagstaff, AZ 86001
(602) 779-5341

Prepaid Card Services
1 Bluehill Plaza, 18th Floor
Pearl River, NY 10965
(914) 620-1414

School Lunch Computer
    Service, Inc.
Village Greene, 150
    Himmelein
Medford, NJ 08055
(609) 654-0664

Sigma Science
10005 Technology Blvd.
    West
Dallas, TX 75220
(214) 350-6800

SNAP Systems
P.O. Box 2410
Santa Monica, CA 90406
(213) 393-9995

Soft Stone International,
    Inc.
742-4 Piedmont Ave. NE
Atlanta, GA 30308
(404) 872-5868

Southern Utah Computer
    Systems, Inc.
291 N. Bluff St.
St. George, UT 84770
(801) 628-4423

Southwest Technical
    Products
199 W. Rhapsody
San Antonio, TX 78216
(512) 344-0241

Top Hat Systems Ltd.
2422 Rand Morgan, Suite E
Corpus Christi, TX 78410
(512) 241-6110

Tri-Com Systems
P.O. Box 12632
Salem, OR 97309
(503) 364-7273

Via Media
6172 E. 20th
Tucson, AZ 85711
(602) 790-3801

BIBLIOGRAPHY

Adams, E. A., and A. M. Messersmith. 1986. "Robots in Food Systems." *Journal of the American Dietetic Association* 86: 1217-23.

Chaban, Joel. 1987. *1987 Directory of Hardware and Software for the Foodservice Industry.* Washington, D.C.: National Restaurant Association.

Decker, Terence. 1984. *Computer Programs for the Kitchen.* Blue Ridge Summit, Pa.: Tab Books.

Dembowski, F., ed. 1983. *Administrative Uses for Microcomputers: Software.* Reston, Va.: Association of School Business Officials.

"Directory of School Food Service Software Vendors." 1989. *School Food Service Journal* 43(2): 47.

Fowler, Karen D. 1986. "Evaluating Foodservice Software: A Suggested Approach." *Journal of the American Dietetic Association* 86(September): 1224-27.

Kasavana, Michael L. 1984. *Computer Systems for Foodservice Operations.* New York: Van Nostrand Reinhold.

Lane, Bruce R. 1989. "Point of Sale and Menu Management Systems." In *Effective Computer Management in Food and Nutrition Services,* edited by Faisal A. Kaud, 58-77. Rockville, Md.: Aspen Publishers.

Luckman, Michael, and Pam Adamson. 1988. "Food Service Enters New Age." *School Food Service Journal* 42(7): 32.

Phillips, T. R. 1987. "Robotics Revolution." *Restaurant Business* 86(8): 169-71.

Pugh, Paul N. 1989. "Computer System Feasibility Study for Public School Food Service." In *Effective Computer Management in Food and Nutrition Services,* edited by Faisal A. Kaud, 159-73. Rockville, Md.: Aspen Publishers.

Woodman, Julie G. 1985. *The IFMA Encyclopedia of the Foodservice Industry.* 5th ed. Chicago: International Foodservice Manufacturers Association.

15

Serving the Community

COMMUNITY NUTRITION CENTERS

The number of people in need is increasing, and more and more communities are finding it necessary to provide nutritious food for larger numbers. The categories of those in need of this kind of help are expanding from the very young to the very old, from the poor to the middle-income family.

By the year 2000, 35 million people will be 65 years old or older. This figure will continue to grow as the baby boom generation reaches its "golden years" (see Table 15-1). Over 60 percent of the mothers of small children will be working outside the home full time, which means an increasing need for day care, extended day care (for those in school), and other types of organized care.

In many urban areas the government has already become involved in providing care for children of working mothers. Public schools are being used to house extended day care programs. Congress is being forced to deal with the need for child care. A logical approach would be to extend the child nutrition programs to include a snack and perhaps a dinner meal for children who have an extended day.

Working mothers are using the school's breakfast program to help them meet the needs of their children. The breakfast program, which had been mainly for the poor, showed large increases in 1988 and 1989, particularly in the paying category.

With labor shortages in the child care field, working mothers are having a difficult time finding full-time child care in the summer months. The summer meal program, sponsored by USDA, which has provided lunch and/or snacks for only the needy, needs to serve those who can pay, too.

Feeding the homeless became a recognized need beginning in the 1980s. Washington was the first state to complete a review of the Community Childhood Hunger Intervention Project (CCHIP), a survey developed by the Food Research and Action Center (FRAC) that measured the extent of hunger in poor communities ("Survey Finds Hunger . . ." 1988).

School foodservice has the opportunity to become a community nutrition center in many communities. This would mean providing food services all year round to a variety of federally funded programs and to different age groups.

A few school districts have discovered these opportunities. Dayton School Food-service (Bender 1987), for example, is providing that community with services that

Table 15-1.   Elderly Population, 1980-2040
(in millions)

	65 and Older	75 and Older	85 and Older
1980	25.7	10.1	2.3
1990	31.8	13.7	3.5
2000	35.0	17.3	5.1
2010	39.3	19.0	6.8
2020	51.4	21.6	7.3
2030	64.3	29.9	8.8
2040	66.6	38.5	12.9

Source: U.S. Bureau of the Census 1984.

generate revenue. Dayton's foodservice operates an efficient central kitchen that is capable of producing more than enough to supply its own school district. As a result, in 1989 this school foodservice was providing preplated meals to more than 62 other sites (parochial and private schools, schools in other districts, day care centers, and recreation sites).

School districts such as Montgomery County, Maryland provide for the elderly and for summer food programs for two different counties. The school district runs a central warehousing and delivery system that stores and distributes food to the needy in cooperation with the social services department. Under a contract with the school district, social services is charged for storage and distribution.

Details on federal requirements for some of these programs are provided below.

CHILD CARE

Private and public day care increased in large numbers in the last ten years because of increasing population and more women working. According to Census Bureau projections, the number of children under age five increased by 16.7 percent between 1980 and 1990. However, their numbers are expected to decrease by 8.2 percent between 1990 and 2000 because of smaller families and an increased number of couples not having any children. State regulations for child care vary from state to state. At least 14 states mandate foodservices at child care centers. Though there will be a decrease in population at day care ages, the child care needs are expected to continue at an increasing level. This is because of the increase in percentage of mothers working.

The federally subsidized Child Care Food Program was created under the Child Nutrition Act of 1966. This program increased by 28 percent between 1983 and 1989, providing a subsidy for approximately 3 million children in day care (about equally divided between day care homes and child care centers).

Eligibility guidelines for free and reduced-priced meals and supplements are the same for the Child Care Food Program and the National School Lunch and Breakfast programs. The cash reimbursement and entitlement commodities are the same also. In addition to

Table 15-2.   Sample Day Care Lunch and
Snack Menus

	Group I	Group II
Lunch		
Crispy Chicken	1 piece	2 pieces
Whipped Potatoes	⅛ cup	¼ cup
Steamed Green Peas	⅛ cup	¼ cup
Roll and Butter	½ piece	1 piece
Fresh Orange Sections	½ fruit	½ fruit
Milk	½ cup	¾ cup
Snack		
Cheese	½ ounce	1 ounce
Saltine Crackers	2 crackers	4 crackers
Juice	½ cup	¾ cup

breakfast and lunch/dinner, the snacks or supplements are subsidized; for example, in 1989-1990 that subsidy amounted to the following:

Paid	$0.0375
Reduced-price	0.21
Free	0.42

The school lunch meal patterns are designed to cover the Child Care Food Program. The school lunch meal patterns for group I (ages 1-2) and group II (ages 3-4) prescribe the portion sizes to be used generally. In some states where kindergarten is not a part of the public schools, group III (ages 5-8) will be used as well. The snack must contain a fruit or vegetable and bread or bread alternate. Table 15-2 provides sample day care lunch and snack menus for groups I and II.

SENIOR CITIZEN FOOD PROGRAMS

It is estimated by the National Council on the Aging that 6.6 million people over the age of 65 in 1989 needed some form of assistance. That number is expected to reach 9 million by the year 2000. Their needs will have to be met by a combination of means. Corporate-managed retirement communities are for those who can afford the cost, and group living is a popular solution when income is tight. It is the people in the group homes, living alone in "granny" apartments, and living with relatives who need foodservice.

There are a number of federally funded programs for the elderly authorized under the Older American Act of 1965 (as amended), and the Nutrition Program for the Elderly Act (Title VII) was signed into law in 1972.

The Administration on Aging (in the U.S. Department of Health and Human Services —see Fig. 15-1) provides meals free to persons age 60 or older and supports the delivery of hot meals to the homebound elderly. The congregate meal program, which serves those

The federal organization that makes the Older Americans Act a reality is the Administration on Aging (AoA). AoA is currently placed in the Office of Human Development Services within the Department of Health and Human Services (OHDS/DHHS). The administrative network reaches through the ten regional offices of DHHS to the 57 State Units on Aging (SUAs) and some 664 Area Agencies on Aging (AAAs).

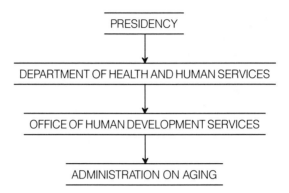

PRESIDENCY

DEPARTMENT OF HEALTH AND HUMAN SERVICES

OFFICE OF HUMAN DEVELOPMENT SERVICES

ADMINISTRATION ON AGING

Recommends policy, develops regulations to implement the Older Americans Act, allocates and administers OAA budget, grants for research, training, model projects, etc.

REGIONAL OFFICES ON AGING
(10 Regions)

Provide technical assistance to states and monitor state aging programs

STATE UNITS ON AGING
(57 Jurisdictions)

Coordinate state-level activities on behalf of older people, develop and administer the state plans on aging, serve as advocates, provide technical assistance to Area Agencies on Aging

AREA AGENCIES ON AGING
(664)

Develop and implement the area plans on aging, serve as advocates for older people, coordinate with other agencies and organizations in the planning and service areas to develop comprehensive aging service systems, administer Older Americans Act programs within their jurisdictions

FIGURE 15-1. The national aging service network. (*Source:* United States Department of Health and Human Resources.)

who are able to meet at designated places, was authorized in 1972 and the home-delivered meals in 1982. The funding for the congregate meals is nearly $400 million and for home-delivered meals, nearly $100 million.

USDA-donated foods are available for use in preparing the meals, or the agent may opt for cash in lieu of the donated foods. The menu for these programs is designed to provide one-third of the Recommended Dietary Allowance (RDA). Therapeutic meals or special diets may be needed.

The cost of a meal in 1990 has been estimated to be as high as $4.12. A break down of costs was as follows: $1.20 to $1.60 for food, $0.25 to $0.30 for paper supplies, $2.24 labor cost, and the remainder for transportation and overhead.

The budget for food for the elderly was set at around $1.5 billion (approximately 57 cents per meal) for 1990. Unfortunately there are no requirements placed on the states for "matching funds."

In 1989, federal funding provided approximately 42 percent of the revenue. The food programs available for senior citizens depend heavily on private donations and client contributions (the expected levels of gratuities are posted at serving lines). The federally funded programs provide approximately 300 million meals per year—69 percent congregate meals and 31 percent home-delivered meals. Greenville, South Carolina, has one of the best-organized area agencies and best-funded programs in the country.

Home-Delivered Meals

Home delivery of meals, often referred to as "meals on wheels," is primarily a volunteer delivery program. Often the meals delivered include a hot lunch and a cold evening meal (see Fig. 15-2). In some cases, a weekend meal is included.

Group Dining

Congregate (group) dining takes place in stand-alone buildings, rooms in the local library or school, or in other available public space. The program provides some activities and

Hot Lunch	*Hot Lunch*
Baked chicken	Fillet of sole
Parsley potatoes	Seasoned noodles
Sliced carrots	Green beans
Lettuce wedge	Red and green cabbage
with dressing	slaw
Bread and margarine	Bread and margarine
Cherry tart	Peach pie
Lowfat milk (2 percent)	Lowfat milk (2 percent)
Cold Meal	*Cold Meal*
Roast beef sandwich	Chicken salad sandwich
Orange gelatin with	Lemon apricot gelatin
pineapple slices	Banana
Lowfat milk (2 percent)	Lowfat milk (2 percent)

FIGURE 15-2. Sample menus for home-delivered meals.

a socialization component as a part of the services, as well as a nutritious meal. Many of the programs provide breakfast as well as lunch. Regulations require that at least one hot meal be served five days out of the week. There are few other guidelines for operating the program.

Union County, New Jersey runs a well-organized senior citizen program. Meals are planned on a six-week menu cycle and are prepared in a central kitchen and transported in insulated boxes throughout the county within two to three hours. One of the weekly menus is shown in Figure 15-3. Clients may request a nutritional analysis, which is provided by a private firm, ~A la Carte Connection™.

PROJECT MENU PLAN NUTRITION PROGRAM FOR THE ELDERLY					
				CONGREGATE HOT: Week #3	
	11-W	12-W	13-W	14-W	15-W
DATE					
MEAT or ALTERNATE 3-oz. Cooked Portion	Veal Cutlet Parmigiana	Hawaiian Ham	Boneless Chicken Cutlet w/Gravy	Roast Beef w/Gravy	Fish Sticks Baked Macaroni & Cheese
VEGETABLES & FRUITS	Green Beans	Carrots, Cauliflower & Broccoli	Chopped Spinach	Stewed Tomatoes & Zucchini	
Two ½ CUP SERVINGS	Spaghetti & Sauce	Glazed Sweet Potatoes	Rice Pilaf	Mashed Potatoes	Harvard Beets
DESSERT ½ CUP	Ice Cream	Cookies	Pineapple Tidbits	Rice Pudding	Fruit Cocktail
BEVERAGE	Pineapple Juice	Apricot Juice	Cr. Mushroom Soup	Minestrone Soup	Beef Noodle Soup
BREAD or ALTERNATE	Italian Bread	Bread	Bread	Dinner Roll	Bread
MARGARINE	Margarine	Margarine	Margarine	Margarine	Margarine
MILK: ½ PT	Milk	Milk	Milk	Milk	Milk

*1989

FIGURE 15-3. Sample menus for congregate dining sites. (*Source:* ~A La Carte Connection™, Cranford, NJ.)

Adult Day Care Foodservice

In 1987, the National School Lunch Act was amended to allow adult day care centers to participate in the Child Care Food Program. Generally, the terms and conditions are the same as for child care centers, with a few exceptions:

1. Federal commodities and cash reimbursements are available to nonprofit centers that provide specialized care services to functionally impaired adults over age 60, for less than 24 hours a day. These can include victims of Alzheimer's disease and other neurological and organic brain disfunctions.

2. The criteria for determining who is eligible for free or reduced-price meals are different from those of child nutrition programs. The only income that has to be considered is the income of the adult and his or her spouse, not the income of anyone else in the household.

3. The meal requirements are the same as for the Child Care Food Program for children ages 6 to 12, with the exception that yogurt or cheese can be substituted for milk. The USDA is expected to develop a meal pattern for this group with larger portions and more flexibility.

The reimbursement rates for this group are the same as for the National School Lunch and Breakfast programs. Since the state may or may not provide subsidies, it is important to determine who will pay the differences between the federal reimbursements and the total costs of providing the service.

SUMMER FOODSERVICE PROGRAM

Over 84 million meals were served under the Summer Foodservice Program in fiscal year 1988 at 17,163 sites. This program, which includes breakfasts, lunches, suppers, and supplements, has continued to increase annually. It was established to ensure that during school vacation, needy children would be able to receive the same nutritious meals provided during the school year.

In most states, summer foodservice is administered by the state department of education. Where states do not administer the program, the regional office of the USDA will administer the program.

The program must have a local sponsoring agent that contracts for foodservices. The sponsoring agent is responsible for submitting claims for reimbursement. Usually, school districts that provide summer foodservice program meals are responsible only for the food, not the distribution or the determination of who qualifies to receive the food.

Children who participate in the program must be under 18 years old. In order for a site to be approved, at least 50 percent of the children in the area it serves, or 50 percent of its enrolled children, must be eligible for free or reduced-price meals, according to U.S. Department of Agriculture income eligibility guidelines.

The prices of the meals, like those for the other programs listed above, should be carefully arrived at, so that all costs are covered. The accountability described above for

Bag or Box Lunch

Ham and Cheese Sandwich	Thinly Sliced Turkey on Bun
with Salad Dressing	with Salad Dressing
Lettuce and Tomato Salad	Chilled Orange Juice
Sliced Peaches	Fresh Grapes
Oatmeal Cookie	Graham Crackers
Milk	Milk

FIGURE 15-4. Sample menus for summer foodservice program.

the Child Care Food Program is applicable also. The federal reimbursement rates for 1990 are shown below.

Operating costs:

Breakfast	$0.995
Lunch or supper	1.785
Supplement	0.45

Administrative costs for meals served at rural or self-preparation sites:

Breakfast	$0.0925
Lunch or supper	0.17
Supplement	0.045

Administrative costs for meals served at other types of sites:

Breakfast	$0.0725
Lunch or supper	0.14
Supplement	0.0375

The meal pattern requirements are the same as for the National School Lunch and National School Breakfast programs. Often bag lunches are provided. A typical menu is shown in Figure 15-4.

CONTRACTS WITH OTHER AGENCIES

Should other agencies be provided foodservices by the public or the private sector? Will school foodservice be unfairly competing? Will sales tax need to be paid? These are some of the questions to be answered when considering an extension of school foodservice to other segments of the community.

The meals for the other school districts and for private and parochial schools are basically the same as far as menus and billing are concerned. In most cases, a school foodservice that provides meals to another school district and to private and parochial schools will do so under a contract. The contract may stipulate the furnishing of just the food or the management of the foodservice program at the school (including service and food). Generally, the school foodservice would bill the group the contract is with,

Office of Food Services
Fairfax County Public Schools
RECEIPT OF MEALS

_____ acknowledges receipt of _____
(day care center/private school)   (number of student meals)

and _____ from _____
            (number of adult meals)   (production school)

Supplies: _____   Signature: _____   ____ ____
            _____   Day Care Center/Head Start   Date
            _____   Senior Citizens
            _____
            _____
            _____   _____   _____
            _____   Production School   Date

Distribution: White copy to Day Care Center/Head Start/Senior Citizens—Yellow copy to Production School file.

Temperature _____° F

FIGURE 15-5. Sample delivery form for contracted services. (_Source:_ Fairfax County, Virginia Public Schools.)

which would be responsible for any claims for reimbursements from federal, state, and/or local sources.

When a school district's foodservice provides meals for any group—federally subsidized day care, senior nutrition programs, or other school districts—a contract should be drawn up with advice from a lawyer. It should address the prices to be charged, the menu pattern, when the bills should be paid, and how both parties can dissolve the contract. These contracts may be with the individual day care provider, senior nutrition site, or school district or with a local government agency or other sponsoring group that administers the programs.

Pricing these services should be considered carefully. The price for the services should reflect the total cost (all costs, even an appropriate share of indirect costs or those paid by a school district). This type of program should not run at any cost to the regular school foodservice programs. The price may also reflect a fee for service (or a profit). For example, if the cost of producing a lunch for a day care program is costing $1.80, the fee for service could be an added 15 cents, bringing the price of the meal to $1.95. This price may exceed the federal reimbursement, in which case the local government or sponsoring group will be subsidizing the program.

Good accountability for all these program is essential. If federal funds are involved, audits can be expected. Also to be remembered are the regulations that a "contractor" (school district) would have to follow in providing the meals and snacks.

The billing at the end of the month or pay period will list the number of meals/snacks by category and the prices charged. The number of meals/snacks received daily should be verified by each of the contracted agents receiving services. A form similar to the one in Figure 15-5 should be used to avoid controversy over the charges.

When providing any contracted services, there is always the possibility that a group or agency will go out of business. This should be addressed in the contract. A deposit equivalent to the cost of services for one month or more may be required. Billing should be done as soon after the first of the month as possible, and the due date should be watched carefully. The cutting off of meals if payment has not been received should be adhered to rather strictly, since the sponsoring group may be having financial trouble. It may be necessary to involve an attorney in the collection of outstanding bills.

BIBLIOGRAPHY

Bender, Betty. 1987. "Dayton Schools Move Toward Entrepreneurship." *School Food Service Journal* 41(4): 80.

"Final Rules: Grant for State and Community Programs on Aging." 1988. *Federal Register* 53, no. 169: 33758-79.

National Association of Area Agencies on Aging. 1987. *Guidelines for Food Purchasing for Nutrition Programs for the Elderly.* Washington, D.C.: National Association of Area Agencies on Aging.

National Association of State Units on Aging. 1985. *An Orientation to the Older Americans Act.* 2d ed., edited by Susan Coombs Ficke. Washington, D.C.: National Association of State Units on Aging.

Subcommittee on Human Services of the House Select Committee on Aging. 1984. *Older Americans Act: A Staff Summary.* Comm. pub. no. 98-482. Washington, D.C.: House Select Committee on Aging.

"Survey Finds Hunger Among Low-Income Kids." 1988. *CNI*, October 20, 2-3.

U.S. Department of Agriculture (USDA). N.d. Series of Six Manuals. Part I, *Nutrition Programs for Elderly in Perspective;* part II, *Purchasing Methods;* part III, *Documents for Formal Bid Purchasing;* part IV, *Reviews and Audits of Contracts;* part V, *Management of Meal Costs;* and part VI, *Meal Production Contracts.* Washington, D.C.: U.S. Department of Agriculture.

U.S. Department of Health and Human Services. 1983. *An Evaluation of the Nutrition Services for the Elderly.* Prepared by Kirschner Associates, Opinion Research Corporation. Washington, D.C.: U.S. Department of Health and Human Services.

Appendix A

National School Lunch Program

Subpart A—General

210.1 General purpose and scope.

(a) *Purpose of the Program.* Section 2 of the National School Lunch Act (42 U.S.C. 1751), states: "It is declared to be the policy of Congress, as a measure of national security, to safeguard the health and well-being of the Nation's children and to encourage the domestic consumption of nutritious agricultural commodities and other food, by assisting the States, through grants-in-aid and other means, in providing an adequate supply of food and other facilities for the establishment, maintenance, operation, and expansion of nonprofit school lunch programs." Pursuant to this act, the Department provides States with general and special cash assistance and donations of foods acquired by the Department to be used to assist schools in serving nutritious lunches to children each school day. In furtherance of Program objectives, participating schools shall serve lunches that are nutritionally adequate, as set forth in these regulations, and shall to the extent practicable, ensure that participating children gain full understanding of the relationship between proper eating and good health.

(b) *Scope of the Regulations.* This part sets forth the requirements for participation in the National School Lunch Commodity School Programs. It specifies Program responsibilities of State and local officials in the areas of Program administration, preparation and service of nutritious lunches, payment of funds, use of Program funds, Program monitoring, and reporting and recordkeeping requirements.

210.2 Definitions.

For the purpose of this part:

"Act" means the National School Lunch Act as amended.

"AIMS" means the Assessment, Improvement and Monitoring System. This is a management improvement system used in the National School Lunch and the Commodity School Programs.

"Child" means—(a) a student of high school grade or under as determined by the State educational agency, who is enrolled in an educational unit of high school grade or under as

---

Final Rule, 7 CFR Part 210 August 2, 1988

described in paragraphs (a) and (b) of the definition of "School," including students who are mentally or physically handicapped as defined by the State and who are participating in a school program established for the mentally or physically handicapped; or (b) a person under 21 chronological years of age who is enrolled in an institution or center as described in paragraphs (c) and (d) of the definition of "School."

"CND" means the Child Nutrition Division of the Food and Nutrition Service of the Department.

"Commodity School Program" means the Program under which participating schools operate a nonprofit lunch program in accordance with this part and receive donated food assistance in lieu of general cash assistance. Schools participating in the Commodity School Program shall also receive special cash and donated food assistance in accordance with 210.4(c).

"Department" means the United States Department of Agriculture.

"Distributing agency" means a State agency which enters into an agreement with the Department for the distribution to schools of donated foods pursuant to Part 250 of this chapter.

"Donated foods" means food commodities donated by the Department for use in nonprofit lunch programs.

"Fiscal year" means a period of 12 calendar months beginning October 1 of any year and ending with September 30 of the following year.

"FNS" means the Food and Nutrition Service, United States Department of Agriculture.

"FNSRO" means the appropriate Regional Office of the Food and Nutrition Service of the Department.

"Food component" means one of the four food groups which compose the reimbursable school lunch, i.e., meat or meat alternate, milk, bread or bread alternate, and vegetable/fruit.

"Food item" means one of the five required foods that compose the reimbursable school lunch, i.e., meat or meat alternate, milk, bread or bread alternate, and two (2) servings of vegetables, fruits, or a combination of both.

"Food service management company" means a commercial enterprise or a nonprofit organization which is or may be contracted with by the school food authority to manage any aspect of the school food service.

"Free lunch" means a lunch served under the Program to a child from a household eligible for such benefits under 7 CFR Part 245 and for which neither the child nor any member of the household pays or is required to work.

"Handicapped student" means any child who has a physical or mental impairment as defined in 15b.3 of the Department's nondiscrimination regulations (7 CFR Part 15b).

"Lunch" means a meal which meets the school lunch pattern for specified age/grade groups of children as designated in 210.10.

"National School Lunch Program" means the Program under which participating schools operate a nonprofit lunch program in accordance with this part. General and special cash assistance and donated food assistance are made available to schools in accordance with this part.

"Net cash resources" means all monies, as determined in accordance with the State agency's established accounting system, that are available to or have accrued to a school food authority's nonprofit school food service at any given time, less cash payable. Such monies may include, but are not limited to, cash on hand, cash receivable, earnings on investments, cash on deposit and the value of stocks, bonds or other negotiable securities.

"Nonprofit," when applied to schools or institutions eligible for the Program, means exempt from income tax under section 501(c)(3) of the Internal Revenue Code of 1954, as amended; or, in the Commonwealth of Puerto Rico, certified as nonprofit by the Governor.

"Nonprofit school food service" means all food service operations conducted by the school food authority principally for the benefit of schoolchildren, all of the revenue from which is used solely for the operation or improvement of such food services.

"OIG" means the Office of the Inspector General of the Department.

"Program" means the National School Lunch Program and the Commodity School Program.

"Reduced price lunch" means a lunch served under the Program: (a) to a child from a household eligible for such benefits under 7 CFR Part 245; (b) for which the price is less than the school food authority designated full price of the lunch and which does not exceed the maximum allowable reduced price specified under 7 CFR Part 245; and (c) for which neither the child or any member of the household is required to work.

"Reimbursement" means Federal cash assistance including advances paid or payable to participating schools for lunches meeting the requirements of 210.10 and served to eligible children.

"Revenue," when applied to nonprofit school food service, means all monies received by or accruing to the nonprofit school food service in accordance with the State agency's established accounting system including, but not limited to, children's payments, earnings on investments, other local revenues, State revenues, and Federal cash reimbursements.

"School" means: (a) An educational unit of high school grade or under, recognized as part of the educational system in the State and operating under public or nonprofit private ownership in a single building or complex of buildings; (b) any public or nonprofit private classes of preprimary grade when they are conducted in the aforementioned schools; (c) any public or nonprofit private residential child care institution, or distinct part of such institution, which operates principally for the care of children, and, if private, is licensed to provide residential child care services under the appropriate licensing code by the State or a subordinate level of government, except for residential summer camps which participate in the Summer Food Service Program for Children, Job Corps centers funded by the Department of Labor, and private foster homes. The term "residential child care institutions" includes, but is not limited to: homes for the mentally, emotionally or physically impaired, and unmarried mothers and their infants; group homes; halfway houses; orphanages; temporary shelters for abused children and for runaway children; long-term care facilities for chronically ill children; and juvenile detention centers. A long-term care facility is a hospital, skilled nursing facility, intermediate care facility, or distinct part thereof, which is intended for the care of children confined for 30 days or more; or (d) with respect to the Commonwealth of Puerto Rico, nonprofit child care centers certified as such by the Governor of Puerto Rico.

"School food authority" means the governing body which is responsible for the administration of one or more schools, and has the legal authority to operate the Program therein or be otherwise approved by FNS to operate the Program.

"School year" means a period of 12 calendar months beginning July 1 of any year and ending June 30 of the following year.

"Secretary" means the Secretary of Agriculture.

"State" means any of the 50 States, District of Columbia, the Commonwealth of Puerto Rico, the Virgin Islands, Guam, American Samoa, the Commonwealth of the Northern

Marianas, or the Federated States of Micronesia, the Republic of the Marshalls, and the Republic of Palau.

"State agency" means (a) the State educational agency; (b) any other agency of the State which has been designated by the Governor or other appropriate executive or legislative authority of the State and approved by the Department to administer the Program in schools, as specified in 210.3 (b); or (c) the FRNSO where the FRNSO administers the Program as specified in 210.3(c).

"State educational agency" means, as the State legislature may determine, (a) the chief State school officer (such as the State Superintendent of Public Instruction, Commissioner of Education, or similar officer), or (b) a board of education controlling the State department of education.

"State food distribution advisory council" means a group which meets to advise the State educational agency with respect to the needs of schools participating in the program concerning the manner of selection and distribution of commodities.

"Subsidized lunch" (paid lunch) means a lunch served to children who are either not eligible for or elect not to receive the free or reduced price benefits offered under 7 CFR Part 245. The Department subsidizes each paid lunch with both general cash assistance and donated foods. Although a paid lunch student pays for a large portion of his or her lunch, the Department's subsidy accounts for a significant portion of the cost for that lunch.

210.3 Administration.

(a) *FNS.* FNS will act on behalf of the Department in the administration of the Program. Within FNS, the CND will be responsible for Program administration.

(b) *States.* Within the States, the responsibility for the administration of the Program in schools, as defined in 210.2, shall be in the State educational agency. If the State educational agency is unable to administer the Program in public or private nonprofit residential child care institutions or nonprofit private schools, then Program administration for such schools may be assumed by FNSRO as provided in paragraph (c) of this section, or such other agency of the State as has been designated by the Governor or other appropriate executive or legislative authority of the State and approved by the Department to administer such schools. Each State agency desiring to administer the Program shall enter into a written agreement with the Department of the Administration of the Program in accordance with the applicable requirements of this part; Part 235; Part 245; Parts 15, 15a, 15b, and 3015 of Departmental regulations; and FNS instructions.

(c) *FNSRO.* The FNSRO will administer the Program in nonprofit private schools or public or nonprofit private residential child care institutions if the State agency is prohibited by law from disbursing Federal funds paid to such schools. In addition, the FNSRO will continue to administer the Program in those States in which nonprofit private schools or public or nonprofit private residential child care institutions have been under continuous FNS administration since October 1, 1980, unless the administration of the Program in such schools is assumed by the State. The FNSRO will, in each State in which it administers the Program, assume all responsibilities of a State agency as set forth in this part and Part 245 of this chapter as appropriate. References in this part to "State agency" include FNSRO, as applicable, when it is the agency administering the Program.

(d) *School Food Authorities.* The school food authority shall be responsible for the administration of the Program in schools. State agencies shall ensure that school food authorities administer the Program in accordance with the applicable requirements of this part; Part 245; Parts 15, 15a, 15b, and 3015 of Departmental regulations; and FNS instructions.

Subpart B—Assistance to States and School Food Authorities

210.4 Cash and donated food assistance to States.

(a) *General.* To the extent funds are available, FNS will make cash assistance available in accordance with the provisions of this section to each State agency for lunches served to children under the National School Lunch and Commodity School Programs. To the extent donated foods are available, FNS will provide donated food assistance to distributing agencies for each lunch served in accordance with the provisions of this part and Part 250 of this chapter.

(b) *Assistance for the National School Lunch Program.* The Secretary will make cash and/or donated food assistance available to each State agency and distributing agency, as appropriate, administering the National School Lunch Program, as follows:

(1) *Cash assistance:* Cash assistance payments are composed of a **general** cash assistance payment, authorized under section 4 of the Act, and a **special** cash assistance payment, authorized under section 11 of the Act. General cash assistance is provided to each State agency for **all** lunches served to children in accordance with the provisions of the National School Lunch Program. Special cash assistance is provided to each State agency for lunches served under the National School Lunch Program to children determined eligible for free or reduced price lunches in accordance with Part 245 of this chapter. The total general cash assistance paid to each State for any fiscal year shall not exceed the lesser of amounts reported to FNS as reimbursed to school food authorities in accordance with 210.5(d)(3) or the total calculated by multiplying the number of lunches reported in accordance with 210.5(d)(1) for each month of service during the fiscal year, by the applicable national average payment rate prescribed by FNS. The total special assistance paid to each State for any fiscal year shall not exceed the lesser of amounts reported to FNS as reimbursed to school food authorities in accordance with 210.5(d)(3) or the total calculated by multiplying the number of free and reduced price lunches reported in accordance with 210.5 (d)(1) for each month of service during the fiscal year by the applicable national average payment rate prescribed by FNS. In accordance with section 11 of the Act, FNS will prescribe annual adjustments to the per meal national average payment rate (general cash assistance) and the special assistance national average payment rates (special cash assistance) which are effective on July 1 of each year. These adjustments, which reflect changes in the food away from home series of the Consumer Price Index for all Urban Consumers, are annually announced by Notice in July of each year in the *Federal Register.* FNS will also establish maximum per meal rates of reimbursement within which a State may vary reimbursement rates to school food authorities. These maximum rates of reimbursement are established at the same time and announced in the same Notice as the national average payment rates.

(2) *Donated food assistance.* For each school year, FNS will provide distributing agencies with donated foods for lunches served under the National School Lunch Program

as provided under Part 250 of this chapter. The per lunch value of donated food assistance is adjusted by the Secretary annually to reflect changes as required under section 6 of the Act. These adjustments, which reflect changes in the Price Index for Foods Used in Schools and Institutions, are effective on July 1 of each year and are announced by Notice in the *Federal Register* in July of each year.

(c) *Assistance for the Commodity School Program.* FNS will make special cash assistance available to each State agency for lunches served in commodity schools in the same manner as special cash assistance is provided in the National School Lunch Program. Payment of such amounts to State agencies is subject to the reporting requirements contained in 210.5(d). FNS will provide donated food assistance in accordance with Part 250 of this chapter. Of the total value of donated food assistance to which it is entitled, the school food authority may elect to receive cash payment of up to 5 cents per lunch served in its commodity school(s) for donated foods processing and handling expenses. Such expenses include any expenses incurred by or on behalf of a commodity school for processing or other aspects of the preparation, delivery, and storage of donated foods. The school food authority may have all or part of these cash payments retained by the State agency for use on its behalf for processing and handling expenses by the State agency or it may authorize the State agency to transfer to the distributing agency all or any part of these payments for use on its behalf for these expenses. Payment of such amounts to State agencies is subject to the reporting requirements contained in 210.5(d). The total value of donated food assistance is calculated on a school year basis by adding:

(1) The applicable national average payment rate (general cash assistance) prescribed by the Secretary for the period of July 1 through June 30 multiplied by the total number of lunches served during the school year under the Commodity School Program; and

(2) The national per lunch average value of donated foods prescribed by the Secretary for the period of July 1 through June 30 multiplied by the total number of lunches served during the school year under the Commodity School Program.

210.5 Payment process to States.

(a) *Grant Award.* FNS will specify the terms and conditions of the State agency's grant in a grant award document and will generally make payments available by means of a Letter of Credit issued in favor of the State agency. The State agency shall obtain funds for reimbursement to participating school food authorities through procedures established by FNS in accordance with 7 CFR Part 3015. State agencies shall limit requests for funds to such times and amounts as will permit prompt payment of claims or authorized advances. The State agency shall disburse funds received from such requests without delay for the purpose for which drawn. FNS may, at its option, reimburse a State agency by Treasury Check. FNS will pay by Treasury Check with funds available in settlement of a valid claim if payment for that claim cannot be made within the grant closeout period specified in paragraph (d) of this section.

(b) *Cash-in-Lieu of Donated Foods.* All federal funds to be paid to any State in place of donated foods will be made available as provided in Part 240 of this chapter.

(c) *Recovery of Funds.* FNS will recover any Federal funds made available to the State agency under this part which are in excess of obligations reported at the end of each fiscal year in accordance with the reconciliation procedures specified in paragraph (d) of this section. Such recoveries shall be reflected by a related adjustment in the State agency's Letter of Credit.

(d) *Substantiation and Reconciliation Process.* Each State agency shall maintain Program records as necessary to support the reimbursement payments made to school food authorities under 210.7 and 210.8 and the reports submitted to FNS under this paragraph. The State agency shall ensure such records are retained for a period of 3 years or as otherwise specified in 210.23(c).

(1) *Monthly report.* Each State agency shall submit a final Report of School Program Operations (FNS-10) to FNS for each month. The final reports shall be limited to claims submitted in accordance with 210.8 and shall be postmarked and/or submitted no later than 90 days following the last day of the month covered by the report. States shall not receive Program funds for any month for which the final report is not submitted within this time limit unless FNS grants an exception. Upward adjustments to a State's report shall not be made after 90 days from the month covered by the report unless authorized by FNS. Downward adjustments to a State's report shall always be made regardless of when it is determined that such adjustments are necessary. FNS authorization is not required for downward adjustments. Any adjustments to a State's report shall be reported to FNS in accordance with procedures established by FNS.

(2) *Quarterly report.* Each state agency shall also submit to FNS a quarterly Financial Status Report (SF-269) on the use of Program funds. Such reports shall be postmarked and/or submitted no later than 30 days after the end of each fiscal year quarter.

(3) *End of year report.* Each state agency shall submit a final Financial Status Report (SF-269) for each fiscal year. This final fiscal year grant closeout report shall be post-marked and/or submitted to FNS within 120 days after the end of each fiscal year or part thereof that the State agency administered the Program. Obligations shall be reported only for the fiscal year in which they occur. FNS will not be responsible for reimbursing Program obligations reported later than 120 days after the close of the fiscal year in which they were incurred. Grant closeout procedures are to be carried out in accordance with 7 CFR Part 3015.

210.6 Use of Federal funds.

General. State agencies shall use Federal funds made available under the Program to reimburse or make advance payments to school food authorities in connection with lunches served in accordance with the provisions of this part; *except that*, with the approval of FNS, any State agency may reserve an amount up to one percent of the funds earned in any fiscal year under this part for use in carrying out special developmental projects. Advance payments to school food authorities may be made at such times and in such amounts as are necessary to meet the current fiscal obligations. All Federal funds paid to any State in place of donated foods shall be used as provided in Part 240 of this chapter.

210.7 Reimbursement for school food authorities.

(a) *General.* Reimbursement payments to finance nonprofit school food service operations shall be made only to school food authorities operating under a written agreement with the State agency. Subject to the provisions of 210.8(b), such payments may be made for lunches served in accordance with provisions of this part and Part 245 in the calendar month preceding the calendar month in which the agreement is executed. These reimbursement payments include general cash assistance for all lunches served to children under the National School Lunch Program and special cash assistance payments for free or reduced price lunches served to children determined eligible for such benefits under the National School Lunch and Commodity School Programs. The school food authority shall not claim reimbursement for any lunches produced in excess of the one lunch per child day limitation specified under 210.10(b). Any excess lunches that are produced may be served, but shall not be claimed for general or special cash assistance provided under 210.4. Nor shall any school food authority claim or be eligible for special cash assistance reimbursement for free or reduced price lunches in each school food authority. Approval shall be in accordance with Part 245 of this chapter.

(b) *Assignment of Rates.* At the beginning of each school year, State agencies shall establish the per meal rates of reimbursement for school food authorities participating in the Program. These rates of reimbursement may be assigned at levels based on financial need; *except that,* the rates are not to exceed the maximum rates of reimbursement established by the Secretary under 210.4(b) and are to permit reimbursement for the total number of lunches in the State from funds available under 210.4. Within each school food authority, the State agency shall assign the same rate of reimbursement from general cash assistance funds for all lunches served to children under the Program. Assigned rates of reimbursement may be changed at any time by the State agency, *provided that* notice of any change is given to the school food authority. The total general and special cash assistance reimbursement paid to any school food authority for lunches served to children during the school year are not to exceed the sum of the products obtained by multiplying the total reported number of lunches, by type, served to eligible children during the school year by the applicable maximum per lunch reimbursements prescribed for the school year for each type of lunch.

210.8 Method of reimbursement.

(a) *Monthly Claims.* To be entitled to reimbursement under this part, each school food authority shall submit to the State agency, a monthly Claim for Reimbursement, as described in paragraph (b) of this section. A final Claim for Reimbursement shall be postmarked or submitted to the State agency not later than 60 days following the last day of the full month covered by the claim. State agencies may establish shorter deadlines at their discretion. Claims not postmarked and/or submitted within 60 days shall not be paid with Program funds unless otherwise authorized by FNS. The State agency shall promptly take corrective action with respect to any Claim for Reimbursement as determined necessary through its claims review process or otherwise. In taking such corrective action, State agencies may make adjustments on claims filed within the 60 day deadline if such adjustments are completed within 90 days of the last day of the claim month and are reflected in the final Report of School Program Operations (FNS-10) for the claim month required under 210.5(d). Upward adjustments in Program funds claimed which are not reflected in the final FNS-10 for the claim month shall not be made unless authorized by FNS. Downward adjustments in amounts claimed shall always be made, without FNS authorization, regardless of when it is determined that such adjustments are necessary.

(b) *Content of Claim.* The Claim for Reimbursement shall include data in sufficient detail to justify the reimbursement claimed and to enable the State agency to provide the Report of School Program Operations required under 210.5(d). The State agency may authorize a school food authority to submit a consolidated Claim for Reimbursement for all schools under its jurisdiction, *provided that* the date on each school's operations required in this section are maintained on file at the local office of the school food authority, and the claim separates consolidated data for commodity schools from data for other schools. Unless otherwise approved by FNS, the Claim for Reimbursement for any month shall include only lunches served in that month except if the first or last month of Program operations for any year contains 10 operating days or less, such month may be combined with the Claim for Reimbursement for the appropriate adjacent month. However, Claims for Reimbursement may not combine operations occurring in two fiscal years.

(c) *Advance Funds.* The State agency may advance funds available for the Program to a school food authority in an amount equal to the amount of reimbursement estimated to be needed for one month's operation. Following the receipt of claims, the State agency shall make adjustments, as necessary, to ensure that the total amount of payments received by the school food authority for the fiscal year does not exceed an amount equal to the number of lunches by reimbursement type served to children times the respective payment rates assigned by the State in accordance with 210.7(b). The State agency shall recover advances of funds to any school food authority failing to comply with the 60-day claim submission requirements in paragraph (a) of this section.

Subpart C—Requirements for School Food Authority Participation

210.9 Agreement with State agency.

(a) *Application.* An official of a school food authority shall make written application to the State agency for any school in which it desires to operate the Program. Applications shall provide the State agency with sufficient information to determine eligibility. The school food authority shall also submit for approval a Free and Reduced Price Policy Statement in accordance with Part 245 of this chapter.

(b) *Annual Agreement.* The school food authority shall annually enter into a written agreement with the State agency. The State agency may allow school food authorities to extend by amendment a previous year's agreement in lieu of taking a new agreement annually *provided that* each year a current written agreement is on file at the State agency. The agreement shall contain a statement to the effect that the "School Food Authority and Participating schools under its jurisdiction, shall comply with all provisions of 7 CFR Parts 210 and 245." This agreement shall provide that each school food authority shall, with respect to participating schools under its jurisdiction:

(1) Maintain a nonprofit school food service and observe the limitations on the use of nonprofit school food service revenues set forth in 210.14(a) and the limitations on any competitive school food service as set forth in 210.11(b);

(2) Limit its net cash resources to an amount that does not exceed 3 months average expenditures for its nonprofit school food service or such other amount as may be approved in accordance with 210.19(a);

(3) Maintain a financial management system as prescribed under 210.14(c);

(4) Comply with the requirements of the Department's regulations regarding financial management (7 CFR Part 3015);

(5) Serve lunches, during the lunch period, which meet the minimum requirements prescribed in 210.10;

(6) Price the lunch as a unit;

(7) Serve lunches free or at a reduced price to all children who are determined by the school food authority to be eligible for such meals under 7 CFR Part 245;

(8) Claim reimbursement at the assigned rates only for lunches served in accordance with the agreement;

(9) Submit Claims for Reimbursement in accordance with 210.8;

(10) Comply with the requirements of the Department's regulations regarding nondiscrimination (7 CFR Parts 15, 15a, 15b);

(11) Make no discrimination against any child because of his or her eligibility for free or reduced price meals in accordance with the approved Free and Reduced Price Policy Statement;

(12) Enter into an agreement to receive donated foods as required by 7 CFR Part 250;

(13) Maintain, in the storage, preparation and service of food, proper sanitation and health standards in conformance with all applicable State and local laws and regulations;

(14) Accept and use, in as large quantities as may be efficiently utilized in its nonprofit school food service, such foods as may be offered as a donation by the Department;

(15) Maintain necessary facilities for storing, preparing and serving food;

(16) Upon request, make all accounts and records pertaining to its school food service available to the State agency and to FNS, for audit or review, at a reasonable time and place. Such records shall be retained for a period of 3 years after the date of the final Claim for Reimbursement for the fiscal year to which they pertain, except that if audit finds have not been resolved, the records shall be retained beyond the 3 year period as long as required for resolution of the issues raised by the audit;

(17) Maintain files of currently approved and denied free and reduced price applications, respectively. If applications are maintained at the school food authority level, they shall be readily retrievable by school;

(18) Retain the individual applications for free and reduced price lunches submitted by families for a period of 3 years after the end of the fiscal year to which they pertain or as otherwise specified under paragraph (b)(16) of this section.

210.10 Lunch components and quantities.

(a) *Meal Pattern Definitions.* For the purpose of this section:

(1) "Infant cereal" means any iron-fortified dry cereal especially formulated and generally recognized as cereal for infants and that is routinely mixed with formula or milk prior to consumption.

(2) "Infant formula" means any iron-fortified formula intended for dietary use solely as a food for normal, healthy infants; excluding those formulas specifically formulated for infants with inborn errors of metabolism or digestive or absorptive problems. Infant formula, as served, must be in liquid state at recommended dilution.

(b) *General.* School food authorities shall ensure that participating schools provide nutritious and well-balanced lunches to children in accordance with the provisions of this section. The requirements and recommendations of this section are designed so that the nutrients of the lunch, averaged over a period of time, *approximate* one-third of the Recommended Dietary Allowances for children of each age/grade group as specified in paragraph (c) of this section. School food authorities shall ensure that each lunch is priced as a unit. Except as otherwise provided herein, school food authorities shall ensure that sufficient quantities of food are planned and produced so that lunches provided contain all the required food items in at least the minimum amounts (see figure 4-2). School food authorities shall ensure that lunches are planned and produced on the basis of participation trends, with the objective of providing one reimbursable lunch per child per day. Production and participation records shall be maintained to demonstrate positive action toward providing one reimbursable lunch per child per day. Any excess lunches that are produced may be served, but shall not be claimed for general or special cash assistance provided under 210.4.

(c) *Minimum Required Lunch Quantities.* Schools that are able to provide quantities of food to children solely on the basis of their ages or grade level should do so. Schools that cannot serve children on the basis of age or grade level shall provide all school age children Group IV portions as specified in Figure 4-2. Schools serving children on the basis of age or grade level shall plan and produce sufficient quantities of food to provide Groups I-IV no less than the amounts specified for those children in Figure 4-2, and sufficient quantities of food to provide Group V no less than the specified amounts for Group IV. It is recommended that such schools plan and produce sufficient quantities of food to provide Group V children the larger amounts specified in the table. Schools that provide increased portion sizes for Group V may comply with children's requests for smaller portion sizes of the food items; however, schools shall plan and produce sufficient quantities of food to at least provide the serving sizes required for Group IV. Schools shall ensure that lunches are served with the objective of providing the per lunch minimums for each age and grade level as specified in Figure 4-2.

(d) *Lunch Components.* This section specifies the basic food components of the school lunch pattern which shall be served as food items in quantities specified in paragraph (c) of this section.

(1) *Milk.* Schools shall offer students fluid whole milk *and* at least one of the following:

(i) Fluid unflavored milk containing two percent or less milk fats;

(ii) Fluid unflavored skim milk; or

(iii) Buttermilk.

All milk served shall be pasteurized fluid types of milk which meet State and local standards for such milk; *except that,* in the meal pattern for infants under 1 year of age, the milk shall be unflavored types of whole fluid milk or an equivalent quantity of reconstituted evaporated milk which meets such standards. All milk shall contain vitamins A and D at levels specified by the Food and Drug Administration and consistent with State and local standards for such milk. School food authorities that served 3/4 cup (6 fluid ounces) of milk to Group III children prior to May 1, 1980, may continue to do so. Such school food authorities shall retain documentation of the date on which they began such service and the reasons for adopting this portion size.

(2) *Meat or meat alternate.* The quantity of meat or meat alternate shall be the quantity of the edible portion as served. When the school determines that the portion size of a meat alternate is excessive, it shall reduce the portion size of that particular meat alternate and supplement it with another meat/meat alternate to meet the full requirement. To be counted as meeting the requirement, the meat or meat alternate shall be served in a main dish or in a main dish and only one other menu item. The Department recommends that if

schools do not offer children choices of meat or meat alternates each day, they serve no one meat alternate of form of meat (e.g., ground, diced, pieces) more than three times in a single week.

(i) Vegetable protein products, cheese alternate products, and enriched macaroni with fortified protein may be used to meet part of the meat or meat alternate requirement when used as specified. An enriched macaroni product with fortified protein may be used as part of a meat alternate or as a bread alternate, but not as both food components in the same meal.

(ii) Nuts and seeds and their butters listed in program guidance are nutritionally comparable to meat or other meat alternates based on available nutritional data. Acorns, chestnuts, and coconuts shall not be used as meat alternates due to their low protein and iron content. Nut and seed meals or flours shall not be used as a meat alternate except as Alternate Foods for Meals. As noted in the School Lunch Pattern (Fig. 4-2), nuts or seeds may be used to meet no more than one-half of the meat/meat alternate requirement. Therefore, nuts and seeds must be used in the meal with another meat/meat alternate to fulfill the requirement.

(3) *Vegetable or fruit.* Full strength vegetable or fruit juice may be counted to meet not more than one-half of the vegetable/fruit requirement. Cooked dry beans or peas may be used as a meat alternate or as a vegetable, but not as both food components in the same meal.

(4) *Bread or bread alternate.* (i) All breads or bread alternates such as bread, biscuits, muffins or rice, macaroni, noodles, other pastas or cereal grains such as bulgar or corn grits, shall be enriched or whole grain or made with enriched or whole grain meal or flour.

(ii) Unlike the other component requirements, the bread requirement is based on minimum daily servings and total servings per week. Schools shall serve daily at least one-half serving of bread or bread alternate to children in Group I and at least one serving to children in Groups II-V. Schools which serve lunch at least 5 days a week shall serve a total of at least five servings of bread or bread alternate to children in Group I and eight servings per week to children in Groups II-V. Schools serving lunch 6 or 7 days per week should increase the weekly quantity by approximately 20 percent (1/5) for each additional day. When schools operate less than 5 days per week, they may decrease the weekly quantity by approximately 20 percent (1/5) for each day less than five. The servings for biscuits, rolls, muffins, and other bread alternates are specified in the *Food Buying Guide for Child Nutrition Programs (PA 1331)*, an FNS publication.

(e) *Offer versus Serve.* Each school shall offer its students all five required food items as set forth in Figure 4-2. Senior high students shall be permitted to decline up to two of the five required food items. At the discretion of the school food authority, students below the senior high level *may* be permitted to decline one or two of the required five food items. The price of a reimbursable lunch shall not be affected if a student declines food items or accepts smaller portions. State educational agencies shall define "senior high."

(f) *Choice.* To provide variety and to encourage consumption and participation, schools should, whenever possible, provide a selection of foods and types of milk from which children may make choices. When a school offers a selection of more than one type of lunch or when it offers a variety of foods and milk for choice within the required lunch pattern, the school shall offer all children the same selection regardless of whether the children are eligible for free or reduced price lunches or pay the school food authority designated full price. The school may establish different unit prices for each type of lunch served provided that the benefits made available to children eligible for free or reduced price lunches are not affected.

(g) *Lunch Period.* At or about mid-day schools shall serve lunches which meet the requirements of this part during a period designated as the lunch period by the school food authority. Such lunch periods shall occur between 10:00 A.M. and 2:00 P.M., unless otherwise exempted by FNS. With State approval, schools that serve children 1-5 years old are encouraged to divide the service of the specified quantities and food items into two distinct service periods. Such schools may divide the quantities and/or food items between these service periods in any combination that they choose.

(h) *Infant Lunch Pattern.* Infants under 1 year of age shall be served an infant lunch as specified in this paragraph when they participate in the Program. Foods within the infant lunch pattern shall be texture and consistency appropriate for the particular age group being served, and shall be served to the infant during a span of time consistent with the infant's eating habits. For infants 4 through 7 months of age, solid foods are optional and should be introduced only when the infant is developmentally ready. Whenever possible the school should consult with the infant's parent in making the decision to introduce solid foods. Solid foods should be introduced one at a time on a gradual basis with the intent of ensuring health and nutritional well-being. For infants 8 through 11 months of age, the total amount of food authorized in the meal patterns set forth below must be provided in order to qualify for reimbursement. Additional foods may be served to infants 4 months of age and older with the intent of improving their overall nutrition. Breast milk provided by the infant's mother may be served in place of infant formula from birth through 11 months of age. However, meals containing only breast milk do not qualify for reimbursement. Meals containing breast milk served to infants 4 months of age or older may be claimed for reimbursement when the other required meal component or components are supplied by the school. Although it is recommended that either breast milk or iron-fortified infant formula be served for the entire first year, whole milk may be served beginning at 8 months of age as long as infants are consuming one-third of their calories as a balanced mixture of cereal, fruits, vegetables, and other foods in order to ensure adequate sources of iron and vitamin C. The infant lunch pattern shall contain, as a minimum, each of the following components in the amounts indicated for the appropriate age group:

(1) Birth through 3 months—4 to 6 fluid ounces of iron-fortified infant formula.

(2) 4 through 7 months—(i) 4 to 8 fluid ounces of iron-fortified infant formula; (ii) 0 to 3 tablespoons of iron-fortified dry infant cereal (optional); and (iii) 0 to 3 tablespoons of fruit or vegetable of appropriate consistency or a combination of both (optional).

(3) 8 through 11 months—(i) 6 to 8 fluid ounces of iron-fortified infant formula or 6 to 8 ounces of whole milk; (ii) 2 to 4 tablespoons of iron-fortified dry infant cereal and/or 1 to 4 tablespoons meat, fish, poultry, egg yolk, or cooked dry beans or peas, or ½ to 2 ounces (weight) of cheese or 1 to 4 ounces (weight or volume) of cottage cheese, cheese food or cheese spread of appropriate consistency; and (iii) 1 to 4 tablespoons of fruit or vegetable of appropriate consistency or a combination of both.

(i) *Exceptions.* Lunches claimed for reimbursement shall meet the school lunch pattern requirements specified in paragraphs (c) and (d) of this section. However, lunches served which accommodate the exceptions and variations authorized under this paragraph are also reimbursable. Exceptions and variations are restricted to the following:

(1) *Medical or dietary needs.* Schools shall make substitutions in foods listed in this section for students who are considered handicapped under 7 CFR Part 15b and whose handicap restricts their diet. Schools may also make substitutions for nonhandicapped students who are unable to consume the regular lunch because of medical or other special dietary needs. Substitutions shall be made on a case by case basis only when supported by a statement of the need for substitutions that includes recommended alternate foods, unless otherwise exempted by FNS. Such statement shall, in the case of a handicapped student, be signed by a physician or, in the case of a nonhandicapped student, by a recognized medical authority.

(2) *Ethnic, religious or economic variations.* FNS may approve variations in the food components of the lunch on an experimental or on a continuing basis in any school where there is evidence that such variations are nutritionally sound and are necessary to meet ethnic, religious, or economic needs.

(3) *Foreign meal patterns.* Schools in American Samoa, Puerto Rico and the Virgin Islands may serve a starchy vegetable such as yams, plantains, or sweet potatoes to meet the bread or bread alternate requirement. For the Commonwealth of the Northern Mariana Islands, FNS has established a meal pattern which is consistent with local food consumption patterns and which, given available food supplies and food service equipment and facilities, provides optimum nutrition consistent with sound dietary habits for participating children. The State agency shall attach to and make a part of the written agreement required under 210.9, the requirements of that pattern.

(4) *Natural disaster.* In the event of a natural disaster or other catastrophe, FNS may temporarily allow schools to serve lunches for reimbursement that do not meet requirements of this section.

(5) *Insufficient milk supply.* The inability of a school to obtain a supply of milk shall not bar it from participation in the Program and is to be resolved as follows:

(i) If emergency conditions temporarily prevent a school that normally has a supply of fluid milk from obtaining delivery of such milk, the State agency may approve the service of lunches during the emergency period with an available alternate form of milk or without milk.

(ii) If a school is unable to obtain a supply of fluid whole milk and fluid unflavored milk containing two percent or less milk fats on a continuing basis, the State agency may approve the service of either fluid whole milk or fluid unflavored milk containing two percent or less milk fats. The Department recommends that the State agency approve for service the available fluid milk with the lowest fat and sugar content. In Alaska, Hawaii, American Samoa, Guam, Puerto Rico, the Commonwealth of the Northern Marianas and the Virgin Islands, if a sufficient supply of fluid milk cannot be obtained, "milk" shall include reconstituted or recombined milk, or as otherwise provided under written exception by FNS.

(iii) If a school is unable to obtain a supply of any type of fluid milk on a continuing basis, the State agency may approve the service of lunches without milk if the school uses an equivalent amount of canned, whole or nonfat dry milk in the preparation of the lunch.

210.11 *Competitive food services.*

(a) *Definitions.* For the purpose of this section:

(1) "Competitive foods" means any foods sold in competition with the Program to children in food service areas during the lunch periods.

(2) "Food of minimal nutritional value" means: (i) In the case of artificially sweetened foods, a food which provides less than five percent of the United States Recommended Dietary Allowances (USRDA) for each of eight specified nutrients per serving; and (ii) in the case of all other foods, a food which provides less than five percent of the USRDA for each of eight specified nutrients per 100 calories and less than five percent of the USRDA for each of eight specified nutrients per serving. The eight nutrients to be assessed for this purpose are—protein, vitamin A, vitamin C, niacin, riboflavin, thiamine, calcium, and iron.

(b) *General.* State agencies and school food authorities shall establish such rules or regulations as are necessary to control the sale of foods in competition with lunches served under the Program. Such rules or regulations shall prohibit the sale of foods of minimal nutritional value in the food service areas during the lunch periods. The sale of other competitive foods may, at the discretion of the State agency and school food authority, be allowed in the food service area during the lunch period only if all income from the sale of such foods accrues to the benefit of the nonprofit school food service or the school or student organizations approved by the school. State agencies and school food authorities may impose additional restrictions on the sale of and income from all foods sold at any time throughout schools participating in the program.

210.12 *Student, parent and community involvement.*

(a) *General.* School food authorities shall promote activities to involve students and parents in the Program. Such activities may include menu planning, enhancement of the eating environment, Program promotion, and related student-community support activities. School food authorities are encouraged to use the school food service program to teach students about good nutrition practices and to involve the school faculty and the general community in activities to enhance the Program.

(b) *Food Service Management Companies.* School food authorities contracting with a food service management company shall comply with the provisions of 210.16(a) regarding the establishment of an advisory board of parents, teachers and students.

(c) *Residential Child Care Institutions.* Residential child care institutions shall comply with the provisions of this section, to the extent possible.

210.13 *Facilities management.*

(a) *Health Standards.* The school food authority shall ensure that food storage, preparation and service is in accordance with the sanitation and health standards established under State and local law and regulations.

(b) *Storage.* The school food authority shall ensure that the necessary facilities for storage, preparation, and service of food are maintained. Facilities for the handling, storage, and distribution of purchased and donated foods shall be such as to properly safeguard against theft, spoilage and other loss.

210.14 Resource management.

(a) *Nonprofit School Food Service.* School food authorities shall maintain a nonprofit school food service. Revenues received by the nonprofit school food service are to be used only for the operation or improvement of such food service, *except that,* such revenues shall not be used to purchase land or buildings, unless otherwise approved by FNS, or to construct buildings. Expenditures of nonprofit school food service revenues shall be in accordance with the financial management system established by the State agency under 210.19(a) of this part. School food authorities may use facilities, equipment, and person-nel supported with nonprofit school food revenues to support a nonprofit nutrition program for the elderly, including a program funded under the Older Americans Act of 1965 (42 U.S.C. 3001 *et seq.*).

(b) *Net Cash Resources.* The school food authority shall limit its net cash resources to an amount that does not exceed 3 months average expenditures for its nonprofit school food service or such other amount as may be approved by the State agency in accordance with 210.19(a).

(c) *Financial Management System.* The school food authority shall maintain a financial management system in accordance with 210.19(a) of this part. School food authorities shall keep records for the nonprofit school food service cited in paragraph (a) of this section separate from records for any other food service which may be operated by the school food authority.

(d) *Use of Donated Foods.* The school food authority shall enter into an agreement with the distributing agency to receive donated foods as required by Part 250 of this chapter. In addition, the school food authority shall accept and use, in as large quantities as may be efficiently utilized in its nonprofit school food service, such foods as may be offered as a donation by the Department.

210.15 Reporting and recordkeeping.

(a) *Reporting Summary.* Participating school food authorities are required to submit forms and reports to the State agency or the distributing agency, as appropriate, to demonstrate compliance with Program requirements. These reports include, but are not limited to:

(1) A claim for Reimbursement as specified by the State agency in accordance with 210.8;

(2) An application and agreeement for Program operations between the school food authority and the State agency, and a Free and Reduced Price Policy Statement as required under 210.9;

(3) Documentation of corrective action taken for any program deficiency found on any review/audit as required under 210.18(k);

(4) A formal corrective action plan whenever AIMS performance standard violations in excess of error tolerances are disclosed on either a first or second review as specified under 210.18 (i);

(5) A written response to AIMS audit findings under 210.18(k);

(6) A commodity school's preference whether to receive part of its donated food alloca-tion in cash for processing and handling of donated foods as required under 210.19(b);

(7) A written response to audit findings pertaining to the school food authority's operation as required under 210.22; and

(8) Information on civil rights complaints, if any, and their resolution as required under 210.23.

(b) *Recordkeeping Summary.* In order to participate in the Program, a school food authority shall maintain records to demonstrate compliance with Program requirements. These records include but are not limited to:

(1) Documentation of participation data by school in support of the Claim for Reimbursement, as required under 210.8(b);

(2) Production and participation records to demonstrate positive action toward providing one lunch per child per day as required under 210.10(b);

(3) Records of revenues and expenditures to demonstrate that the food service is being operated on a nonprofit basis, as required under 210.14(a) including net cash resources, or the information necessary for the State to compute net cash resources through a review or audit as specified under 210.18(b); and

(4) Currently approved and denied applications for free and reduced price lunches and a description of the verification activities, as required under 7 CFR Part 245.

210.16 *Food service management companies.*

(a) *General.* Any school food authority (including a State agency acting in the capacity of a school food authority) may contract with a food service management company to manage its food service operation in one or more of its schools. However, no school or school food authority may contract with a food service management company to operate an a la carte food service unless the company agrees to offer free, reduced price and paid reimbursable lunches to all eligible children. Any school food authority that employs a food service management company in the operation of its nonprofit school service shall:

(1) Adhere to the procurement standards specified in 210.21 when contracting with the food service management company.

(2) Ensure that the food service operation is in conformance with the school food authority's agreement under the Program;

(3) Monitor the food service operation through periodic on-site visits;

(4) Retain control of the quality, extent, and general nature of its food service, and the prices to be charged the children for meals;

(5) Retain signature authority on the State agency-school food authority agreement, free and reduced price policy statement and claims;

(6) Ensure that all federally donated foods received by the school food authority and made available to the food service management company accrue only to the benefit of the school food authority's nonprofit school food service and are fully utilized therein;

(7) Maintain applicable health certification and assure that all State and local regulations are being met by a food service management company preparing or serving meals at a school food authority facility; and

(8) Establish an advisory board composed of parents, teachers, and students to assist in menu planning.

(b) *Invitation to Bid.* In addition to adhering to the procurement standards under 210.21, school food authorities contracting with food service management companies shall ensure that:

(1) The invitation to bid or request for proposal contains a 21-day cycle menu to be used as a standard for the purpose of basing bids or estimating average cost per meal. If a

school food authority has no capability to prepare a cycle menu, it may, with State agency approval, request that a 21-day cycle menu be developed and submitted by each food service management company which intends to submit a bid or proposal to the school food authority. The food service management company must adhere to the cycle for the first 21 days of meal service. Changes thereafter may be made with the approval of the school food authority.

(2) Any invitation to bid or request for proposal indicate that nonperformance subjects the food service management company to specified sanctions in instances where the food service management company violates or breaches contract terms. The school food authority shall indicate these sanctions in accordance with the procurement provisions stated in 210.21.

(c) *Contracts.* Contracts that permit all income and expenses to accrue to the food service management company and "cost-plus-a-percentage-of-cost" and "cost-plus-a-percentage-of-income" contracts are prohibited. Contracts that provide for fixed fees such as those that provide for management fees established on a per meal basis are allowed. Contractual agreements with food service management companies shall include provisions which ensure that the requirements of this section are met. Such agreements shall also include the following:

(1) The food service management company shall maintain such records as the school food authority will need to support its Claim for Reimbursement under this part, and shall, at a minimum, report claim information to the school food authority promptly at the end of each month. Such records shall be made available to the school food authority, upon request, and shall be retained in accordance with 210.23(c).

(2) The food service management company shall have State or local health certification for any facility outside the school in which it proposes to prepare meals and the food service management company shall maintain this health certification for the duration of the contract.

(3) No payment is to be made for meals that are spoiled or unwholesome at time of delivery, do not meet detailed specifications as developed by the school food authority for each food component specified in 210.10, or do not otherwise meet the requirements of the contract. Specifications shall cover items such as grade, purchase units, style, condition, weight, ingredients, formulations, and delivery time.

(d) *Duration of Contract.* The contract between a school food authority and food service management company shall be of a duration of no longer than 1 year; and options for the yearly renewal of a contract signed after February 16, 1988, may not exceed 4 additional years. All contracts shall include a termination clause whereby either party may cancel for cause with 60-day notification.

Subpart D—Requirements for State Agency Participation

210.17 Matching Federal funds.

(a) *State Revenue Matching.* For each school year, the amount of State revenues appropriated or used specifically by the State for program purposes shall not be less than 30 percent of the funds received by such State under section 4 of the National School Lunch Act during the school year beginning July 1, 1980; *provided that,* the State revenues derived from the operation of such programs and State Revenues expended for salaries and administrative expenses of such programs at the State level are not considered in this computation. However, if the per capita income of any State is less than the per capita income of the United States, the matching requirements so computed shall be decreased by the percentage by which the State per capita income is below the per capita income of the United States.

(b) *Private School Exemption.* No State in which the State agency is prohibited by law from disbursing State appropriated funds to nonpublic schools shall be required to match general cash assistance funds expended for meals served in such schools, or to disburse to such schools any of the State Revenues required to meet the requirements of paragraph (a) of this section. Furthermore, the requirements of this section do not apply to schools in which the Program is administered by a FNSRO.

(c) *Territorial Waiver.* American Samoa and the Commonwealth of the Northern Mariana Islands shall be exempted from the matching requirements of paragraph (a) of this section if their respective matching requirements are under $100,000.

(d) *Applicable Revenues.* The following State revenues, appropriated or used specifically for program purposes, which are expended for any school year shall be eligible for meeting the applicable percentage of the matching requirements prescribed in paragraph (a) of this section for that school year:

(1) State revenues disbursed by the State agency to school food authorities for program purposes, including revenue disbursed to nonprofit private schools where the State administers the program in such schools;

(2) State revenues made available to school food authorities and transferred by the school food authorities to the nonprofit school food service accounts or otherwise expended by the school food authorities in connection with the nonprofit school food service program; and

(3) State revenues used to finance the costs (other than State salaries or other State level administrative costs) of the nonprofit school food service program, i.e.:

(i) Local program supervision;

(ii) Operating the program in participating schools; and

(iii) The intrastate distribution of foods donated under Part 250 of this chapter to schools participating in the program.

(e) *Distribution of Matching Revenues.* All State revenues made available under paragraph (a) of this section are to be disbursed to school food authorities participating in the Program, *except as* provided for under paragraph (b) of this section. Distribution of matching revenues may be made with respect to a class of school food authorities as well as with respect to individual school food authorities.

(f) *Failure to Match.* If, in any school year, a State fails to meet the State revenue matching requirement, as prescribed in paragraph (a) of this section, the general cash assistance funds utilized by the State during that school year shall be subject to recall by and repayment to FNS.

(g) *Reports.* Within 120 days after the end of each school year, each State agency shall submit an Annual Report of Revenues (FNS-13) to FNS. This report identifies the State revenues to be counted toward the State revenue matching requirements specified in paragraph (a) of this section.

(h) *Accounting System.* The State agency shall establish or cause to be established a system whereby all expended State revenues counted in meeting the matching requirements prescribed in paragraph (a) of this section are properly documented and accounted for.

210.18 Monitoring responsibilities.

(a) *General Program Compliance.* Each State agency shall require that school food authorities comply with the applicable provisions of this part. The State agency shall ensure compliance through audits, supervisory assistance reviews, visits to participating schools, or by other means.

(b) *Net Cash Resources.* Each State agency shall monitor through review or audit or by other means, the net cash resources of the nonprofit school food service in each school food authority participating in the Program. In the event that such resources exceed 3 months average expenditures for the school food authority's nonprofit school food service or such other amount as may be approved in accordance with 210.19(a), the State agency may require the school food authority to reduce the price children are charged for meals, improve food quality or take other action designed to improve the nonprofit school food service. In the absence of any such action, the State agency shall make adjustments in the rate of reimbursement under the Program.

(c) *Improved Management.* The State agency shall work with the school food authority toward improving the school food authority's management practices where the State agency has found poor food service management practices leading to decreasing or low student participation and/or poor student acceptance of the Program or of foods served. Poor student acceptance may be indicated by a substantial number of students who routinely and over a period of time:

(1) Do not favorably accept a particular menu item;

(2) Return foods; or

(3) Choose less than all five food items as authorized under 210.10(e).

(d) *Food Service Management Companies.* Each State agency shall annually review each contract between any school food authority and food service management company to ensure compliance with all the provisions and standards set forth in 210.16. Each State agency shall perform an on-site review of each school food authority contracting with a food service management company at least once during each 4-year period. Such reviews shall include an assessment of the school food authority's compliance with 210.16. The State agency may require that all food service management companies that wish to contract for food service with any school food authority in the State must register with the State agency. State agencies shall provide assistance upon request of a school food authority to assure compliance with Program requirements.

(e) *Investigations.* Each State agency shall promptly investigate complaints received or irregularities noted in connection with the operation of the Program, and shall take appropriate action to correct any irregularities. State agencies shall maintain on file evidence of such investigations and actions. FNS and OIG may make investigations at the request of the State agency or where FNS or OIG determines investigations are appropriate.

(f) *Assessment, Improvement and Monitoring System (AIMS).* Each State agency shall perform AIMS reviews, audits or a combination thereof of all school food authorities participating in the Program in accordance with the provisions of this section; or a State agency may develop an alternate monitoring system as specified in paragraph (n) of this section.

(g) *AIMS Definitions.* The following definitions are provided in order to clarify AIMS requirements:

(1) "AIMS audits" means on site evaluations of school food authorities participating in the Program for compliance with AIMS performance standards, by State auditors or State contracted auditors once every 2 years, in accordance with USDA's guide or an audit guide approved by FNS and USDA's OIG.

(2) "AIMS error tolerance level" means the degree of error of an AIMS performance standard as specified in paragraph (i)(4) of this section which, if exceeded in a reviewed school food authority, triggers a second AIMS review in all large school food authorities and in at least 25 percent of those small school food authorities which exceed error tolerance levels on a first AIMS review.

(3) "AIMS performance standards" means the following standards which measure compliance with Program regulations:

(i) Performance Standard 1—Certification—Within the school food authority, each child's application for free and reduced price meals is correctly approved or denied in accordance with the applicable provisions of Part 245.

(ii) Performance Standard 2—Claims—The numbers of free and reduced price meals claimed for reimbursement by each school for any review period are, in each case, less than or equal to the number of children in that school correctly approved for free and reduced price meals, respectively for the review period, times the days of operation for the review period.

(iii) Performance Standard 3—Counting—The *system* used for counting and recording meal totals, by type, claimed for reimbursement at both food authority and school levels yields correct claims.

(iv) Performance Standard 4—Components—Meals claimed for reimbursement within the school food authority contained food items as required by 210.10.

(4) "AIMS reviews" means on-site evaluation, of all school food authorities participating in the Program during each 4-year AIMS review period, by the State agency or State auditors for compliance with the AIMS performance standards and follow-up reviews, as required.

(5) "Corrective action plan" means the written description a school food authority submits to the State agency to explain how and when a program deficiency will be corrected.

(6) "Large school food authority" means, in any State:

(i) All school food authorities that participate in the Program and have enrollments of 40,000 students or more each; and

(ii) The two largest school food authorities that participate in the Program and have enrollments of 2,000 students or more each.

(7) "Small school food authority" means, in any State, a school food authority that participates in the Program and is not a large school food authority.

(h) *Number of Schools Reviewed or Audited Under AIMS.* The number of schools within the school food authority which must be included in a review or audit is dependent upon the total number of schools in the school food authority. The minimum number of schools the State agency shall review or audit is illustrated in Table A-1.

(i) *AIMS Reviews.* States performing AIMS reviews shall monitor compliance with the AIMS performance standards described in paragraph (g) of this section. On the first AIMS

Table A-1

Number of Schools in the School Food Authority	Minimum[a]
1 to 5	1
6 to 10	2
11 to 20	3
21 to 40	4
41 to 60	6
61 to 80	8
81 to 100	10
101 or more	12[b]

[a]Minimum number of schools to be reviewed or audited.
[b]Twelve plus 5 percent of the number of schools over 100.
Fractions shall be rounded to the nearest whole number.

review, the State agency shall review the school food authority for Performance Standards 1-4. On second AIMS reviews, the State agency shall, at a minimum, review the school food authority for the performance standards which exceeded error tolerance in the first review.

(1) *Scope of AIMS reviews.* In reviewing performance standards:

(i) The State agency shall analyze and determine the adequacy of local approval procedures for free and reduced price meals by examining the eligibility determinations made within the school food authority. The State agency shall review the applications for all children for whom application was made attending the reviewed schools, or a statistically valid sample of the applications for such children. The State agency shall also ensure that the system to update the application file is adequate. If the State agency chooses to review a statistically valid sample of applications, the State agency shall ensure that the sample size is large enough so that there is a 95 percent chance that the actual error rate for all applications is not less than 2 percentage points less than the error rate found in the sample (i.e., the lower bound of the one-sided 95 percent confidence interval is no more than 2 percentage points less than the point estimate). In addition, the State agency shall determine the need for a second review and base fiscal action upon the error rate found in the sample.

(ii) The State agency shall ensure that, at a minimum, for each school reviewed, the number of free meals claimed in the school food authority's most recent Claim for Reimbursement does not exceed the number of children correctly approved for free meals for the claim period times the days of operation of that school, as reported to the school food authority for the claim month. The State agency shall apply the same procedure to the claim for reduced price meals.

(iii) The State agency shall ensure that each school reviewed has an adequate system for counting and recording meals served by reimbursement type and that the school food authority properly consolidates meals counts from its schools.

(iv) The State agency shall determine by observation of a representative sample of meals that meals contain food items as required in 210.10.

(2) *Timing of AIMS reviews.* During each 4-year AIMS review period, the first AIMS review of a school food authority shall be completed within the school year in which the review was begun. A second AIMS review, when required, is recommended to be conducted in the same school year as the first review and is required to be conducted no later than December 31 of the school year following the first review.

(3) *Method of selecting school food authorities and schools to review.*

(i) Each school year, the State agency shall use its own criteria to select school food authorities for AIMS review; *provided that* all participating school food authorities are reviewed at least once every 4 years and that school food authorities found on the first review to exceed error tolerance levels are subject to second reviews as specified in paragraph (i)(4) of this section.

(ii) On a first AIMS review of a school food authority, the State agency shall select, to the extent practicable, the required minimum number of schools to review on a proportionate basis from each type of attendance unit (e.g., elementary school, middle school, high school), and shall select schools within attendance unit grouping either randomly or by using State agency criteria which shall be kept on file at the State agency. If using its own criteria, the State agency shall ensure that some of the schools selected are chosen because of the likelihood of problems. On a second AIMS review, the State agency shall choose schools using State agency criteria, which may include random selection. State agency criteria for selecting schools for second AIMS reviews shall also be kept on file. The minimum number of schools to be selected and reviewed during a first or second AIMS review of a school food authority is specified in paragraph (h) of this section.

(4) *Error tolerance for AIMS review.* State agencies shall ensure that corrective action plans are completed by all school food authorities which are found on first reviews to exceed the error tolerance described below. Further, State agencies shall conduct second reviews of: all large school food authorities found to exceed such tolerances on first reviews; and at least 25 percent of small school food authorities found to exceed such tolerance on first reviews. An error tolerance is exceeded when:

(i) For AIMS Performance Standard 1, 10 percent or more (but not less than 10 children) of the children listed on reviewed applications and attending reviewed schools in a school food authority are incorrectly approved or denied for free or reduced price meal benefits; and/or

(ii) For AIMS Performance Standard 3, a number of schools reviewed in a school food authority, as specified in Table A-2 of paragraph (i)(5), claim reimbursement for more free or more reduced price meals, respectively, than the number of children correctly approved for such meals for the test period times the days of operation for the period; and/or

(iii) For AIMS Performance Standard 3, a number of schools reviewed in a school food authority, as specified in Table A-2 of paragraph (i)(5), have an inadequate system for counting and recording meal totals by type claimed for reimbursement, or the school food authority does not use valid procedures for consolidating claims; and/or

(iv) For AIMS Performance Standard 4, 10 percent or more of the total meals observed in a school food authority are missing one or more required food items.

(5) *Performance Standards 2 and 3 tolerances.* Table A-2 indicates the number of schools violating Performance Standards 2 or 3, thus necessitating a corrective action plan in the applicable school food authority and a second review in a large school

Table A-2

Number of Schools Reviewed	Number of Schools[a]
1 to 10	1
11 to 20	2
21 to 30	3
31 to 40	4
41 to 50	5
51 to 60	6
61 to 70	7
71 to 80	8
81 to 90	9
91 to 100	10
101 or more	10[b]

[a]Number of schools violating Performance Standards 2 or 3 respectively, thus necessitating a second review of the school food authority.
[b]10 plus the number identified above for the appropriate increment.

authorities and at least 25 percent of the small school food authorities which exceed error tolerance levels on a first AIMS review.

(6) *Corrective action plans for AIMS reviews.* Corrective action plans are required to address AIMS performance standard deficiencies exceeding the error tolerance levels described in this section. The following procedures shall be followed to develop a corrective action plan:

(i) The State agency shall assist the school food authority in developing a mutually agreed upon corrective action plan.

(ii) The corrective action plan shall identify the corrective actions and timeframes needed to correct the deficiencies found during the review. Corrective action shall include all necessary fiscal actions as described in 210.19(c), including adjusting data to be used in preparing the Claim for Reimbursement.

(iii) The plan shall be written, signed by the proper official of the school food authority, and submitted to and approved by the State agency within 60 days following the exit conference of a review. State agencies may extend this deadline to 90 days. Extensions beyond 90 days may be made, for cause, with written justification to and approval by FNSRO.

(iv) The State agency shall require the school food authority to implement an amended or extended corrective action plan when error tolerance levels are exceeded on a second AIMS review.

(7) *New violations found on a second AIMS review.* If, during the course of a second AIMS review, a performance standard violation is found that has not been noted on a previous AIMS review, the State agency shall institute and document appropriate corrective action. If the violation exceeds the error tolerance level, the State agency shall require a corrective action plan and the completion of corrective action. The State agency shall

take fiscal action as described in 210.19(c) of this part for any degree of violation of AIMS Performance Standards 2, 3, and 4.

(j) *AIMS Audits*. Audits by State agency, State or State-contracted auditors may be used as an alternative to AIMS reviews. If the State agency chooses this option, the audit must ensure that the four performance standards listed under paragraph (g) of this section are being complied with by the audited school food authority. This includes performing all activities described in paragraph (i)(1) of this section. Additionally, a State using AIMS audits in place of AIMS reviews shall:

(1) Audit school food authorities once every 2 years;

(2) Take fiscal action in accordance with 210.19 (c);

(3) Have a documented system for achieving corrective action;

(4) Select schools within a school food authority based upon generally accepted audit principles; and

(5) Use a State audit guide approved by FNS. A State agency shall submit its guide to FNSRO by February 1 of each year; except that portions of the guide which do not change annually need not be resubmitted. State agencies shall provide the title of the sections that remain unchanged, as well as the year of the last guide in which the sections were submitted.

(k) *AIMS Exit Conference, Notification and Corrective Action*. The State agency and the school food authority shall hold an exit conference at the close of an AIMS review or audit to discuss the deficiencies observed, the extent of the deficiencies and the corrective action needed to correct the deficiencies. If a corrective action plan is required as described in paragraph (i) (6) of this section, it shall be discussed during the exit conference. After every AIMS review or audit, the State shall provide written notification of the review or audit findings to the school food authority's superintendent or authorized representative who signed the State agency/school food authority agreement or who is otherwise authorized to represent the superintendent. The State shall require that the school food authority take and document corrective action for any program deficiency found on any review or audit. Corrective action may include training, assistance, recalculation of data to ensure the correctness of any claim that the school food authority is preparing at the time of the review, or other actions.

(l) *AIMS Reporting*. Each State agency shall report to FNSRO:

(1) The name of any school food authority which exceeds an error tolerance level on a second AIMS review in any review period and the type and extent of the regulatory violations; and

(2) Beginning March 1, 1989, the results of AIMS reviews/audits by March 1 of each school year, on a form designated by FNS. In such annual reports, the State agency shall include the results of all AIMS review/audits conducted in the preceding school year and any consequent second AIMS reviews performed in the preceding school year or by December 31 of the current school year.

(m) *AIMS Recordkeeping*. Each State agency shall keep records which document the details of all AIMS reviews or audits and demonstrate the degree of compliance with AIMS Performance Standards. AIMS records shall be kept on file by the State agency for a minimum of 3 years after the end of the school year in which the review or audit was conducted or after school year in which problems have been resolved, whichever is later.

Such records shall include documentation of AIMS first reviews and any consequent second reviews. When necessary, the records must include a corrective action plan as described in this section. Additionally, the State agency must have on file:

(1) Criteria for selecting schools on first and second reviews, if the selection is not random;

(2) Its system for selecting small school food authorities for second reviews; and

(3) Documentation demonstrating compliance with the statistical sampling requirements specified in 210.18 (i).

(n) *State Alternate to AIMS.* Any State developed monitoring system shall:

(1) Be equivalent to AIMS in scope;

(2) Monitor compliance with AIMS Performance Standards 1-4;

(3) Include on-site visits of all school food authorities on a cyclical basis;

(4) Require that corrective action be taken and documented for any Program deficiency found;

(5) Provide for fiscal action and set forth the State agency's criteria for taking such action;

(6) Provide for the maintenance of a detailed description of the system and records of all monitoring visits and activities which demonstrate the degree of compliance with AIMS performance standards, corrective action needed and taken, and fiscal action taken;

(7) Receive approval by the appropriate FNSRO prior to implementation; and

(8) Beginning March 1, 1989, submit annual reports of the results of such alternate State monitoring reviews to FNSRO on a form designated by FNS.

210.19 Additional responsibilities

(a) *General Program Management.* Each State agency shall provide an adequate number of consultative, technical and managerial personnel to administer programs and monitor performance in complying with all program requirements. Such personnel shall, at a minimum, visit participating schools to monitor for compliance with Program regulations and instructions, the Department's nondiscrimination regulations (7 CFR Parts 15, 15a and 15b), and the Department's Uniform Federal Assistance Regulations (7 CFR Part 3015). Each State agency shall establish a financial management system under which school food authorities shall account for all revenues and expenditures of their nonprofit school food service. The system shall prescribe the allowability of nonprofit school food service expenditures in accordance with this part, and, as applicable 7 CFR Part 3015. The system shall permit determination of school food service net cash resources, and shall include any criteria for approval of net cash resources in excess of 3 months' average expenditures.

(b) *Commodity Distribution Information.* The State agency shall periodically assess school needs for donated foods under 7 CFR Part 250, notify the distributing agency of the schools' commodity needs, and recommend appropriate variations in rate of distribution. In assessing the commodity needs of schools, usage history and existing donated food inventories should be considered. As early as practicable each school year, but later than September 1, the State agency shall forward to the distributing agency and FNSRO an estimate of the average daily number of Program lunches to be served by school food authorities; an estimate of the average daily number of lunches to be served by commodity schools; and the amount of any cash payments in lieu of commodities for donated food processing and handling expenses to be received by or on behalf of commodity schools in accordance with 240.5 of this chapter. That State agency shall promptly revise the information required by this paragraph to reflect additions or deletions of eligible schools and provide any necessary adjustment in the number of lunches served.

(c) *Fiscal Action.* Fiscal action includes, but is not limited to, the recovery of overpayments through direct assessment or offset of future claims; disallowance of overclaims as reflected in unpaid Claims for Reimbursement; and correction of records to ensure that unfiled Claims for Reimbursement are corrected when filed. State agencies are responsible for ensuring program integrity at the school food authority level. As such, they shall take fiscal action against school food authorities for Claims for Reimbursement that are not properly payable under this part. In taking fiscal action, State agencies shall use their own procedures, within the constraints of this part, and shall maintain all records pertaining to action taken under this section. The State shall determine the extent of fiscal action based on the severity and longevity of the problems. The State agency may refer to FNS for assistance in making a claims determination under this paragraph.

(1) *AIMS.* When a State agency chooses to conduct AIMS reviews, as described in 210.18 (i), fiscal action may be taken on a first review; *except* fiscal action shall be taken when, under Performance Standard 3, the number of meals claimed for school food authority reimbursement has been incorrectly aggregated from individual school reports so that an excessive number of meals has been claimed. State agencies shall take fiscal action on the second review for any degree of violation of AIMS Performance Standards 2, 3 and 4. When a State agency chooses to conduct AIMS audits, as described in 210.18 (j), fiscal action shall be assessed for any degree of violation of Performance Standards 2, 3 and 4. When a State agency develops its own compliance monitoring system in accordance with 210.18 (n), fiscal action shall be taken in accordance with the criteria established under that system. The criteria shall be consistent in principle with the fiscal action requirements for AIMS reviews and audits as set forth in this section.

(2) *Failure to collect.* If a State agency fails to disallow a claim or recover an overpayment from a school food authority, as described in this section, FNS will notify the State agency that a claim may be assessed against the State agency. In all such cases, the State agency shall have full opportunity to submit evidence concerning overpayment. If after considering all available information, FNS determines that a claim is warranted, FNS will assess a claim in the amount of such overpayment against the State agency. If the State agency fails to pay any such demand for funds promptly, FNS will reduce the State agency's Letter of Credit by the sum due in accordance with FNS' existing offset procedures for Letter of Credit. In such event, the State agency shall provide the funds necessary to maintain Program operations at the level of earnings from a source other than the Program.

(3) *Interest charge.* If an agreement cannot be reached with the State agency for payment of its debts or for offset of debts on its current Letter of Credit, interest will be charged against the State agency from the date the demand letter was sent, at the rate established by the Secretary of Treasury.

(4) *Use of recovered payment.* The amounts recovered by the State agency from school food authorities may be utilized during the fiscal year for which the funds were initially available, first, to make payments to school food authorities for the purposes of the Program; and second, to repay any State funds expended in the reimbursement of claims

under the Program and not otherwise repaid. Any amounts recovered which are not so utilized shall be returned to FNS in accordance with the requirements of this part.

(5) *Exception.* In the event that the State agency finds, during a State review or State audit, that a school food authority is failing to meet the quantities for each food item required under the meal pattern in 210.10, the State agency need not disallow payment or collect an overpayment arising out of such failure, if the State agency takes such other action as, in its opinion, will have a corrective effect.

(6) *Claims adjustment.* FNS will have the authority to determine the amount of, to settle, and to adjust any claim arising under the Program, and to compromise or deny such claim or any part thereof. FNS will also have the authority to waive such claims if FNS determines that to do so would serve the purposes of the Program. This provision shall not diminish the authority of the Attorney General of the United States under section 516 of Title 28, U.S. Code, to conduct litigation on behalf of the United States.

(d) *Management Evaluations.* Each State agency shall provide FNS with full opportunity to conduct management evaluations of all State agency Program operations and shall provide OIG with full opportunity to conduct audits of all State agency Program operations. Each State agency shall make available its records, including records of the receipt and disbursement of funds under the Program and records of any claim compromised in accordance with paragraph (d)(1) of this section, upon a reasonable request by FNS, OIG, or the Comptroller General of the United States. FNS and OIG retain the right to visit schools and OIG also has the right to make audits of the records and operations of any school.

(1) *Disregard overpayment.* In conducting management evaluations or audits for any fiscal year, the State agency, FNS, or OIG may disregard any overpayment which does not exceed $35 or, in the case of State agency administered programs, does not exceed the amount established under State law, regulations, or procedure as a minimum amount for which claim will be made for State losses. However, no overpayment is to be disregarded where there are unpaid claims of the same fiscal year from which the overpayment can be deducted or there is substantial evidence of violations of criminal law or civil fraud statutes.

(2) *AIMS.* As a part of its management evaluation of a State agency, FNS will evaluate the State's progress in effectively meeting the AIMS requirements consistent with administrative responsibilities placed upon the State agency by this part.

(e) *Additional Requirements.* Nothing contained in this part shall prevent a State agency from imposing additional requirements for participation in the Program which are not inconsistent with the provisions of this part.

210.20 Reporting and recordkeeping

(a) *Reporting Summary.* Participating State agencies shall submit forms and reports to FNS to demonstrate compliance with Program requirements. The reports include but are not limited to:

(1) Requests for cash to make reimbursement payments to school food authorities as required under 210.5(a);

(2) Information on the amounts of Federal Program funds expended and obligated to date (SF-269) as required under 210.5(d);

(3) Statewide totals on Program participation (FNS-10) as required under 210.5(d);

(4) Information on State funds provided by the State to meet the State matching requirements (FNS-13) specified under 210.17 (g);

(5) Names of school food authorities found in violation of AIMS performance standards on AIMS second reviews, together with information on the type and extent of violations, as required under 210.18(1);

(6) Result of AIMS reviews/audits as required under 210.18(1); and

(7) Results of the commodity preference survey and recommendations for commodity purchases as required under 210.27(d).

(b) *Recordkeeping Summary.* Participating State agencies are required to maintain records to demonstrate compliance with Program requirements. The records include but are not limited to:

(1) Accounting records and source documents to control the receipt, custody and disbursement of Federal Program funds as required under 210.5(a);

(2) Documentation supporting all school food authority claims paid by the State agency as required under 210.5(d);

(3) Documentation to support the amount the State agency reported having used for State revenue matching as required under 210.17(h);

(4) Records supporting the State agency's review of net cash resources as required under 210.18(b);

(5) Reports on the results of investigations of complaints received or irregularities noted in connection with Program operations as required under 210.18(e);

(6) Confirmation of a State agency's approval of a school food authority's AIMS corrective action plan as required under 210.18(i) and records of all AIMS reviews and audits, including records of action taken to correct program deficiencies as required under 210.18(m);

(7) State agency criteria, for selecting schools for AIMS reviews and small school food authorities for AIMS second reviews as required under 210.18(m);

(8) Documentation of action taken to disallow improper claims submitted by school food authorities, as required by 210.19(c) and as determined through claims processing, resulting from actions such as AIMS reviews, AIMS audits, and USDA audits;

(9) Records of USDA audit findings, State agency's and school food authorities' responses to them and of corrective action taken as required by 210.22(a);

(10) Records pertaining to civil rights responsibilities as defined under 210.23(b); and

(11) Records pertaining to the annual food preference survey of school food authorities as required by 210.27(d).

Subpart E—State Agency and School Food Authority Responsibilities

210.21 Procurement.

(a) *General.* State agencies and school food authorities shall comply with the requirements of 7 CFR Part 3015 concerning the procurement of supplies, food, equipment and other services with Program funds. These requirements ensure that such materials and services are obtained for the Program efficiently and economically and in compliance with applicable laws and executive orders.

(b) *Contractual Responsibilities.* The standards contained in CFR Part 3015 do not relieve the State agency or school food authority of any contractual responsibilities under its contracts. The State agency or school food authority is the responsible authority, without recourse to FNS, regarding the settlement and satisfaction of all contractual and administrative issues arising out of procurements entered into in connection with the Program. This includes, but is not limited to source evaluation, protests, disputes, claims, or other matters of a contractual nature. Matters concerning violation of law are to be referred to the local, State, or Federal authority that has proper jurisdiction.

(c) *Procurement Procedure.* The State agency or school food authority may use its own procurement procedures which reflect applicable State and local laws and regulations *provided that* procurements made with Program funds adhere to the standards set forth in 7 CFR Part 3015.

210.22 Audits.

(a) *General.* State agencies and school food authorities shall comply with the requirements of 7 CFR Part 3015 concerning the audit requirements for recipients and subrecipients of the Department's financial assistance.

(b) *Audit Procedure.* These requirements call for organization-wide financial and compliance audits to ascertain whether financial operations are conducted properly; financial statements are presented fairly; recipients and subrecipients comply with the laws and regulations that affect the expenditures of Federal funds; recipients and subrecipients have established procedures to meet the objectives of federally assisted programs; and recipients and subrecipients are providing accurate and reliable information concerning grant funds. States and school food authorities shall use their own procedures to arrange for and prescribe the scope of independent audits, provided that such audits comply with the requirements set forth in 7 CFR Part 3015.

210.23 Other responsibilities.

(a) *Free and Reduced Price Lunches.* State agencies and school food authorities shall ensure that lunches are made available free or at a reduced price to all children who are determined by the school food authority to be eligible for such benefits. The determination of a child's eligibility for free or reduced price lunches is to be made in accordance with 7 CFR Part 245.

(b) *Civil Rights.* In the operation of the Program, no child shall be denied benefits or be otherwise discriminated against because of race, color, national origin, age, sex, or handicap. State agencies and school food authorities shall comply with the requirements of: Title VI of the Civil Rights Act of 1964; Title IX of the Education Amendments of 1972; Section 504 of the Rehabilitation Act of 1973; the Age Discrimination Act of 1975; Department of Agriculture regulations on nondiscrimination (7 CFR Parts 15, 15a, and 15b); and FNS Instruction 113-6.

(c) *Retention of Records.* State agencies and school food authorities may retain necessary records in their original form or on microfilm. State agency records shall be retained for a period of 3 years after the date of submission of the final Financial Status Report for the fiscal year. School food authority records shall be retained for a period of 3 years after submission of the final Claim for Reimbursement of the fiscal year. In either case, if audit findings have not been resolved, the records shall be retained beyond the 3-year period as long as required for the resolution of the issues raised by the audit.

Subpart F—Additional Provisions

210.24 Suspension, termination and grant closeout procedures.

Whenever it is determined that a State agency has materially failed to comply with the provisions of this part, or with FNS guidelines and instructions, FNS may suspend or terminate the Program in whole, or in part, or take any other action as may be available and appropriate. A State agency may also terminate the Program by mutual agreement with FNS. FNS and the State agency shall comply with the provisions of the Department's Uniform Federal Assistance Regulations, 7 CFR Part 3015, Subpart N concerning grant suspension, termination and closeout procedures. Furthermore, the State agency shall apply these provisions to suspension or termination of the Program in school food authorities.

210.25 Penalties.

Whoever embezzles, willfully misapplies, steals, or obtains by fraud any funds, assets, or property provided under this part whether received directly or indirectly from the Department, shall if such funds, assets, or property are of a value of $100 or more, be fined no more than $10,000 or imprisoned not more than 5 years or both; or if such funds, assets, or property are of a value of less than $100, be fined not more than $1,000 or imprisoned not more than 1 year or both. Whoever receives, conceals, or retains for personal use or gain, funds, assets, or property provided under this part, whether received directly or indirectly from the Department, knowing such funds, assets, or property have been embezzled, willfully misapplied, stolen, or obtained by fraud, shall be subject to the same penalties.

210.26 Educational prohibitions.

In carrying out the provisions of the Act, neither the Department nor the State agency shall impose any requirements with respect to teaching personnel, curriculum, instruction, methods of instruction, or materials of instruction in any school as a condition for participation in the Program.

210.27 State Food Distribution Advisory Council.

(a) *Council Composition.* Each State educational agency, in cooperation with the State distributing agency, shall establish a State Food Distribution (SFD) Advisory Council which is composed of at least five representatives, excluding ex officio representatives, of schools which participate in the Program in the State. The State should make every effort to appoint individuals who represent large urban public schools; small rural public schools; residential child care institutions; private schools; parent teacher organizations; students from junior or senior high schools; nutritionists; school administrators; and teachers. These representatives shall be appointed for not more than 3 years.

(b) *Council Leadership.* The Chairman and Vice Chairman of the SFD Advisory Council shall be elected by members of the Council. The Chief State School Officer, or designee, shall be an ex officio member of SFD Advisory Council acting in an advisory capacity and a non-voting member. The Chief Officer of the State distributing agency which distributes USDA donated foods to schools within the State, or designee will be an ex officio member of the SFD Advisory Council also acting in an advisory capacity and as a non-voting member. If the State educational agency and the State distributing agency are the same entity within the State, the ex officio member of the SFD Advisory Council shall be the Chief Food Distribution Officer of the State educational agency, or designee.

(c) *Council Timeframe.* The Council shall meet at least once a year and shall report to the State educational agency and State distributing agency, if it is a different entity, no later than March 30 of each year, recommendations concerning the manner of selection and distribution of commodity assistance for the next school year. The State educational agency shall inform FNSRO of the Council's recommendations no later than April 30 of each year.

(d) *Council Responsibilities.* Major responsibilities of the Council include providing the State educational and distributing agencies with information concerning the most desired foods and the least desired foods. This information shall be obtained in a survey of school food authorities within the State. The Council shall also advise the State educational and distributing agencies on the types and amounts of available donated food items to order, the preferred available package size, and donated foods school food authorities would like processed and desired end products. The Council may also advise the State educational and distributing agency on intra State distribution systems, delivery schedules, and State food distribution program operations. Recommendations for the Department regarding national purchasing practices, changes in donated food specifications and packaging improvements may also be included in the report.

(e) *State Responsibilities.* In reporting the Council's recommendations to FNSRO, the State educational agency shall include the number of school food authorities providing the required information to the Council; the average daily number of lunches served by schools in these school food authorities during April of the previous year; and the average daily number of lunches served by all food authorities within the State during April of the previous year.

(f) *State Recordkeeping.* The State educational agency shall maintain records concerning the survey of school food authorities including, at a minimum, a description of survey methods and a copy of the format used to obtain food preferences; the name and address of each school food authority included in the survey; and a record of the data obtained from each school food authority.

(g) *Expenses.* The State educational agency may make payment for justified expenses incurred for or by the SFD Advisory Council from State Administrative Expense funds. In instances when State Administrative Expense funds are used, payments shall be made in accordance with Part 235 of this chapter. State agencies which are the same entity as the State distributing agency may also use food distribution assessment funds as provided for in 250.6(i) and (j) of this chapter. Members of the SFD Advisory Council shall serve without compensation. The State educational agency shall provide compensation for necessary travel and subsistence expenses incurred by Council members in the performance of Council duties. Parent and student participant members, in addition to necessary travel and subsistence expenses, shall be compensated for personal expenses related to participation on the Council, such as child care expenses and lost wages during scheduled Council meetings. The State educational agency shall establish a system whereby expenses are paid in advance for any member who indicates that they cannot financially afford to meet any of the allowed expenses. In instances where members can meet these expenses, a reimbursement shall be provided in a timely manner.

Appendix B

Excerpts from the Child Nutrition Act of 1966

Declaration of Purpose

SEC. 2. [(42 U.S.C. 1771)] In recognition of the demonstrated relationship between food and good nutrition and the capacity of children to develop and learn, based on the years of cumulative successful experience under the national school lunch program with its significant contributions in the field of applied nutrition research, it is hereby declared to be the policy of Congress that these efforts shall be extended, expanded, and strengthened under the authority of the Secretary of Agriculture as a measure to safeguard the health and well-being of the Nation's children, and to encourage the domestic consumption of agricultural and other foods, by assisting States, through grants-in-aid and other means, to meet more effectively the nutritional needs of our children.

Special Milk Program Authorization

SEC. 3. (a)(1) There is hereby authorized to be appropriated for the fiscal year ending June 30, 1970, and for each succeeding fiscal year such sums as may be necessary to enable the Secretary of Agriculture, under such rules and regulations as he may deem in the public interest, to encourage consumption of fluid milk by children in the United States in (A) nonprofit schools of high school grade and under, except as provided in paragraph (2), which do not participate in a meal service program authorized under this Act or the National School Lunch Act and (B) nonprofit nursery schools, child-care centers, settlement houses, summer camps, and similar nonprofit institutions devoted to the care and training of children, which do not participate in a meal service program authorized under this Act or the National School Lunch Act.

(2) The limitation imposed under paragraph (1)(A) for participation of nonprofit schools in the special milk program shall not apply to split-session kindergarten programs conducted in schools in which children do not have access to the meal service program

Public Law 89-642 as amended through July 1, 1989.

operating in schools the children attend as authorized under this Act or the National School Lunch Act.

(3) For the purposes of this section "United States" means the fifty States, Guam, the Commonwealth of Puerto Rico, the Virgin Islands, American Samoa, the Trust Territory of the Pacific Islands, and the District of Columbia.

(4) The Secretary shall administer the special milk program provided for by this section to the maximum extent practicable in the same manner as he administered the special milk program provided for by Public Law 89-642, as amended, during the fiscal year ending June 30, 1969.

(5) Any school or nonprofit child care institution which does not participate in a meal service program authorized under this Act or the National School Lunch Act shall receive the special milk program upon their request.

(6) Children who qualify for free lunches under guidelines established by the Secretary shall, at the option of the school involved (or of the local educational agency involved in the case of a public school), be eligible for free milk upon their request.

(7) For the fiscal year ending June 30, 1975, and for subsequent school years, the minimum rate of reimbursement for a half-pint of milk served in schools and other eligible institutions shall not be less than 5 cents per half-pint served to eligible children, and such minimum rate of reimbursement shall be adjusted on an annual basis each school year to reflect changes in the Producer Price Index for Fresh Processed Milk published by the Bureau of Labor Statistics of the Department of Labor.

(8) Such adjustment shall be computed to the nearest one-fourth cent.

(9) Notwithstanding any other provision of this section, in no event shall the minimum rate of reimbursement exceed the cost to the school or institution of milk served to children.

(b) Commodity only schools shall not be eligible to participate in the special milk program under this section. For the purposes of the preceding sentence, the term "commodity only schools" means schools that do not participate in the school lunch program under the National School Lunch Act, but which receive commodities made available by the Secretary for use by such schools in nonprofit lunch programs.

School Breakfast Program Authorization

SEC. 4. (a) There is hereby authorized to be appropriated such sums as are necessary to enable the Secretary to carry out a program to assist the States and the Department of Defense through grants-in-aid and other means to initiate, maintain, or expand nonprofit breakfast programs in all schools which make application for assistance and agree to carry out a nonprofit breakfast program in accordance with this Act. Appropriations and expenditures for this Act shall be considered Health and Human Services functions for budget purposes rather than functions of Agriculture.

Apportionment to States

(b)(1)(A) The Secretary shall make breakfast assistance payments to each State educational agency each fiscal year, at such times as the Secretary may determine, from the sums appropriated for such purpose, in an amount equal to the product obtained by multiplying—

(i) the number of breakfasts served during such fiscal year to children in schools in such States which participate in the school breakfast program under agreements with such State educational agency; by

(ii) the national average breakfast payment for free breakfasts, for reduced-price breakfasts, or for breakfasts served to children not eligible for free or reduced-price meals, as appropriate, as prescribed in clause (B) of this paragraph.

(B) The national average payment for each free breakfast shall be 57 cents (as adjusted pursuant to section 11(a) of the National School Lunch Act). The national average payment for each reduced-price breakfast shall be one-half of the national average payment for each free breakfast, adjusted to the nearest one-fourth cent, except that in no case shall the difference between the amount of the national average payment for a free breakfast and the national average payment for a reduced-price breakfast exceed 30 cents. The national average payment for each breakfast served to a child not eligible for free or reduced-price meals shall be 8.25 cents (as adjusted pursuant to section 11(a) of the National School Lunch Act).

(C) No school which receives breakfast assistant payments under this section may charge a price of more than 30 cents for a reduced-price breakfast.

(D) No breakfast assistance payment may be made under this subsection for any breakfast served by a school unless such breakfast consists of a combination of foods which meet the minimum nutritional requirements prescribed by the Secretary under subsection (e) of this section.

(2)(A) The Secretary shall make additional payments for breakfasts served to children qualifying for a free or reduced-price meal at schools that are in severe need.

(B) The maximum payment for each such free breakfast shall be the higher of—

(i) the national average payment established by the Secretary for free breakfasts plus 10 cents, or

(ii) 45 cents, which shall be adjusted on an annual basis each July 1 to the nearest one-fourth cent in accordance with changes in the series for food away from home of the Consumer Price Index published by the Bureau of Labor Statistics of the Department of Labor for the most recent twelve-month period for which such data are available, except that the initial such adjustment shall be made on January 1, 1978, and shall reflect the change in the series of food away from home during the period November 1, 1976, to October 31, 1977.

(C) The maximum payment for each such reduced-price breakfast shall be 30 cents less than the maximum payment for each free breakfast as determined under clause (B) of this paragraph.

(3) The Secretary shall increase by *6 cents** the annually adjusted payment for each breakfast served under this Act and section 17 of the National School Lunch Act. These funds shall be used to assist States, to the extent feasible, in improving the nutritional quality of the breakfasts.

---

*Became effective on July 1, 1989.

(4) Notwithstanding any other provision of law, whenever stocks of agricultural commodities are acquired by the Secretary or the Commodity Credit Corporation and are not likely to be sold by the Secretary or the Commodity Credit Corporation or otherwise used in programs of commodity sale or distribution, the Secretary shall make such commodities available to school food authorities and eligible institutions serving breakfasts under this Act in a quantity equal in value to not less than 3 cents for each breakfast served under this Act and section 17 of the National School Lunch Act.

(5) Expenditures of funds from State and local sources for the maintenance of the breakfast program shall not be diminished as a result of funds or commodities received under paragraph (3) or (4).

State Disbursement to Schools

(c) Funds apportioned and paid to any State for the purpose of this section shall be disbursed by the State educational agency to schools selected by the State educational agency to assist such schools in operating a breakfast program and for the purpose of subsection (d). Disbursement to schools shall be made at such rates per meal or on such other basis as the Secretary shall prescribe. In selecting schools for participation, the State educational agency shall, to the extent practicable, give first consideration to those schools drawing attendance from areas in which poor economic conditions exist, to those schools in which a substantial proportion of the children enrolled must travel long distances daily, and to those schools in which there is a special need for improving the nutrition and dietary practices of children of working mothers and children from low-income families. Breakfast assistance disbursements to schools under this section may be made in advance or by way of reimbursement in accordance with procedures prescribed by the Secretary.

(Severe Need Assistance)

(d)(1) Each State educational agency shall provide additional assistance to schools in severe need, which shall include only—

(A) those schools in which the service of breakfasts is required pursuant to State law; and

(B) those schools (having a breakfast program or desiring to initiate a breakfast program) in which, during the most recent second preceding school year for which lunches were served, 40 percent or more of the lunches served to students at the school were served free or at a reduced-price, and in which the rate per meal established by the Secretary is insufficient to cover the costs of the breakfast program. The provision of eligibility specified in clause (A) of this paragraph shall terminate effective July 1, 1983, for schools in States where the State legislatures meet annually and shall terminate effective July 1, 1984, for schools in States where the State legislatures meet biennially.

(2) A school, upon the submission of appropriate documentation about the need circumstances in that school and the school's eligibility for additional assistance, shall be entitled to receive 100 percent of the operating costs of the breakfast program, including

the costs of obtaining, preparing, and serving food, or the meal reimbursement rate specified in paragraph (2) of section 4(b) of this Act, whichever is less.

Nutritional and Other Program Requirements

(e)(1) Breakfasts served by schools participating in the school breakfast program under this section shall consist of a combination of foods and shall meet minimum nutritional requirements prescribed by the Secretary on the basis of tested nutritional research. Such breakfasts shall be served free or at a reduced price to children in school under the same terms and conditions as are set forth with respect to the service of lunches free or at a reduced price in section 9 of the National School Lunch Act.

(2) At the option of a local school food authority, a student in a school under the authority that participates in the school breakfast program under this Act may be allowed to refuse not more than one item of a breakfast that the student does not intend to consume. A refusal of an offered food item shall not affect the full charge to the student for a breakfast meeting the requirements of this section or the amount of payments made under this Act to a school for the breakfast.

(Expansion of Program)

(f) As a national nutrition and health policy, it is the purpose and intent of the Congress that the school breakfast program be made available in all schools where it is needed to provide adequate nutrition for children in attendance. The Secretary is hereby directed, in cooperation with State educational agencies, to carry out a program of information in furtherance of this policy. Within 4 months after the enactment of this subsection [enacted on October 7, 1975], the Secretary shall report to the committees of jurisdiction in the Congress his plans and those of the cooperating State agencies to bring about the needed expansion in the school breakfast program.

State Administrative Expenses

SEC. 7. (a)(1) Each fiscal year, the Secretary shall make available to the States for their administrative costs an amount equal to not less than 1½ percent of the Federal funds expended under sections 4, 11, and 17 of the National School Lunch Act and sections 3 and 4 of this Act during the second preceding fiscal year. The Secretary shall allocate the funds so provided in accordance with paragraphs (2), (3), and (4) of this subsection. There are hereby authorized to be appropriated such sums as may be necessary to carry out the purposes of this section.

(2) The Secretary shall allocate to each State for administrative costs incurred in any fiscal year in connection with the programs authorized under the National School Lunch Act or under this Act, except for the programs authorized under section 13 or 17 of the National School Lunch Act or under section 17 of this Act, an amount equal to not less than 1 percent and not more than 1½ percent of the funds expended by each State under sections 4 and 11 of the National School Lunch Act and sections 3 and 4 of this Act during the second preceding fiscal year. In no case shall the grant available to any State under this

subsection be less than the amount such State was allocated in the fiscal year ending September 30, 1981, or $100,000, whichever is larger.

(3) The Secretary shall allocate to each State for its administrative costs incurred under the program authorized by section 17 of the National School Lunch Act in any fiscal year an amount, based upon funds expended under that program in the second preceding fiscal year, equal to (A) 20 percent of the first $50,000, (B) 10 percent of the next $100,000, (C) 5 percent of the next $250,000, and (D) 2½ percent of any remaining funds. The Secretary may adjust any State's allocation to reflect changes in the size of its program.

(4) The remaining funds appropriated under this section shall be allocated among the States by the Secretary in amounts the Secretary determines necessary for the improvement in the States of the administration of the programs authorized under the National School Lunch Act and this Act, except for section 17 of this Act, including, but not limited to, improved program integrity and the quality of meals served to children.

(5) Funds available to States under this subsection and under section 13(k)(1) of the National School Lunch Act shall be used for the costs of administration of the programs for which the allocations are made, except that States may transfer up to 10 percent of any of the amounts allocated among such programs.

(6) Where the Secretary is responsible for the administration of programs under this Act or the National School Lunch Act, the amount of funds that would be allocated to the State agency under this section and under section 13(k)(1) of the National School Lunch Act shall be retained by the Secretary for the Secretary's use in the administration of such programs.

(b) Funds paid to a State under subsection (a) of this section may be used to pay salaries, including employee benefits and travel expenses, for administrative and supervisory personnel; for support services; for office equipment; and for staff development.

(c) If any State agency agrees to assume responsibility for the administration of food service programs in nonprofit private schools or child care institutions that were previously administered by the Secretary, an appropriate adjustment shall be made in the administrative funds paid under this section to the State not later than the succeeding fiscal year.

(d) Notwithstanding any other provision of law, funds made available to each State under this section shall remain available for obligation and expenditure by that State during the fiscal year immediately following the fiscal year for which such funds were made available. For each fiscal year the Secretary shall establish a date by which each State shall submit to the Secretary a plan for the disbursement of funds provided under this section for each such year, and the Secretary shall reallocate any unused funds, as evidenced by such plans, to other States as the Secretary considers appropriate.

(e) The State may use a portion of the funds available under this section to assist in the administration of the commodity distribution program.

(f) Each State shall submit to the Secretary for approval by October 1 of each year an annual plan for the use of State administrative expense funds, including a staff formula for State personnel, system level supervisory and operating personnel, and school level personnel.

(g) Payments of funds under this section shall be made only to States that agree to maintain a level of funding out of State revenues, for administrative costs in connection with programs under this Act (except section 17 of this Act) and the National School Lunch Act (except section 13 of that Act), not less than the amount expended or obligated in fiscal year 1977.

(h) For the fiscal years beginning October 1, 1977, and ending September 30, 1989, there are hereby authorized to be appropriated such sums as may be necessary for the purposes of this section.

Utilization of Foods

SEC. 8. Each school participating under section 4 of this Act shall, insofar as practicable, utilize in its program foods designated from time to time by the Secretary as being in abundance, either nationally or in the school area, or foods donated by the Secretary. Foods available under section 416 of the Agricultural Act of 1949, as amended, or purchased under section 32 of the Act of August 24, 1935, as amended, or section 709 of the Food and Agriculture Act of 1965, may be donated by the Secretary to schools, in accordance with the needs as determined by local school authorities, for utilization in their feeding programs under this Act.

Nonprofit Programs

SEC. 9. The food and milk service programs in schools and nonprofit institutions receiving assistance under this Act shall be conducted on a nonprofit basis.

Regulations

SEC. 10. The Secretary shall prescribe such regulations as he may deem necessary to carry out this Act and the National School Lunch Act including regulations relating to the service of food in participating schools and service institutions in competition with the programs authorized under this Act and the National School Lunch Act. Such regulations shall not prohibit the sale of competitive foods approved by the Secretary in food service facilities or areas during the time of service of food under this Act or the National School Lunch Act if the proceeds from the sales of such foods will inure to the benefit of the schools or of organizations of students approved by the schools. In such regulations the Secretary may provide for the transfer of funds by any State between the programs authorized under this Act and the National School Lunch Act on the basis of an approved State plan of operation for the use of the funds and may provide for the reserve of up to 1 per centum of the funds available for apportionment to any State to carry out special developmental projects.

Preschool Programs

SEC. 12. The Secretary may extend the benefits of all school feeding programs conducted and supervised by the Department of Agriculture to include preschool programs operated as part of the school system.

Accounts and Records

SEC. 16. (a) States, State educational agencies, schools, and nonprofit institutions participating in programs under this Act shall keep such accounts and records as may be necessary to enable the Secretary to determine whether there has been compliance with this Act and the regulations hereunder. Such accounts and records shall at all times be available for inspection and audit by representatives of the Secretary and shall be preserved for such period of time, not in excess of three years, as the Secretary determines is necessary.

(b) With regard to any claim arising under this Act or under the National School Lunch Act, the Secretary shall have the authority to determine the amount of, to settle and to adjust any such claim, and to compromise or deny such claim or any part thereof. The Secretary shall also have the authority to waive such claims if the Secretary determines that to do so would serve the purposes of either such Act. Nothing contained in this subsection shall be construed to diminish the authority of the Attorney General of the United States under section 516 of title 28, United States Code, to conduct litigation on behalf of the United States.

Cash Grants for Nutrition Education

SEC. 18. (a) The Secretary is hereby authorized and directed to make cash grants to State educational agencies for the purpose of conducting experimental or demonstration projects to teach schoolchildren the nutritional value of foods and the relationship of nutrition to human health.

(b) In order to carry out the program, provided for in subsection (a) of this section, there is hereby authorized to be appropriated not to exceed $1,000,000 annually. The Secretary shall withhold not less than 1 per centum of any funds appropriated under this section and shall expend these funds to carry out research and development projects relevant to the purpose of this section, particularly to develop materials and techniques for the innovative presentation of nutritional information.

Nutrition Education and Training

SEC. 19. (a) Congress finds that—

(1) the proper nutrition of the Nation's children is a matter of highest priority;

(2) the lack of understanding of the principles of good nutrition and their relationship to health can contribute to a child's rejection of highly nutritious foods and consequent plate waste in school food service operations;

(3) many school food service personnel have not had adequate training in food service management skills and principles, and many teachers and school food service operators have not had adequate training in the fundamentals of nutrition or how to convey this information so as to motivate children to practice sound eating habits;

(4) parents exert a significant influence on children in the development of nutritional habits and lack of nutritional knowledge on the part of parents can have detrimental effects on children's nutritional development; and

(5) there is a need to create opportunities for children to learn about the importance of the principles of good nutrition in their daily lives and how these principles are applied in the school cafeteria.

Purpose

(b) It is the purpose of this section to encourage effective dissemination of scientifically valid information to children participating or eligible to participate in the school lunch and related child nutrition programs by establishing a system of grants to State educational agencies for the development of comprehensive nutrition information and education programs. Such nutrition education programs shall fully use as a learning laboratory the school lunch and child nutrition programs.

Definitions

(c) For purposes of this section, the term "nutrition information and education program" means a multidisciplinary program by which scientifically valid information about foods and nutrients is imparted in a manner that individuals receiving such information will understand the principles of nutrition and seek to maximize their well-being through food consumption practices. Nutrition education programs shall include, but not be limited to, (A) instructing students with regard to the nutritional value of foods and the relationship between food and human health; (B) training school food service personnel in the principles and practices of food service management; (C) instructing teachers in sound principles of nutrition education; and (D) developing and using classroom materials and curricula.

Nutrition Information and Training

(d)(1) The Secretary is authorized to formulate and carry out a nutrition information and education program, through a system of grants to State educational agencies, to provide for (A) the nutritional training of educational and food service personnel, (B) the food service management training of school food service personnel, and (C) the conduct of nutrition education activities in schools and child care institutions.

(2) The program is to be coordinated at the State level with other nutrition activities conducted by education, health, and State Cooperative Extension Service agencies. In formulating the program, the Secretary and the State may solicit the advice and recommendations of the National Advisory Council on Child Nutrition; State educational agencies; the Department of Health and Human Services; and other interested groups and individuals concerned with improvement of child nutrition.

(3) If a State educational agency is conducting or applying to conduct a health education program which includes a school-related nutrition education component as defined by the Secretary, and that health education program is eligible for funds under programs administered by the Department of Health and Human Services, the Secretary may make funds authorized in this section available to the Department of Health and

Human Services to fund the nutrition education component of the State program without requiring an additional grant application.

(4) The Secretary, in carrying out the provisions of this subsection, shall make grants to State educational agencies who, in turn, may contract with land-grant colleges eligible to receive funds under the Act of July 2, 1862, or the Act of August 30, 1890, including the Tuskegee Institute, other institutions of higher education, and nonprofit organizations and agencies, for the training of educational and school food service personnel with respect to providing nutrition education programs in schools and the training of school food service personnel in school food service management. Such grants may be used to develop and conduct training programs for early childhood, elementary, and secondary educational personnel and food service personnel with respect to the relationship between food, nutrition, and health; educational methods and techniques, and issues relating to nutrition education; and principles and skills of food service management for cafeteria personnel.

(5) The State, in carrying out the provisions of this subsection, may contract with State and local educational agencies, land-grant colleges eligible to receive funds under the Act of July 2, 1862, or the Act of August 30, 1890, including the Tuskegee Institute, other institutions of higher education, and other public or private nonprofit educational or research agencies, institutions, or organizations to pay the cost of pilot demonstration projects in elementary and secondary schools with respect to nutrition education. Such projects may include, but are not limited to, projects for the development, demonstration, testing, and evaluation of curricula for use in early childhood, elementary, and secondary education programs.

Agreements with State Agencies

(e) The Secretary is authorized to enter into agreements with State educational agencies incorporating the provisions of this section, and issue such regulations as are necessary to implement this section.

Use of Funds

(f)(1) The funds available under this section may, under guidelines established by the Secretary, be used by State educational agencies for (A) employing a nutrition education specialist to coordinate the program, including travel and related personnel costs; (B) undertaking an assessment of the nutrition education needs of the State; (C) developing a State plan of operation and management for nutrition education; (D) applying for and carrying out planning and assessment grants; (E) pilot projects and related purposes; (F) the planning, development, and conduct of nutrition education programs and workshops for food service and educational personnel; (G) coordinating and promoting nutrition information and education activities in local school districts (incorporating, to the maximum extent practicable, as a learning laboratory, the child nutrition programs); (H) contracting with public and private nonprofit educational institutions for the conduct of nutrition education instruction and programs relating to the purposes of this section; and (I) related nutrition education purposes, including the preparation, testing, distribution, and evaluation of visual aids and other informational and educational materials.

(2) Any State desiring to receive grants authorized by this section may, from the funds appropriated to carry out this section, receive a planning and assessment grant for the purposes of carrying out the responsibilities described in clauses (A), (B), (C), and (D) of paragraph (1) of this subsection. Any State receiving a planning and assessment grant, may, during the first year of participation, be advanced a portion of the funds necessary to carry out such responsibilities: *Provided*, That in order to receive additional funding, the State must carry out such responsibilities.

(3) An amount not to exceed 15 percent of each State's grant may be used for up to 50 percent of the expenditures for overall administrative and supervisory purposes in connection with the program authorized under this section.

(4) Nothing in this section shall prohibit State or local educational agencies from making available or distributing to adults nutrition education materials, resources, activities, or programs authorized under this section.

Accounts, Records, and Reports

(g)(1) State educational agencies participating in programs under this section shall keep such accounts and records as may be necessary to enable the Secretary to determine whether there has been compliance with this section and the regulations issued hereunder. Such accounts and records shall at all times be available for inspection and audit by representatives of the Secretary and shall be preserved for such period of time, not in excess of five years, as the Secretary determines to be necessary.

(2) State educational agencies shall provide reports on expenditures of Federal funds, program participation, program costs, and related matters, in such form and at such times as the Secretary may prescribe.

State Coordinators for Nutrition; State Plan

(h)(1) In order to be eligible for assistance under this section, a State shall appoint a nutrition education specialist to serve as a State coordinator for school nutrition education. It shall be the responsibility of the State coordinator to make an assessment of the nutrition education needs in the State as provided in paragraph (2) of this subsection, prepare a State plan as provided in paragraph (3) of this subsection, and coordinate programs under this Act with all other nutrition education programs provided by the State with Federal or State funds.

(2) Upon receipt of funds authorized by this section, the State coordinator shall prepare an itemized budget and assess the nutrition education needs of the State. Such assessment shall include, but not be limited to, the identification and location of all students in need of nutrition education. The assessment shall also identify State and local individual, group, and institutional resources within the State for materials, facilities, staffs, and methods related to nutrition education.

(3) Within nine months after the award of the planning and assessment grant, the State coordinator shall develop, prepare, and furnish the Secretary, for approval, a comprehensive plan for nutrition education within such State. The Secretary shall act on such plan not later than sixty days after it is received. Each such plan shall describe (A) the findings of the nutrition education needs assessment within the State; (B) provisions for coordi-

nating the nutrition education program carried out with funds made available under this section with any related publicly supported programs being carried out within the State; (C) plans for soliciting the advice and recommendations of the National Advisory Council on Child Nutrition, the State educational agency, interested teachers, food nutrition professionals and paraprofessionals, school food service personnel, administrators, representatives from consumer groups, parents, and other individuals concerned with the improvement of child nutrition; (D) plans for reaching all students in the State with instruction in the nutritional value of foods and the relationships among food, nutrition, and health, for training food service personnel in the principles and skills of food service management, and for instructing teachers in sound principles of nutrition education; and (E) plans for using, on a priority basis, the resources of the land-grant colleges eligible to receive funds under the Act of July 2, 1862, or the Act of August 30, 1890, including the Tuskegee Institute. To the maximum extent practicable, the State's performance under such plan shall be reviewed and evaluated by the Secretary on a regular basis, including the use of public hearings.

Department of Defense Overseas Dependents' Schools

SEC. 20. (a) For the purpose of obtaining Federal payments and commodities in conjunction with the provision of breakfasts to students attending Department of Defense dependents' schools which are located outside the United States, its territories or possessions, the Secretary of Agriculture shall make available to the Department of Defense, from funds appropriated for such purpose, the same payments and commodities as are provided to States for schools participating in the school breakfast program in the United States.

(b) The Secretary of Defense shall administer breakfast programs authorized by this section and shall determine eligibility for free and reduced-price breakfasts under the criteria published by the Secretary of Agriculture, except that the Secretary of Defense shall prescribe regulations governing computation of income eligibility standards for families of students participating in the school breakfast program under this section.

(c) The Secretary of Defense shall be required to offer meals meeting nutritional standards prescribed by the Secretary of Agriculture; however, the Secretary of Defense may authorize deviations from Department of Agriculture prescribed meal patterns and fluid milk requirements when local conditions preclude strict compliance or when such compliance is highly impracticable.

(d) Funds are hereby authorized to be appropriated for any fiscal year in such amounts as may be necessary for the administrative expenses of the Department of Defense under this section.

(e) The Secretary of Agriculture shall provide the Secretary of Defense with technical assistance in the administration of the school breakfast programs authorized in this section.

Glossary

AccuClaim. Nationwide project legislated by Congress to promote effective and accurate meal counts and claims for reimbursement in the National School Lunch and Breakfast programs. Considered by school districts as "federal audits."

ADA. Average daily attendance.

ADP. Average daily participation.

AIMS. Assessment, improvement, and monitoring system; management improvement system used in the National School Lunch Program during the 1980s.

A la Carte. The sale of food items individually, separate from a complete meal.

Amend. To change a bill or regulation or part of a bill or regulation.

Appropriation. Money allocated by the federal government for various Child Nutrition programs.

ASBO. Association of School Business Officials.

ASFSA. American School Food Service Association.

Attendance factor. The average number of students present at the school. If the school's attendance factor is not available, the national attendance factor is used.

Audit. System used to evaluate operation of Child Nutrition programs for compliance with laws and regulations.

Audit trail. A procedure that traces through all stages of an accounting system or data-processing operation, starting from the source document (at point of sale) and ending with the final report (monthly state claim).

Balance sheet. A financial statement that shows the financial condition of a fund at a given point.

Bar code. A product information code that is made up of vertical bars of different thickness that can be read by an optical scanner.

Base kitchen. A kitchen located in a school that prepares food for serving on-site and for other schools to serve.

Bill. New legislation introduced in the House or Senate.

Bloc grant. Specific amount of money that is not earmarked for specific programs.

Bon Appetit. Computer software program marketed by IBM.

Break-even point (BEP). The amount of revenue necessary to cover costs.

Cash in lieu of commodities. Monies issued for purchase of foods instead of donated commodities.

Cash reimbursement rates. Monies received for serving meals that meet the federal meal requirements.

CBORD Menu Management. Computer software program developed at Cornell University and marketed by CBORD, Inc., Ithaca, New York.

Central kitchen. Facility that prepares meals for delivery to other sites. Sometimes referred to as a *commissary.*

Claim assessment. Action taken by reviewers (auditors) to recover overpayment of federal funds made to school districts; referred to as "fiscal action."

CLOC. Commodity letter of credit issued for purchase of specified foods instead of donated commodities.

CN label. Child Nutrition Labeling Program, providing USDA statement identifying the specific contribution that a food product makes toward meeting the requirements of the meal pattern.

CNA. Child Nutrition Act of 1966.

Comment period. Amount of time (number of days) given by USDA for interested persons to comment on proposed or interim regulations.

Commodity only school. Schools not participating in the National School Lunch Program, but receiving commodities for a nonprofit lunch program.

Competitive foods. Foods sold to students at school during the breakfast or lunch periods in competition with the School Lunch or School Breakfast programs.

COMPUTRITION. Computer software programs marketed by Computrition, Chatworth, California.

Congressional hearings. Opportunity for interested persons and/or organizations to present testimony before a Congressional committee.

Congressional Record. Verbatim account of happenings on the floors of the House and Senate, issued daily when Congress is in session. Available in most libraries.

Continuing resolution. Resolution adopted by the House and Senate that would continue funding for various programs for a specified period of time if new legislation has not been adopted by the end of the fiscal year.

Convenience food. Food items that have been processed before being received at the school and may or may not require additional preparation before serving.

Delaney clause. A provision of the federal Food, Drug, and Cosmetic Act that prohibits the use of food additives shown to be carcinogenic in animals or humans.

Disposable service. Utensils, trays, plates, and cups that can be disposed of after use; referred to also as *single service.*

Donated commodities or **donated foods.** Agricultural food items made available by the Department of Agriculture to Child Nutrition programs.

Dry storage area. The space provided for the storage of consumable and nonconsumable items not requiring refrigeration.

ECR. Electronic cash register.

Efficiency rate. The ratio of actual performance time to standard performance time under good conditions.

Eligible child. One who qualifies for free or reduced-price meals under the federal guidelines.

Error-prone school. One that claims a high percentage of those who qualify for free and reduced-price meals.

Escalator clause. Automatic increase or decrease of reimbursement rate based on the Consumer Price Index for food away from home.

Fair Labor laws. Laws that protect the employee in the workplace.

Federal Hazard Communication Standard. Law that requires that employees be protected against harm and requires inservice training and information for all employees who handle or use potentially hazardous chemicals; referred to as the "Right-to-Know Law."

Federal Register. Document that provides a uniform system for making available to the public regulations (proposed, interim, and final) and legal notices issued by federal agencies.

Finishing kitchen. Kitchen that receives pre-prepared foods for reconstituting or heating, assembling, portioning, and serving on-site.

Fixed costs (FM). Those costs that stay relatively constant.

FNS. Food and Nutrition Service of the USDA.

Focused sampling. Selection process of federal free and reduced-price meal applications for verification by the local school district under federal regulations; based on 1 percent or 1,000 (the lesser) approved applications, plus 0.5 percent or 500 (lesser) of approved applications based on food stamp/AFDC (Aid to Dependent Families with Children) case number.

Food stamps. Coupons used for increasing the food purchasing power of eligible households.

Free meals. Meals served to students at no cost to the recipient because they qualify for free meals in accordance with federal guidelines.

FY. The federal government's fiscal year beginning October 1 and ending September 30.

GAO. Government Accounting Office. Audits each department of the federal government.

GRAS. "Generally recognized as safe." A designation for substances under the federal Food, Drug, and Cosmetic Act.

Group dining. Senior nutrition program subsidized by the federal government; referred to as *congregate dining.*

HR. Bills introduced in the House of Representatives are identified by HR before the bill number.

IMPS. Institutional Meat Purchase Specifications.

Income eligibility. Range of income within which students qualify for free or reduced-price meals.

Indirect cost. Those costs that cannot be directly identified because the amount is prorated across several programs; for example, utilities.

Interface. The ability of circuitry or software to allow two devices to send information to each other.

Interim regulation. Rule or regulation that has the effect of a final rule or regulation until the comment period is ended and the final rule or regulation is published.

Law. A bill that has been passed by both Houses of Congress and signed by the president. A bill may also become law without the president's signature if not signed within 10 working days after receipt.

Lobby. A group seeking to influence the passage or defeat of legislation or attempting to create a climate of favorable opinion toward legislation.

Loss leader. Items priced at a low price for a reason; for example, French fries at a fast food restaurant priced low to increase the amount of money spent by the customer.

Main frame. The central processing unit of a computer; the main part of the computer.

Management companies. Commercial enterprises that contract with a school board to operate foodservice programs.

Mandate. Legislation and/or regulation that demands something be done.

MAPS. Computer software program developed and marketed by MAPS, Inc., Columbia, Mississippi.

Markup. The amending of a bill according to information obtained at a hearing or at the request of committee members.

"Master-Slave" electronic cash register (ECR) configuration. A configuration where one cash register with a central processor unit acts as the "master," accumulating the data from the "slaves" through an interface of the cash registers.

Matching requirements. Federal funds must be matched by state funds as follows: (1) Three parts state or local money (including student payment) to one part Section 4 funds for paid meals, and (2) 10 percent of the product of all Section 4 funds multiplied by three.

Meals on wheels. A volunteer food delivery program for those people confined to the home. Referred to as *home-delivered meals.*

MPLH. Meals per labor hour. A means of rating the productivity of employees.

MSDS. Material safety data sheet required by OSHA for hazardous substances in the workplace.

National Advisory Council for Child Nutrition Programs. Council appointed by the secretary of agriculture. Its purpose is to make a continuing study of the operation of programs included in the National School Lunch Act and Child Nutrition Act of 1966.

National School Breakfast Meal Pattern. Made up of foods and portion sizes required by USDA regulations.

National School Lunch Meal Pattern. Formerly called the *Type A Pattern.* Made up of foods and portion sizes required by USDA regulations.

NCP. National Commodity Processing system for making USDA-donated commodities available to schools in processed form.

NET. Nutrition Education and Training.

Networking. The ability of different hardware, software, operating systems, and users to communicate.

Nonprofit lunch program. Foodservice program maintained by a school for the benefit of children. All income from this program is used solely for the operation or improvement of the foodservice.

NSF. National Sanitation Foundation.

NSLP. National School Lunch Program.

Offer versus serve. Provision of NSLP and Child Nutrition Program under which students must be offered a complete meal for the meal to qualify for federal subsidy, but students may select less—three of the five items offered for lunch; three of the four items offered for breakfast.

OIG. Office of the Inspector General.

OMB. Office of Management and Budget.

On-site preparation. Food prepared and served in individual school kitchens; sometimes referred to as *self-contained* and *traditional system.*

Optical character reader-recognition (OCR) device. A device that identifies printed characters or stripes through the use of light-sensitive devices.

OSHA. Occupational Safety and Health Act.

Paid students. Refers to meals sold to children other than free and reduced-price meals.

Participation. Number of students eating meals or taking part in the special milk program.

Performance funding. Guaranteed federal reimbursement for every meal that meets the requirements in the school lunch and breakfast programs.

Perpetual inventory. An inventory system that maintains a count on each item in stock.

Physical inventory. A physical count of all items in inventory.

PL. Public law.

Plate waste. Food taken but not eaten.

Polling. The surveying of the activities of another computer from a remote location by means of telecommunication devices.

POS. Point of sale. The point in the serving line where determination can accurately be made that an eligible lunch or breakfast has been served to an eligible child.

Processing contracts. An agreement entered into by the state or USDA to turn donated commodities into another or similar product (e.g., ground beef into hamburger patties or burritos).

Productivity rate. The rate of output per unit of time.

Profit and loss statement. An operating statement that shows the financial results at the end of an accounting period; if expenditures exceed the income, the statement would show a deficit or loss.

Proposed regulations. Regulations written for public comments; they are not enforceable.

Random sampling. This applies to verification procedures, the lesser of 3 percent or 3,000 of approved applications, selected at random.

RDA. Recommended Dietary Allowances.

Reauthorization. Programs that have been authorized for a specified period of time, at the end of which they may be continued by legislation.

Rebate system. Method by which the education agency or school food authority receives cash from the processor to cover the cost of commodities in foods purchased.

Receiving kitchen. The school kitchen that receives already prepared and portioned foods from another preparation site.

Reconciliation bill. The budget bill reported out of a conference committee that is a compromise between House and Senate budget bills.

Reduced-price meals. Meals served to students who do not qualify because of family income for free meals but who do not need to pay full charges.

Regulations. Instructions for implementing public laws.

Reimbursable meal. A meal, meeting the USDA meal pattern, that is served to a school child, priced as an entire meal, and qualifies for reimbursement under federal regulations.

Reimbursement. Financial assistance received from the federal government for meals served that meet federal requirements. The amount received is based on type of meal served.

Revenue sharing. Consolidation of federal funds for several federal programs.

RFP. Request for proposal for a contract by the USDA or a local school district.

S. S precedes the number in all bills introduced in the Senate.

SAE. State administrative expense.

Satellite foodservice. Food prepared and transported from one school or central kitchen to other schools to serve.

SBP. School breakfast program.

School food authority (SFA). The governing body responsible for the administration of school foodservice.

School year. Period from July 1 to June 30 as defined.

SEA. State education agency.

Section 6 commodities. (National School Lunch Act of 1946.) Commodities purchased with federal funds appropriated for all lunches; usually called *general assistance funds* (NSLA).

Section 32 commodities. (Public Law 320 of 1935, as amended.) Commodities purchased with federal funds appropriated for free and/or reduced-price meals; usually called *special assistance funds* (NSLA).

Section 416 commodities. (Agricultural Act of 1949, as amended.) Commodities purchased with funds received by the Secretary of Agriculture from 30 percent of the custom receipts.

Section 709 commodities. (Food and Agriculture Act of 1965.)

SNAP. School Nutrition Accountability Program. Computer software program developed and marketed by SNAP Systems, Inc., Santa Monica, California.

Software. A collection of instructions, systems, applications, programs, and documentation required for operating hardware (microprocessor), referred to as a *software package.*

Standard of identity. The official federal description of a processed food product; available from the Superintendent of Documents.

State Advisory Council for Commodity Distribution. Council composed of representatives from schools in the state that participate in the school lunch program. The council's purpose is to advise the state agency as to the manner of selection and distribution of commodity assistance.

State agency. That agency in the state that has jurisdiction over Child Nutrition programs (always in the department of education).

Statement of change. A financial statement that shows the fund balances.

Subsidy. Monetary or commodity assistance given by the USDA to school foodservice programs.

Testimony. Written statement stating an official position on legislation or regulations concerning Child Nutrition programs presented before congressional committees in Washington.

Time and motion economy principles. The rules that apply to human motions for the optimum output in a given period of time.

UCS. Universal Communications Standard. Developed by the Uniform Code Council to standardize the computerization of order placing through on-line communications and billing of products ordered.

UPC. Universal Product Code. A national system of product identification using a bar-code reader.

USDA. United States Department of Agriculture.

Variable costs (VC). Those costs that vary with the number served.

Verification. The confirmation of income or food stamp eligibility for free and reduced-price benefits under the National School Lunch Program or National School Breakfast Program.

Work center or station. The area with the equipment used to do similar work.

Index